Brian,
Thank you for
the tour.

Jack Ondrack
2013

Gold Medalist: the Annotated Autobiography of Leone McGregor Hellstedt

MD, MSc, PhD, Med.lic., DSc

Copyright Jack Ondrack, 2013

ISBN 978-0-9919147-0-8

Alberta Bound Books Ltd., Edmonton, Alberta, Canada, 2013

albertaboundbook@tbwifi.ca

Gold Medalist: the Annotated Autobiography of
Leone McGregor Hellstedt, MD, MSc, PhD, Med.lic., DSc

CONTENTS

Autobiography in bold type; notes in plain type.

PREFACE

Along the wall of a corridor in the Walter C. Mackenzie Health Sciences Centre are portraits of the graduating classes of the University of Alberta's Faculty of Medicine. The first group to receive MDs, in 1925, is small: ten men and one woman. A few years ago I came to be looking at that class photo following a visit to a sick friend. In a contemplative mood, I looked at the woman in the picture and wondered: what was it like for her in that male-dominated profession? in that male-dominated era? who was she? She's good looking. I'll bet she was some interesting person. Someday I'll ask about her.

When my odometer rolled over three score and ten, I took the hints from my business colleagues and retired. No regrets - I was keen to get on with my hobbies of motor racing, golf and reading. Along the way I had learned through casual conversations that the lady in the Class of '25 picture, "... might be the one who became a psychoanalyst in Sweden." Now she sounded *really* interesting. I had long read Freud for pleasure; two retirement goals were to shoot my age on a nice easy golf course and to read Freud in the original German.

From a 732-page history of the Faculty of Medicine (2008, Dr. Robert Lampard) I learned that Leone McGregor was the gold medalist in the class of 1925 (half a sentence on page 251); and from a 13-page section devoted to Dr. Mary Percy Jackson, a footnote concerning Jackson's colleague Dr. Margaret Owens, citing "Women Physicians of the World", edited by Leone G. (sic) Hellstedt, "Dr. Owens was President of the Medical Women's International Association, as was Dr. Leone Hellstedt, the gold medalist in the first U of A MD class of 1925." (p.355) I found it odd that such an apparently distinguished graduate should receive so little attention: two partial sentences in 732 pages.

The main University of Alberta history (Ellen Schoeck, 757 pages, 2006) yielded two pages under the heading, "The Faculty of Medicine's First Graduate", along with a photo of a university women's hockey team, Leone McGregor goaltender, seated in the middle. Most of the text concerned

Lorne Tyrrell's social encounter with Leone McGregor when Dr. Tyrrell (later Dean of the Faculty) was doing postgraduate study in Stockholm. Again I had found a surprising lack of information about a distinguished University of Alberta graduate.

Internet searches yielded a book edited by Leone McGregor Hellstedt, *Women Physicians of the World.* In it are 91 autobiographies of female physicians from 27 nations, including a six page autobiography of Dr. Hellstedt. Here I learned that Leone was born in almost the same time and place as my own mother: early in the year 1900 in a little house on the prairie a ways from the nearest town with a hospital, Winnipeg.

Two afternoons in the University of Alberta Archives, seeking Leone McGregor lore, were followed by a conversation with Katherine Captain, administrative officer in the University of Alberta Faculty of Medicine and Dentistry, who told me about the upcoming celebration of the 100th anniversary of the Faculty. My debt to the Faculty is considerable: in two instances graduates of this school saved my life. Moreover, the education I received from the University of Alberta has enriched my life immeasurably. I owe the U of A. The natural outcome was an offer to produce a biography of the Faculty of Medicine's first graduate as a contribution to the celebration of the Faculty's 100th anniversary (which Katherine welcomed).

Since that conversation in early 2011 the enigmatic Leone has occupied me in active research or preoccupied me in reflection every day. Much is known about her; more is unknown, as it must be for someone who died 36 years ago. In addition to the brief autobiography in *Women Physicians of the World*, the Medical Women's International Association (MWIA) archives yielded 548 letters to and from Leone during the period 1968-1975. Her children Monica (now Dr. Mona Theorell of Stockholm, Sweden) and Donald McGregor (now Donald McGregor Hellstedt of Lucerne, Switzerland) generously provided information about their mother and father, including the 77-page typescript autobiography which Leone wrote in 1969 at the request of the Hon. Ethel Wilson, Minister Without Portfolio in the Alberta government. I was able to find copies of some of her speeches and some newspaper articles which mentioned Leone. The longest article was written by Matthew Halton, also a graduate of the University of Alberta.

Matthew Halton, in 1928 the editor of the University of Alberta student newspaper, The Gateway, left his home in Pincher Creek in 1929 to take up a fellowship at London University and to begin a career as a foreign correspondent for The Toronto Star. He became the voice of Canada during WW2 via the BBC and CBC. On the front page of The Toronto Star of December 20, 1933 over his byline was an article about an interview with "... the beautiful and brilliant Canadian girl who was the first woman to graduate in medicine from the University of Alberta and one of the few women to get her name on that register of fame called 'American Men of Science'." The article mainly concerned contemporary findings in genetics and pathology and Leone's qualifications to explain them (an Alberta MD, an MSc and a PhD from the University of Minnesota, postdoctoral studies at Harvard Medical, at the Eppendorfer Krankenhaus in Hamburg and at the Karolinska Institut in Stockholm).

Much of Matthew Halton's journalistic success could be attributed to the colour he gave his reports:
"Considering all she has achieved, Dr. Leone Hellstadt (sic) is audaciously young as well as audaciously good looking.";
"... said Dr. Hellstadt, leaning eager, radiant and charming before my fireplace.";
" 'By experimenting with various irritants' , said the lady - after stopping long enough to engage in an argument with someone on her other side about the new Germany, of which Dr. Hellstadt is, to put it mildly, enamored."

I don't know if Halton's aside about Nazi Germany was a factor, but in at least three letters to her MWIA colleagues in Vienna ~40 years later Leone mentioned her mistrust of books by journalists.

Leone McGregor lived in Hamburg during the winter of 1930-1931, doing post-doctoral study at the Eppendorfer Krankenhaus. She was aware of the strikes and street riots between Nazis and Communists which led to the election of a Nationalsozialistische deutsche Arbeiterpartei (NSDAP, Nazi party) majority on the Bergedorf (a suburb of Hamburg) town council in January of 1931. In April, 1932, as a result of the unemployment crisis, voters made the NSDAP the strongest party in Hamburg.

In 1932, newly married, Leone moved to Stockholm with her husband, Ernst Folke Hellstedt; but he remained chairman of the board of Bergedorfer Eisenwerk. Meeting in London shortly before Christmas, 1933 were three friends from the University of Alberta, probably enjoying debate buoyed by Christmas cheer, well informed about the new Germany, and expressing contrary opinions.   According to Matthew Halton, Leone was not on the side of the angels. Her story was not a linear, virtuous progression in the Horatio Alger vein as it might have been in another, simpler setting, but perhaps understandable only in the light of the epic events, political contortions and moral ambiguity of Sweden during the Nazi era.

Why do I find Leone's story compelling? Why spend thousands of hours in research and writing on a topic which has apparently not had similar appeal to anyone else?   The fact that Leone was born in the same time and region as my mother raises psychoanalytic eyebrows - in light of the Oedipus complex. More superficially, I would not be the first to take an interest in the times and places of my ancestors.

Or does Leone speak to me because I'm an Alberta chauvinist? Guilty. I was born and raised in Alberta and consider it the best place in the world. Okay, it is cold and dark for a few months each year. But apart from that, the beauty, the natural resources and the history of the people are justifiably a source of pride for those privileged to live here. Leone was an Albertan; the idioms and humour in her English language correspondence 50 years after she left this province were still redolent of Alberta. She and her friends from obscure and humble Alberta backgrounds were actors with unusual, intertwined roles in the greatest dramas of the 20th century, the Great Depression and WW2, on the center stage, Europe.

The valid reason for this book: I think many readers will find Leone not only interesting, but enigmatic and perhaps inspiring. She was a girl with magnificent natural endowment in a burgeoning scientific career, who at mid-life abruptly changed direction to become an ordinary wife and mother, in the most extraordinary social situation, the practical and moral trials of Sweden before and during WW2. Then late in life she devoted her considerable energy and talent to the advancement of others.

Thus there were three phases in Leone's life: first, a youth of striving to take advantage of the new opportunities for women, resulting in a career in medical science; second, abandonment of this career in favour of the role of wife and mother in the stultifying environment of wartime Sweden; third, resumption of career - as a practising psychoanalyst and a leader in the worldwide movement to expand the role of women in medicine.

To convey an understanding of Leone this book develops four major themes: one, her life history, her childhood, family, education, work - who, where and when; two, a description of the societal developments which made Leone's life history possible, mainly the movement toward women's equality and its particular expression in science and medicine; three, the events which shaped her mid-life in Germany and Sweden; and four, when her children reached adulthood, her contribution to society as a practising psychoanalyst and leader of the Medical Women's International Association. The elaboration of these themes should tell us who Leone was when she received an honorary doctorate from the University in Alberta at Spring Convocation, 1977, a few weeks before her death.

ACKNOWLEDGEMENTS

Naming all the individuals and organizations that helped produce this book would be impossible. They are too numerous. However, there are some whose contributions were such that they must be thanked explicitly.

In more or less alphabetical order: The overall impetus for the book was provided by the University of Alberta Faculty of Medicine and Dentistry - the celebration of its 100th anniversary. From the University of Alberta Press, Peter Midgely made valuable suggestions. Librarians at the University of Alberta Archives were most helpful; they supplied critical information, as did those of another archive, that of the Bergedorf Museum. From nearby Denmark, Dorthe Stamp drove to Bergedorf and was more successful than I in finding interesting information in the Bergedorf Museum Archives. Librarians at the Drexel University Library, notably Matthew Herbison and Alexander Miller, led me to and through the archives of the Medical Women's International Association. Dr. Shelley Ross, Secretary General of the Medical Women's International Association, granted permission to use the MWIA archive material. The Edmonton Journal, the Glenbow Foundation and The Toronto Star were valuable sources.

For an inquiring mind, Abebooks, Amazon and ebay are heaven-sent. Nearly all of the hundreds of books that I consulted in order to write this one were obtained quickly and painlessly via these modern marvels. The book one wants could be in a used book store in Anchorage, Auckland … Bergedorf, Berlin … Zürich. With a few mouse-clicks one can find the book and have it in one's hands a week later – no more driving to a city library, finding a parking spot, rummaging in card catalogues, etc. Similarly, internet sources like Wikipedia are radically more efficient than historical library systems. The curious, those who think that life is too short to learn all that they would like to know, should give thanks.

An incomplete list of the individuals I wish to thank: Katherine Captain, Eugene Cholod, David Halton, Donald Hellstedt, Marmie Hess, Stephanie Hellstedt, Manfred Kets de Vries, Rod McDaniel, Karen Mills Might, Dagmar Mueller, Ole

Nielsen, George Oake, Esther Ondrack, Jody Paulson, Shawnna Robert, Jill Rubinson, Bill Selby, Shirley Stinson, Mona Theorell, Ian Winchester and Verna Yiu.

Special thanks are due George Oake and Ian Winchester for reading drafts, contributing their ideas and finally their opinions of the manuscript.

Without the help of Leone's children, Dr. Mona Theorell and Donald McGregor Hellstedt, this book would not have been possible.

Extra special thanks are due Esther Ondrack, for proof-reading and much more.

Chapter 1

Leone Arrived With The Twentieth Century

Assiniboia, The Northwest Territories, Canada, began the 20th century inauspiciously. The mean temperature for the months of January and February, 1900, was minus 17 degrees C, most nights fell below minus 25 and the temperature did not rise above freezing during the entire month of February.

By far the warmest day during this period was January 19. The remnants of a *chinook*, the warm wind from the Pacific Ocean that occasionally releases parts of Alberta from the grip of winter, touched Assiniboia. Before the day was out, however, a severe storm arrived. The village of Carnduff was besieged by cold and snow for weeks thereafter. By way of compensation, perhaps, that evening the village saw the birth of a genius.

Clara Leone McGregor was born in the first month of the first year of the 20th century. From a humble beginning in a crude homestead, her prodigious intelligence, courage and determination took her on a life's journey which tracked the major themes of her generation. Her life unfolded at the frontiers of 20th century developments: mass education; women's equality/liberation; the ascendance of science over religion; the creation of wealth - science, technology and social innovations combined to raise material standards to unprecedented levels; medical science and social evolution produced a population which exceeds the earth's carrying capacity; and Leone lived through the Great War, the Great Depression, World War Two and the Cold War in the eye of the political storm around the moral dilemmas of western civilization ... what is the value of freedom? of excellence? should the weak, who are the majority, inherit the earth? what is the value of human life? of the individual?

Born a Canadian, raised in freedom-loving Alberta, Leone strove for and achieved excellence. She respected and supported others of exceptional ability. She loved the opera. Her friends were intellectuals. She valued excellence in material things as well. Yet she lived most of her life in Sweden, complaining about the high taxes and a succession of governments catering to the lowest common denominator.

A few years before she died she renounced her Canadian citizenship.

Leone spent her last days soliciting and editing autobiographies of women physicians. After her term as president of the Medical Women's International Association, 1970-1972, she followed through on her idea that the stories of women around the world who had succeeded in becoming physicians could inspire girls to do the same; she took the initiative, pressing busy women to take the time to tell their stories; and she collected and edited the results.[1]

In order to appreciate what is remarkable or unremarkable about anyone, it is necessary to know about their times, their social context. In Leone's case particularly, because she was herself an innovator, it is important to understand her environment. It is hard to know where to stop in describing background: if one has been to an outdoor toilet in minus 30 degree darkness, Leone's gratitude for luxurious apartments in Hamburg and Stockholm will not require elucidation; if one has sold encyclopaedias door to door to finance tuition and board, Leone's medical school summers as a Chautauqua promoter will be especially meaningful. Yet these examples I considered not worthy of much elaboration - most of us can appreciate their unpleasantness without extensive description. The situation in Sweden during the Nazi era, however, was complicated morally, economically and politically; Leone was greatly affected by it, as were some of her friends from the University of Alberta; as of the year 2012, historians are still unravelling threads; therefore it has been given considerable attention.

A life like Leone's would have been impossible except **when** it occurred - the first three quarters of the twentieth century.

The CPR Estevan-Brandon branch line reached Carnduff, Assiniboia,
Northwest Territories in 1891 and fostered a village.

Where Leone Was Born

The western Canadian prairie, now the provinces of Manitoba,
Saskatchewan and Alberta, was more or less unchanged for the 5,000 years
prior to 1730. A herd of buffalo was commonly attended by a pack of
wolves and a tribe of nomadic Indians. Plains Indians, as they gained
proficiency in use of the descendants of the horses introduced by the
Spaniards, and in the use of firearms supplied by fur traders, became much
more efficient at killing the buffalo which provided their food, clothing and
shelter. Horses and *travois* allowed them to travel more easily, to carry
more goods than was possible the old way using dogs and women. Because
less time was required for pure survival, social life became more extensive
and arts and crafts flourished. Buffalo constituted the base of their
economy, however. The new hunting technology used by Indians inevitably
reduced the buffalo population - by 1850 the economic base was narrow.
When white men came to kill buffalo - for tongues and for the hides that
were made into drive belts for the burgeoning industry of the east - it
narrowed further and the superstructure collapsed. With the buffalo gone,
Plains Indians were reduced to poverty and a promising line of cultural
development was extinguished.

Queen Victoria's concern regarding the incursions of armed and ambitious American Civil War veterans prompted attention to the Canadian west. Confederation came in 1867 along with mobilization of a new force, the North-West Mounted Police, to see that the U.S. border, the 49th parallel, was respected. Construction of a transcontinental railway began - the last spike was driven in British Columbia in 1885.

Treaty Number Two of 1871 governed the relations of whites and Indians in the Carnduff area: Indians were confined to reservations; and white men, by the terms of the Dominion Land Act of 1872, could obtain 160-acre homesteads in exchange for a nominal payment and some work on the land.[2]

Following the Battle of the Little Big Horn in the summer of 1876, thousands of Sioux and Lakota fled across the "medicine line". Carnduff is about 20 km from the U.S. border, less than a day's ride on open prairie. Manitoba is 30 km distant. When Manitoba became a province in 1870, many Métis migrated west - for more freedom of movement and to hunt the remaining buffalo. Treaty Number Four in 1874 made most of southern Saskatchewan available for homesteading. The social turmoil attending the uncertain status of Métis, the chaotic resettlement of Indians driven from the U.S. onto Canadian reservations, white people's diseases and the hardships attending extinction of the buffalo was expressed in events such as the Frog Lake Massacre and the Riel Rebellion of 1885. By the end of the "Gay Nineties", however, the Indian and Métis populations of the Northwest Territories had been suppressed. Homesteads were being snapped up quickly. Between 1900 and 1905, when Saskatchewan became a province, the population of this 588,276 sq km (bigger than France, more than twice the area of Britain) doubled, from 85,000 to 170,000. Enormous vistas of prairie, grass trimmed by elk and a million buffalo, had been transformed into brushy plots, intermittently broken ground, barbed wire fences and primitive dwellings. Its former inhabitants, defeated, were confined to reservations; or alcoholic, lived in the slums of Winnipeg or the seamy centres of new towns like Carnduff.

With a little understanding of the "when" and "where" of Leone's origin, we can proceed to the "who" - luckily, with Leone to tell us about it.

4

Leone's Draft Autobiography Dated January 1970

Most valuable among the sources of information in compiling Leone's story were her autobiographies: six pages in "Women Physicians of the World", written in 1976; and a 77-page typescript prepared in 1969 apparently at the request of the Hon. Ethel Wilson, a minister in the Alberta government. Oddly, the library of the Alberta Legislative Assembly and the library of the University of Alberta listed this manuscript as being in their collections, but librarians at both were unable to find a copy. Fortunately Leone's daughter Dr. Mona Theorell found, to her surprise, this typescript in her mother's papers while she was seeking answers to my questions. When I visited Mona in Stockholm in August, 2012, she kindly gave me a copy for use in this book. It is a typescript with many errors and stroked-out lines, i.e. obviously a draft. Apparently it was never edited or published.

In the course of this book the entirety of Leone's typescript is presented with a minimum of editing. The facts or ideas she mentioned have not been altered, nor has her wording. Such things as her habit of expressing numbers unpredictably - sometimes as a numeral and sometimes as a word - has been tampered with to the extent of complying with the convention of using a word for a single digit number and numerals for 10 or more. Typographical, spelling and punctuation errors have been tidied up, disregarding their significance as Freudian slips in favour of rhetorical flow.

It is important to remember that her recollections of childhood are those of a psychoanalyst, someone who has thoroughly searched her memory, conscious and unconscious, with the help of a training psychoanalyst. As such they should be deeper, wider and more accurate than those one would expect from a psychological civilian. Nevertheless, I sought independent confirmation of facts; nearly all the examples I found vindicated Leone.

When Leone wrote this autobiography she was a 70-year old psychoanalyst of classical Freudian persuasion. Accordingly she organized her thoughts along Freudian lines. I have followed this pattern in their presentation. The first two years of life, before the emergence of self identity and symbolic capacity, are behind an amnesic barrier, inaccessible to the adult who experienced them. Although crucial for personality development, an understanding of the developmental features of this period must be inferred from study of the mother's behaviour and the child's biological inheritance.

Accordingly Chapter One contains Leone's history of her mother and father. Chapter Two contains Leone's account of the oedipal phase, wherein the child wishes to possess the parent of the opposite sex and fears its rival in this enterprise, the other parent. Normally the oedipal phase is considered to be age two to six; Leone was precocious intellectually and probably in her emotional development as well. Chapter Three deals with Leone's latency period, during which guilt from the oedipal phase is repressed and the child forms attachments and learns to function in groups outside the immediate family. Chapter Four contains Leone's account of her adolescence, the reappearance of sexuality in the centre of experience in the form of puberty and the orgasmic experience, and the turbulence of relationships within the family characteristic of this period. Chapter Five reviews and discusses Leone's account of her history. Chapters Six and later deal with Leone as an adult, from the age of sixteen self-supporting economically and psychologically.

Background and experiences of a girl born in Carnduff Saskatchewan in January 1900. The choice and course of her career in medicine.

Leone McGregor Hellstedt   January 1970   Stockholm

CONTENTS

My mother's family

My mother's life up to her marriage

My father's family

My father's life up to his marriage

My childhood
   Birthplace. Ontario. Carnduff. Tilston. Nobleford. Calgary.

My mother's family

The village of Monk Fryston in Yorkshire is near Selby, not far from the Humber River, and is famous for its stone. The parish registers, the oldest in Yorkshire, show that William Roadhouse (the original form of the name was Rhodus) (1740-1831) moved to Monk Fryston with his wife Sarah Sykes and children in 1770. There he was a skilled artisan and stone engraver. The inscription on his tombstone reads "Here lieth William Roadhouse, a man of great moral worth, who departed this life April 3, 1831, aged 90 years, also Sarah, his wife, who died December 17, 1778, and Rebecca, his second wife." His son with Rebecca became a clergyman and his grandson a surgeon, both remaining in England. His two sons with Sarah emigrated to Canada. One of these, William Roadhouse (1774-1857) and his wife Elizabeth Crissey (1774-1864), both born in Monk Fryston, sailed from Liverpool with nine of their children on the ship "Evergreen" for New York on May 26, 1819. They travelled to Albany and arrived at York (Upper Canada), now Toronto, on August 12, 1819. William had already received in England a Crown Grant of 200 acres in Albion Township in what is now Peel County. The official survey had been completed that year but consisted of some lines on a map in a government office in Toronto, then known as York. An attempt to find this land that summer failed so the family had to spend the winter at what is now Aurora. A surveyor found and blazed the lines in December and in April the family was able to move in. By the fall of 1820 some grain and vegetables had been grown for winter provisions. In the next few years a nephew, Benjamin, as well as a younger brother, Henry, each with large families arrived and bought up land concessions. William and Elizabeth's second son Samuel (1798-1884) did not emigrate with his father but married Sarah Farrell (1801-1861) of London, England, and came 12 years later to the Niagara district near Grimsby. One of their sons, Robert Roadhouse (1846-1911) married Ann Jane Taylor (1855-1929) and they became my maternal grandparents. Ann was the daughter of Thomas Taylor (1770-1834), born in Lincoln County, England and Honora O'Connor (1812-1876) of Limerick, Ireland. Thomas Taylor owned and operated a mill at Millfield, Ontario on the canal there. Honora had brought with her from Limerick a small but good library of English classics. She was a broad-minded Catholic who read her bible and prayer books daily. After she became a widow, she lived with her daughter Ann Jane and Robert Roadhouse and helped to bring up my mother. She had been a practical nurse and was well educated for her day. My grandmother Ann Jane who had married at 16 and had my mother at 17 was fully occupied caring for the four boys and the girl who followed. Honora read aloud the English classics and the bible as history to my mother and taught her to read and write before she was five years old. They studied the bible stories with maps and were very interested in all the missionary work. This Catholic great-grandmother was convinced that all missionaries should be medical doctors. She was very tolerant and her religion caused no discussion in the family. Her daughter Ann Jane had joined the Church of England when she married Robert Roadhouse and had no difficulty in bring up her children in this faith.

My mother's life up to her marriage

My mother, Mary Roadhouse, born in 1872, was the eldest of six children and was her father's favourite child. It was he who protected her from her four teasing brothers. It was he who always told her that if she studied hard in school, she could became anything she wanted to. He was optimistic, kind and tolerant. From him she inherited her interest and appreciation of music. Every evening he took her on his knee and discussed with her all she had learned that day. Mama's character was formed by her father and her grandmother Honora. In this Catholic-Protestant home there were no religious problems and my mother was never intolerant in regard to different religions. Her father was conservative in politics and as both he and her grandmother read everything available to them on world affairs, Mama very early became interested in these matters.

Mama enjoyed her school years immensely. When she finished public school, it was far to the nearest High School in Caledonia. She had to row across a creek and walk eight miles twice daily but she was happy to have the opportunity and did not feel at all sorry for herself. Graduating from High School at 16, she taught school on a permit for six months, saved her money and went off to Toronto to the Normal School for one year. There she did well and made many permanent friendships. Most of her girl friends married in the east but during all her life they came out west to visit her in the summers. After teaching for three years in Ontario, she and two girl friends in 1896 decided on a great adventure and applied for schools in the North West Territories. They were all accepted in districts near Arcola (now Saskatchewan).

MARY ROADHOUSE   ARCOLA 1895

Mama taught 20 children in a small log schoolhouse and boarded on a large farm with a charming family from Ontario by the name of Taylor. Mr. Taylor was chairman of the school board and a well-to-do gentleman farmer. Life was very gay out in the west in those days and these three young girls were much sought after. Whole groups of families went picknicking on the weekends, especially in the summer months, where there were wild berries to be found in the nearby foothills. There were lots of barn dances and plenty of unmarried young men students from the east to compete with the local admirers.

Mama's salary at this time enabled her to buy herself an elegant raccoon fur coat, a Persian lamb muff and stole, an organ of her own and she was able to order from a dressmaker all the dresses she desired. At that time dresses were fully lined and fitted tightly. Mama was tall and slim with a perfect figure so she looked very distinguished. She was the first of her friends to have any colour on her black dresses. This was a narrow red chiffon frill around the cuffs and the top of the high-standing collar and the result was regarded as almost daring.

The first summer there arrived a student clergyman who was also allowed to board at the Taylors as they had the largest and finest home in the district. This clergyman's name was Matthew McGregor. He and my mother fell in love with each other and married within a year.

MARY ROADHOUSE   Toronto 1807

My father's family

James McGregor and his wife Elizabeth Hinchey, both born in the north of Ireland of Scottish parents, had sailed from Ireland in 1840 and settled near Belleville, Ontario, where their second child Thomas, my grandfather, was born two years later. Thomas (1842-1917) married in 1863 Sarah Ann Teskey (1844-1927), whose family, originally Tessier, had fled as Huguenots from the Palatinate to Limerick, Ireland, and had later emigrated to Kingston, Ontario. Thomas and Sarah Ann, my paternal grandparents, then in their turn sold their Ontario farm and moved to the North West Territories, now Carnduff, Saskatchewan, with their seven children in 1889. My father, the fourth of six sons, was born near Belleville, Ontario. He was 18 years old and had just finished High School when the family came west. They very soon acquired rather large areas of prairie land. My grandfather was appointed government weed inspector. He lived in Carnduff and made weekly trips throughout the countryside in a buggy with two black horses. He was tall, handsome and distinguished-looking and I was very proud of him. The few times I was allowed to keep him company on his shorter trips and before I had started to school, I found it most thrilling to be taught the names of all the wild flowers, the grain in the fields and the weeds. I learned that one should never pluck a wild flower and I almost never have.

My father's life up to his marriage

Soon after my grandparents had settled in Carnduff, each of the sons became established in different enterprises and the farm lands were rented out to still newer arrivals from the east. Two sons went off to Winnipeg in 1893 to continue their education. One of them, my father, at that time wanted to be a missionary to China, so he entered Wesley College to study for the ministry.

As a child my uncles all seemed to me unbelievably gay and carefree, but my father later told me that they were very strictly brought up with much corporal punishment from their father. Their one sister Tressie became a very dear friend of my mother's, as did my Uncle Henry who was a teacher.

At that time, it was the custom for theology students to take summer jobs as clergymen while the regular clergymen were on holiday or absent for some other reason. My father followed this custom and it was at Clare (now Arcola), Saskatchewan, that he spent the summer when he met my mother. As a result, Matthew McGregor (1871-1951) and my mother Mary Roadhouse (1872-1953) were married at 28 and 26 years of age in Carnduff, Saskatchewan (sic - then NWT), in December, 1898.

Both the McGregor and the Teskey families had been Presbyterians but in the early years in Carnduff my grandmother disapproved of the conduct of the local Presbyterian clergyman and decided to attend the Methodist church. Her husband and the children followed her in this actually most courageous action. In this way my father's denomination became Methodist. My mother, although having been brought up in the Church of England, was not at all religious and had only a historical interest in churches and faiths. She was by nature skeptical and when she and Papa fell in love, she told him that she could never be a clergyman's wife and did not wish to be. Papa adored Mama from the first moment he met her and remained in love with her all his life. His father had recently divided up all the farms between the sons and Papa had received two. He decided to quit his studies at Wesley College and marry and live on one of the two farms only two miles out of Carnduff. Mama had no desire to live on a farm but there seemed to be no other solution.

Matthew McGregor   1897

[1] Hellstedt, Leone McGregor, *Women Physicians of the World: autobiographies of medical pioneers*, Hemisphere Publishing Corporation, Washington & London, 1978.
[2] At the time Leone's father Matthew was qualifying his homestead, single women were excluded. The situation in 1910 described by Georgina Binnie-Clark: *I have watched many women work their way through every sort of agricultural labour in connection with grain-raising, and firmly believe that a large percentage of women are, with very little training, perfectly able to seed, and harrow, harvest and market the crop, and to plough and cultivate the land. But every woman who wants a 160-acre field in Canada - no matter how competent she may be to work it - must buy it at the current price per acre, which is no longer inconsiderable; but every man who wants a 160-acre field in Canada - no matter how incompetent he may be to work it - can have it for the asking.* From the chapter, "Land and the Woman in Canada" in *A Flannel Shirt and Liberty: British Emigrant Gentlewomen in the Canadian West*, edited by Susan Jackel, University of British Columbia Press, Vancouver and London, 1982, p. 179.

MAMA, PAPA AND LEONE   CARNDUFF 1900

Chapter 2   1900 - 1905

My Childhood

Birthplace. Ontario. Carnduff. Tilston. Nobleford. Calgary.

Papa soon discovered that he was not happy on a farm and despite
Mama's protests, he accepted a student post as clergyman in Ronneby,
Minnesota, until shortly before I was born. I arrived on January 19,
1900 on a farm outside Carnduff in a terrible snow storm just before
Dr. Lockhart could get there. I was a wanted baby and Mama always
told me that she taught me all she knew before I was two years old. She
was given no rest, however, for Papa accepted another post as
temporary clergyman in Jacksonville, Oregon, and we of course
accompanied him. My first memories are my daily morning walks with
my father in this beautiful mountain town. He too tried to teach me all
he knew. Mama was not well and was unwillingly expecting a new
baby. Papa also became ill and we were obliged to take the train back
to Carnduff, through the beautiful Rocky Mountains, Papa with severe
headaches of then unknown origin and Mama in the last months of her
second pregnancy. I remember being unable to accept the fact that I
could see the peaks of the highest mountains from the train windows.
My parents had told me that mountains were so high that one could not
see their tops.

My sister Phyllis arrived on March 19, 1902, on the farm outside
Carnduff and was ushered in to the world by Dr. Lockhart. I do not
remember this event. My first memory of her is a hot, windy summer
day when Papa was away in town and Mama detected a prairie fire in
the distance. She had been told what to do in such an emergency. She
placed Phyllis in the baby carriage in the center of a fairly large, newly
ploughed field with me on guard. Then she rushed to the stable and
fetched out the four horses. I can still see her drawing the buggy out to
the middle of that field. I wanted her to fetch the tiny chickens and hens
from the coops but she refused. As luck was, the wind changed and the
fire went past without touching us. I found it all very exciting and could
hardly wait to tell Papa all about it when he returned from town in the

democrat. I remember thinking how brave Mama was, for she had shown no sign of fear.

My mother was soon expecting a third baby. She was always nauseated throughout her pregnancies. This symptom bothered her very much for she was otherwise an unusually healthy woman. I remember her at this time lying on a couch and me sitting on the floor on a cushion nearby with a Big Ben alarm clock on my lap. Phyllis was close by also and Mama was trying to teach me to tell the time. This is a happy memory in many ways. I had Mama's complete attention and I felt very superior to Phyllis about the clock (she was only a little over a year old). I still love clocks and don't feel at all at home unless there is one ticking in every room.[1]

The baby Robert arrived on a beautiful summer day. Mama's best friend from her High School days was a trained nurse who now came out from Ontario to help her. The nurse sent me out to play and told me to keep Phyllis away from the house. I felt that this was very dull and I can still see and hear the crackle of her starched white uniform. When Dr. Lockhart drove up in his buggy with two black horses, two sad little girls (3 ½ and 1 ½ years old) were sitting on the back porch feeling very neglected. Soon, however, we were invited in to see the little baby boy lying beside our mother who looked very happy and gave us permission to pat his head. I tried to satisfy her but I was not pleased. He had so little hair on his head. The nurse stayed on for two weeks and it seemed as if I had lost my mother. They were always together or else Mama was with the baby.

Then came the great tragedy of all of our lives. The baby Robert developed an acute dysentery at six weeks of age and died. There was an epidemic and some seven other babies died at about the same time. My mother was crushed. I did not understand why. I remember Papa lifting me up to see the sweet little boy in a white coffin with a pink rosebud in his hand. Mama could not endure the fact that a healthy baby could become ill and die. We were all very upset. Papa decided to rent out the farm, to move to town and to study law. He became articled in the Gordon law office as was the custom at that time and read law for the next two years. Mama was very happy over this decision. She had never wanted to be a clergyman's wife nor to live on a farm. However, she still could not get over the loss of her baby, so Papa sent us all three to Hamilton, Ontario, to her parents for six months.

The journey was a fascinating experience for me. We slept, ate and lived in the train for three days and three nights. All the passengers in our car talked to Phyllis and me and entertained us. It was the first time I remember being envious of Phyllis. She had already become an entertaining little creature with quite a few of our father's talents in this respect and I soon noticed that the other passengers were more amused by her than by me. I was more serious and more obedient. Mama did not allow us to accept money or candy from anyone. Phyllis could very easily break such rules and be forgiven after she had thrown her arms around Mama's neck. No one could resist her or so I thought.

LEONE AND PHYLLIS   HAMILTON 1904

When we arrived at my grandparents, my grandfather was confined to bed with some minor illness, but I took to him immediately. Mama was thrilled to be in her own home again and with her father. Her brothers were now all grown up and still unmarried so they made a tremendous fuss over us. One uncle used to carry me on his shoulder every evening after dinner down the street about a block away where a monkey sat on a pillar and did various tricks. Another uncle gave me a copper (one cent) every day. With this I was always able to buy a whole chocolate bar after my afternoon sleep and rather much against Mama's wishes. Once I was taken to a big department store where we rode up and down an escalator (this was in 1904). We lived not far from Dundern Castle and walked through the park each day. There I saw my first sailboats and my first formal beds of flowers. I remember very little about my grandmother except how kind she was to beggars who came to the kitchen door. She always gave them a plate of food to eat out in the back garden. Here there were large fruit trees which I had learned to climb. Phyllis was still too small for that. I did not ever want to leave Hamilton but I wanted to see my father again and he was longing for us all, so home we went. I remember the tears on Mama's cheeks as we left Hamilton in the train, and the tears in my grandmother's eyes on the platform outside. I could not understand it all but Mama said I would when I grew up.

Some Thoughts On These Formative Years

Leone's early memories included enjoying walking with her father holding her hand. During the normal time for intense rivalry with the mother for the father's affection, her father was absent for half a year. To an extent Leone transferred that attachment to her grandfather. In addition, she would have understood that her father was deficient - from the behaviour of her mother and the sympathy accorded by her mother's family. In Hamilton, away from her father, everything was better: the house was bigger, the surroundings less primitive, the material things were clean and orderly; the conversational atmosphere must have been more congenial without the tension between Papa's earnest religious talk and Mama's lack of interest in religion; Mama was happy in Hamilton and was forced to return to Carnduff, where at last report she had been miserable. The inability of Leone's father to gratify her mother's wishes for economic security and intellectual companionship, his impotence in these matters, was a factor in Leone's development of a feminist orientation.[2]

A "striking" feature of Leone's childhood was the corporal punishment administered by her mother. Before Leone was one year old she had been spanked for making noise in church. Mama was a strict disciplinarian, not averse to corporal punishment. Her rules were clear; depending on the nature of the offense, a second recurrence (third offence) merited a spanking or isolation in bed. Papa never raised his hand to the children and he sometimes prevailed upon Mama to forbear. A demanding and punitive mother, according to Anna Freud, often elicits the defense mechanism "identification with the aggressor" in a daughter. [3]

Leone identified with her mother, unquestionably. And her mother had identified with Leone's grandmother - in her enthusiasm for education, her polite tolerance for religion and her promulgation of the idea that women could achieve as much as men. By learning to read and write by the age of four, by excelling in school and becoming a schoolteacher, Leone obviously followed her mother. Leone's interest in clothing and fashion, and her lack of interest in religion were characteristic of her mother. The forbearance and courage Mama displayed appeared in Leone's character - her daughter Mona told me that courage was the preeminent quality of her mother. Mama's unhappiness was largely attributable to the weaknesses of Papa. Leone would later become accomplished at making herself attractive to strong, decisive, successful men. As a parent, Leone maintained the pattern: for her daughter she set high standards, was strict and demanding; and her daughter also became a physician.[4]

Sibling rivalry is a strong theme in Leone's childhood. Phyllis was a charming child who became an exceptionally beautiful woman. Leone was obedient; she lacked the ability of her sister to break rules with impunity. Phyllis had more musical talent than Leone, and the confidence and grace which those of rare physical beauty, accustomed to admiration, develop easily. Such a formidable rival for parental approval called for a strong response, and Leone strove to be equal to the task.

[1] Leone's daughter Mona told me that there was at least one clock in each of the twelve rooms of their apartment at Strandvägan 53, Stockholm. Leone strongly believed that clocks should have round faces.

[2] According to the criteria for normality/mental health/freedom from neurosis summarized by Freud and widely adopted since, "The ability to love and to work", Leone was an outstanding success. Her passage through infancy was likely normal, including the typical bout of penis envy which psychoanalysts tell us occurs at age 16-19 months when genital awareness emerges, the infant adopts a sexual identity and recognizes that boys have a penis and girls do not. Freud's conception of penis envy has been attributed to his Austrian Jewish background: *Schmuck* in German means "ornament"; in Yiddish it also means "penis". Similarly from Yiddish we get the expression "the family jewels". Some feminists object to psychoanalysis on the basis of the concept of penis envy, although psychoanalysts have established it as a normal phenomenon, observed in children under the age of two years. Fine, Reuben, *Narcissism, the Self, and Society,* Columbia University Press, New York, 1986, p. 237.

[3] Freud, Anna, *The Ego and the Mechanisms of Defense,* translated by Cecil Baines, rev. ed. International Universities Press, Inc., 13th paperback printing, 1966, pp. 109-121.

[4] None of Leone's grandchildren are physicians, although Mona's daughter Leonie made two starts at medical school before changing courses and becoming a lawyer.

Chapter 3   1905 – 1912   Latency

Carnduff in the new Province of Saskatchewan 1905

When we arrived in Carnduff, Papa was at the train to meet us and I was happy again. Phyllis had forgotten him and cried when he picked her up. We were scarcely settled down in our house and garden when Mama fell one day on the cellar steps. Our cooler was in the cellar under the house. She had cut quite a gash in her leg and had to keep her foot up on a stool for several weeks. Dr. Lockhart took care of her but the wound healed very slowly and I was very worried seeing my active, healthy mother so incapacitated. She was quite worried herself but kept busy embroidering and teaching me to read. She was very thorough and quite strict. She had a blackboard on a stand with the words I should know and new ones were added each day. Each time I came in from play, I had to read through the list. At the same time I was learning to write on a slate. This was easier and I was soon proficient. A friend of Mama's used to come in each day to help her with the necessary housework. Phyllis became so fond of this friend who had no children that she one day said to Mama, "I am going to take my nightie and live at Auntie's." I was very shocked and especially as Mama did not protest but let her go. I can still see that little curly-headed morsel walking away with her nightie rolled up under her arm and not even looking back at us. She was always a brave child and became a very brave woman. Fortunately she did not go all the way to Auntie's but came back within 10 minutes.

About this time I celebrated my fourth birthday. Mama had a party for me with a long table set for 28 children. She sent me around to the different homes a week ahead to invite my guests. I was rather diffident but she assured me that I was a brave little girl and that it was the right thing to do. I can still see myself ringing those front door bells. The party was a great success. We played games in the garden and there were lots of presents. One little boy brought me a wash-tub on legs and a washboard for doll's clothes. I remember the long white tablecloth with an orange peeled to look like a flower in front of each plate.[1]

Soon afterwards Papa sold our farm and bought a very pretty cottage with a still larger garden, lots of trees and a very high swing. Phyllis and I each had a small garden of our own which we planted, weeded and watered diligently. Mama's father sent her dahlias from Ontario but the frost destroyed them the first winter. In one corner of the garden was a woodshed with wood shavings on the floor and a lovely odor. Here I learned to skip and also bounce a tennis ball on a racquet up to 110 times. My Ontario grandparents sent barrels of apples, sacks of chestnuts, tins of maple syrup and kegs of salt herring. This woodshed was my paradise. The cottage was almost new and the previous owners had covered the living room, dining room and two bedrooms with wall-to-wall carpeting. I thought this was lovely and was so disappointed that Mama found it unsanitary. She did not like the dust when she had to sweep and there were no vacuum cleaners in those days.

Our mother had a favourite rule that other children were welcome to play in our yard but that we should not go to other children's yards. This we found very unjust but Mama was adamant. There were large windows all around our cottage and she kept an eye on us all the time. We also had a very large attic where Mama kept trunks of her old clothes which she allowed us to dress up in. One day we were permitted to go across the street to play with my cousin Tressie in her yard. Tressie, six months older than I and much more advanced, suggested that we dress up in her mother's clothes just as we did at our house. I apparently did not know the difference between clothes to play games in and clothes Aunt Lottie was accustomed to wear. I chose her best black taffeta dress to tear around in. Quite unaware of the crime I had committed, I went home serenely and had my dinner. After dinner Aunt Lottie arrived to tell Mama the sad tale. Mama could hardly believe her ears and came in to my bed to ask me if I had really played games in Aunt Lottie's best dress. I was so terrified by something in her voice that I said "No." This was the first time I had lied to her. She realized this and was very disappointed in me.

About this time Aunt Lottie was expecting her third child and Tressie was as usual worldly wise and full of knowledge. She had been able to roller skate at five years of age. She was unafraid of anyone or anything and always had a ready answer. One day while playing in our yard, she told me that she had chosen the night before in Eaton's catalogue the baby that was to come, and that she and her father were going to fetch it in two weeks either at the post office or at the railway station. Mama had told me the facts of life but as I listened to Tressie and feebly tried to argue with her, my doubts accumulated. That evening Mama assured me once again that babies grow in mothers' abdomens, that Tressie was quite mistaken and that it was wisest not to discuss these matters with other children. However, I still felt unsure and pondered about the matter. Finally, in what I believed was a very casual voice, I said, "Mama, how do parents decide if the baby is a boy or girl?" Mama looked at me seriously and said, "But you know better than that." Whereupon I remembered and blushed and resolved to find out more about the subject in some other way.

That winter there was a diphtheria epidemic and Phyllis and I were found to have positive throat swabs so we were quarantined with Mama for six weeks. We were not at all ill but as several children had died, the quarantine rules were very strict and for a whole month we were not allowed even to go outdoors or to play in our wonderful big yard. Mama was bored to death with the life and we scarcely saw Papa. He lived with his parents and came every day or so to the gate and called to us. Dr. Lockhart and the delivery boys were almost our only contact with the outside world. It seemed like heaven when we could go out and play again and Papa came home.

After the diphtheria scare Dr. Lockhart decided to remove my tonsils. This was done on a table in the large kitchen in our cottage. It seems to me that this was my first really major fright. I had already been afraid of large dogs on the street but not as I remember of anything else. Mama explained ahead of time about the operation and the narcosis. Dr. Lockhart and a nurse arrived. One of them put a mask over my face and poured on the chloroform. I though I was going to choke to death and that they did not realize the danger so I fought like a lion. Someone held my feet and hands and Mama tried to calm me. My fright was really terrible. To my surprise my throat did not bother me much when I came out of the anaesthetic. I was, however, nauseated for several days and I still don't like the smell of chloroform.

The next medical event was my vaccination against smallpox. This was done on my arm and I developed a terrific reaction. There were several visits to Dr. Lockhart and quite a lot of misery.

By now I could read quite well and borrowed books from the Sunday School library. I of course skipped many words but managed to enjoy the books anyway. I had a lovely Sunday School teacher whom I admired very much. Suddenly, however, a scandal broke out. She was expecting a baby and neither she nor her family wanted her to marry the man. He had crept into bed with her and her sister, and had told them that everyone did such things. The whole story was a great puzzle to me and I never succeeded in understanding the answers given me. All I observed was that she no longer taught in the Sunday School, that she sat in the back pew at church and that many people stopped greeting her. In this respect my mother was an exception and was always nice to her.

Another tragedy occurred in Carnduff about this time. A young girl of 16 on a farm chased her father with a butcher knife and was arrested and put in the one cell in the town courthouse. I remember so clearly that red-headed girl sitting in the window of her room behind an iron grille, watching the people pass on the street. I felt terribly sorry for her and puzzled much over why she had so behaved. I loved my father so much that I could not understand her.

At this point Phyllis, who loved to push baby carriages up and down the street or to take care of children smaller than herself, came down with the measles and Dr. Lockhart ordered Mama to put me to bed in the same room with her so that I would be sure to catch them. The blinds were to be drawn down and altogether I felt very abused and that life was most unfair. Neither of us became very sick so we had a horrible, boring two weeks.

Mama's best friend during these years and for long after was Phoebe Gordon, the wife of the lawyer (later judge) where Papa was reading law. She had been a childhood friend of Papa's in Ontario. She had no children, a horse and buggy of her own and lots of time on her hands. She and Mama read every general cultural book available and had great discussions. They were both very interested in politics and every Sunday, at our house after morning church, there were exciting arguments. Mama and Aunt Phoebe were all out for votes for women. Papa was not opposed but he thought it might be dangerous. When Mama and Aunt Phoebe cornered him he always managed to switch the discussion over to religious problems, such as whether or not there was any truth in predestination. Mama was also of course in favour of birth control and, while Papa conformed to her wishes to the extent of their knowledge at the time, I think he still felt that God ought to have some say in the matter. Mama and Aunt Phoebe met every Thursday afternoon, weather permitting, and drove out two or three miles to a charming creek, banked with trees, where they made a little fire and drank tea. Mama always provided the thin sandwiches and cake because Aunt Phoebe had the horse and buggy. I was very envious of those afternoons and was almost never allowed to accompany them. I remember once picking wild strawberries and feeling very grown up listening to their conversation about books.

Mama's other best friend, Laura, was a beauty who gave me music lessons. She was engaged to an Englishman, the owner of the largest general store in town. They were often at our home for Sunday dinner, she wearing her engagement ring and seeming very happy. Suddenly the fiancé began to show signs of trying to escape from the engagement. Mama was indignant with him. Aunt Laura had her trousseau ready and even her wedding dress. Tragedy was in the air. Years later she married a much nicer and more suitable man but I remember her as a case of a broken heart.

There must have been a general election about this time. Papa and Mama were conservative although Mama leaned towards the liberal side of conservatism. Papa always campaigned for the conservative candidates all his life. He was an excellent speaker and could hold an audience fascinated. He remembered everything he had ever learned and jokes as well, so the candidates were glad to have his support. He subscribed to Hansard most of his life and read the Canadian papers thoroughly. I was indoctrinated very early. At that time a teasing name for the Liberals was Grits. Grits was also a word for cream of wheat porridge. During elections all school children took part just as intensely as the adults. In the play hour we Conservatives called the liberal children "grits' and felt that we were really humiliating them. Imagine our chagrin when it almost always turned out that the Liberals won the elections. In my mind this catastrophe became vaguely associated with the weather and farming. Every year I heard the crop discussed and each time great hopes were stimulated. Yet it seemed to me that each year the crop was ruined either by hail, frost or wind. Before I started school I had already drawn the general conclusions that crops and the Conservative party were hopeless undertakings. The weather, particularly during the winter, was always very much discussed. The prognosis in the papers was made by a man named Foster. However, before I was able to read the papers and to understand that Foster was a man, I fully believed that Foster was a magnificent machine and I gaily told my playmates that "the Foster" as I called it, had shown that we would have such and such weather the next day. It was years before I discovered the truth about this instrument which I pictured as some sort of thermometer.

Mama had a habit of telling Phyllis and me Bible stories after our daily evening bath and I loved this hour. Phyllis sat on Mama's knee and I sat on a small chair beside her, both of us in white flannel nighties with long sleeves. I was very envious of Phyllis's position on Mama's lap. As I remember it, we were bathed in the kitchen in a large round zinc tub. There was always a splendid fire in the kitchen range and the oven door was wide open with hot air puffing out. The cottage was heated by a furnace in the basement and although we had a pump and sink in the kitchen, the cold water had to be heated on the stove or in its reservoir. After the Bible story was finished we said our prayers and were put to bed.

One day in 1905 my mother said to me in the morning, "This is a day you must remember all your life. From now on we live in the Province of Saskatchewan." The name was easy to say but it was hard to spell. Mama showed me on a map the shape of the three newly created provinces and I felt very proud. For some reason, however, I was ashamed to write only the short form (Sask.) on an envelope, so on each letter I addressed, I tried to spell the name out in full and with disastrous results. Many years later in Sweden I discovered that children here put the accent on the "che" (chay) which makes it quite easy for them to spell.

I cannot remember my first days at school, which seems very odd to me now. I must have been very disappointed. My teacher, Nellie Medd, was a childhood playmate of Papa's from Ontario, a very gifted woman who wrote short stories, plays and even tried her luck at books. She was musical and loved putting on school concerts of all sorts. She taught the cottage school beginners (Grade I, six years old). Perhaps I was bored because I could already read and write. At any rate my first school memory is of how I hated certain fairy tales which she read to us. I particularly detested Jack and the Bean Stalk. I discovered that if I put up my hand and said, "Please may I leave the room?" which I otherwise never asked to do, that I could go out and sit in the schoolyard anywhere until I judged that the horrible tale was finished. Towards the end of the first year she asked us to write a story on any subject at all. I chose "The Garden of Eden." Ordinarily we did most of our school work on slates but on this momentous occasion I took a large piece of brown wrapping paper which I happened to have folded up in my school desk and proceeded to write my first masterpiece. I can still see the writing, sloping either up or down, I am not sure which. I had often asked Mama for details about the Garden of Eden and she had always answered, "Everything beautiful in the world is there." In this rather long composition I included everything I knew about that was beautiful. Apparently the result was rather amazing. In any case a few days later I was sent for the principal of the big school nearby and asked to read aloud my composition to the grade eights. He was so nice about it that I did not feel a bit embarrassed and quite enjoyed my own performance. Mama and Papa did not believe in flattering children so I was totally unaccustomed to praise.

In my second school year I was in a large building and of course with a new teacher. I did not like it as well there. The boys pulled my curls on the way to and from school and I had no idea how to defend myself. Mama said "Hit them on the nose", but I did not dare. The worse problems arose on the way home to lunch. The boys were wildest then.

We had to pass my grandparents' house so I often hid in their garden until the boys were at least a block away. Neither my parents nor my grandparents understood my fear at all. Most of the girls in my class had braids or straight hair which I longed for and even prayed for each evening. Phyllis and I both had short brown curls which were apparently different and an incitement to teasing. I do not remember being happy with this teacher. We did most of our work on slates and I always had extra slates at home. If we did extra sums at home any evening and brought our slates to school, they were corrected and we were given special stars. One Saturday and Sunday I filled four large slates with sums out of a book at home and presented them to my teacher on Monday morning. She asked me, "And when did you do all these?", and I answered in all innocence, "Yesterday" (Sunday). Whereupon to my astonishment she said, "But that is very wicked. No one should work on Sunday.", and gave me back my slates with no extra marks or stars and I was disgraced in front of all the class. This attitude about Sundays must have been rather prevalent at that time. I was utterly confounded and very hurt. I knew that it was allowed to sit on our swing on Sundays but not to swing. If we played games we were not to sing. It was best to sit still and read. But no one had ever forbidden me to <u>work</u> on Sunday. I complained about this to my grandmother McGregor who told me that when she was a child in Ontario, there were many families who did not milk their cows on Sunday and how she as a little girl had felt sorry for the cows with their bursting udders.

As far as Sunday School was concerned, we children were usually in groups of up to 10 of our own age with a nice teacher, who told us Bible stories and arranged picnics for us in summer and entertainments in the winter. Our only duty as far as I can remember was that we had to read our Bible lesson during the week and that we should sign the temperance pledge before we were 10 years old. This I did with pleasure as I had already seen several men on the streets under the influence of liquor and I was terrified of them. My temperance pledge hung on the wall at the head of my bed. It was about 6x8 inches in size with a nice large gold seal and I thought it was very good looking.

Otherwise Sundays were always a bore. Phyllis and I had to be sure that our voices were soft and no noisy games were allowed. I remember once when we were on our teeter-totter in the garden, some of our playmates came in and taught us to chant "teeter-totter holy water' in time to the teetering. Papa heard us and was very shocked at the use of the words, "holy water" in a game and it was of course totally forbidden. My mother was not strict in these matters but Papa felt that he and his family ought to set a good example.

At Xmas in my second year in school about 10 of the best in the class were passed up into the next grade. To my astonishment and horror I was not included. I had believed until then that I was very good in my work. Since that day I never took any chances in school. I have always tried to learn more than what is required. It was perhaps a blessing that I learned this lesson so early. When I was finally promoted to grade III I had a lovely teacher and I remember being very much in love with a boy in the class named Ewart. I drew sunflowers, folded them into little notes and sent them to him in school. I don't think I ever exchanged a word with him. Most of the other girls and boys were in love, too. It was a sort of epidemic. From Grade III on, I never had any trouble in school again in my life. I was blessed with good fortune in regard to teachers and I loved school all the way through.

It was about that time that three boys in my class came down with polio. Two recovered almost completely, but the most daring one, who loved to pull my curls, remained partially paralyzed in one leg. As far as I could judge, the whole school and even many grown-ups believed that the polio had come because the boys had gone swimming in the creek outside town on a Sunday. To swim on Sunday was strictly forbidden for everyone. Mama and Papa did not share this superstition as to the cause of polio but I doubted very much the correctness of their judgement on this point.

I was apparently already very interested in all problems which had to do with accidents or diseases. The station in Carnduff was across the tracks from the town and one day a woman whom I knew by sight was caught between two trains one evening when she went to meet her husband. She had to have a leg amputated and walked thereafter with a crutch. I was horrified.

We all used coal-oil lamps. They had pretty coloured bowls and either hung from the ceiling or were placed on tables. Phyllis and I were never allowed near them. One evening a whole house burned down not far from us. A widow with two children had let a lamp tip over on a tablecloth and was unable to put out the fire. She was badly burned and it was a great tragedy.

It must have been at this time that Phyllis fell ill with fever and pain in her left arm lasting for several weeks and Dr. Lockhart could not discover the cause. From then on all her life she has had intermittent severe pains day and night in that left arm. Mama was worried very much about this but no one knew what to do. Phyllis always looked so healthy, for she had a fair skin and very rosy cheeks while I was the olive-skinned type. Many years later her arm condition was diagnosed as syringomyelia. Fortunately the condition has not progressed.

In those days Mama put turpentine on all scratches and cuts after washing them and this we disliked intensely. Any other symptoms such as headache or tummy ache were immediately treated with a dose of senna tea which was terribly nauseating. As we were on the whole very healthy I did not have to swallow senna tea often. Mama was modern as to the correct diet for children and put all her energy into the matter. We were given cod liver oil daily and liked it, which now seems unbelievable. No candies or sweets were ever allowed between meals and no cakes, only bread and butter after school. However, the bread was homemade and was delicious. Tea and coffee were forbidden until we were 14 and there were no exceptions. On Xmas day, however, we could eat anything in the house, which we did, and were always sick at our stomachs that evening.

We usually spent Xmas with someone of the large McGregor clan. My sixth Xmas was at the home of Papa's sister, Aunt Tressie, in Carrievale. As it was winter, we drove there in a cutter with two horses. Mama was delighted as she loved Papa's only sister. There were lots of children and presents and good food and everything was very gay. Aunt Tressie was very well-to-do and had marvellous toys for my cousins. One dappled rocking horse was larger than we were and had a real hair tail and mane. They also had a phonograph, the first I had seen. There was a mistletoe and the cousins of the same age were supposed to kiss each other under it. Tressie was quite willing but I was too shy and Harry my cousin did not insist.

Mama was also very fond of two families who were relatives of my father and lived on large adjacent farms outside Deloraine in Manitoba. The district is very beautiful and one summer Mama and Phyllis and I went to visit them. I was five and Phyllis three. I had never seen such a large house as that of my Great Uncle Ben. They had an enormous family which even included a nursing baby. It was the fourth child in this family who later studied medicine at Toronto and became Dr. Isabella Ayer and in some indirect way perhaps influenced my own choice of a profession. However, I do not even remember seeing her on this visit. There were thousands of things to do on such a big farm, for it was really enormous. We played in the hay lofts and jumped down into the mangers. We picked berries of all types in the garden and stuffed ourselves whilst so doing. Most of the cousins were older and very enterprising so I learned a lot. One day when all the grown-ups were off in town, about six of us played hide and seek through the whole upstairs of 10 bedrooms. We jumped up and down on the white bedspreads and had a wonderful time. When Aunt Christie and Mama returned, they were naturally shocked at the disorder they found and Mama felt compelled to spank me with her silver hair brush in front of the whole family. It was the only time she had ever punished me publicly and I was insulted and furious as well as ashamed. The game had after all not been my idea alone, but no one else was punished publicly.

In Carnduff at that period the social life of the town centered around the church. The nicest people were there. Everyone dressed up to go to church. The women wore their pretty hats and I thought Mama's were wonderful. I remember clearly two straw hats, one with red cherries under the rim on one side and the other packed with lovely roses on one side. Mama had taught us not to fidget in church but we found this very difficult. Now and then one of the women fainted during the service and then everyone realized that she was expecting a baby. I did not understand the connection but I soon discovered the truth of the conclusion.

People took babies to church in those days. If the baby cried, the mother took it out in the vestry until it quieted down. Mama always said she had had me perfectly trained in this respect by the time I was eight months old. A little spanking in the vestry had helped. As Phyllis and I grew older we all went to church on Sunday mornings. Papa often went Sunday evenings as well. We were never obliged to go. Usually friends of our parents came home to lunch after church and there were great discussions on religious beliefs and political questions. I had such an overdose of these discussions as a child that I have never interested myself in either problem as an adult and much less discussed them.

Our mother was very strict with us and our father very lenient. He never once punished me in any way. Mama had no inhibition in this respect. There were always two warnings and then the third offence was punished with a whipping or by being sent to bed for the rest of the day. This latter punishment I found just too awful, so I became a very obedient child.

When I was eight years old we moved to Tilston, Manitoba, a very small town with a hardware store which Papa bought and ran with two clerks. I do not know exactly why Papa gave up his law studies. He said it was too difficult to live with a family on such a limited income when he saw the opportunity to do better. I only know that this moving from place to place was a symptom which he was unable to surmount all his life. Each time the reasons he gave seemed logical. He earnestly believed that he would be able to earn more money and do more for us. Mama opposed each move, even with weeping which was quite foreign to her, but apparently not with sufficient intensity. Papa was always too optimistic and his way of life in this respect was foreign to her.

We drove to Tilston in two cutters on a sunny cold winter day with deep snow. We ate lunch at a stopping lodge from where I have a memory of a woman nursing a baby in the parlor in front of us all, while we waited to be called in to eat. Apparently I was curious and stood very close to the nursing mother until Mama called me back to her side. I felt very corrected and have been furious with snoopy people ever since. On the next stage of the journey my hands were cold so Mama lent me her Persian lamb muff. When we arrived in Tilston it was missing. I had lost it and I was devastated.

The following summer in Tilston was beautiful. There were small sloughs surrounded by trees all around the district and many song birds. It was the fad in that epoch for children to make collections of birds' eggs. The nests were easily accessible and I soon became interested in having a good collection. We pricked each end of the egg, blew out the contents and then placed the shell carefully in a cardboard box filled with shredded white tissue paper. There were very nice pocket bird books to help identify the eggs. I was fascinated with this whole project until the season advanced and I began every now and then to blow out a bird embryo instead of an egg yolk. This nauseated me so much that I stopped collecting.

Papa bought us at this stage a lovely collie puppie called Nellie. Phyllis appropriated her and loved her and she grew so fast that she was soon bigger than her mistress. I was so very sad that she preferred Phyllis that Mama arranged for me to have music lessons on her organ to comfort me. This also turned out tragically because although I got the lessons, Phyllis learned to play much better and more quickly, almost without lessons.

By now I was wanting to stay up in the evenings when Mama and Papa played tennis with other couples, but I usually had to go to bed at the same time as Phyllis. I soon managed, however, to learn the rules of the game and to handle a racquet fairly well for my age, so that when a fourth was missing they would accept me to fill in. I think it was via tennis that I began to feel a little bit grown up.

The next winter our collie, Nellie, was run over by a huge sled loaded with coal. Her leg was so badly broken that she had to be shot. I heard the shot in the evening, for Mama had prepared me, but it still hurts me. I have never wanted to have a dog since then.

I do not remember our schoolteacher in Tilston. I know that I envied the country children who came to school in vans. I thought it must be wonderful to live on a farm and ride back and forth to school in a van. My chief school memory in Tilston is from the day Phyllis put a pussy willow up her nose and could not get it out. She began to cry and both she and the teacher were terrified and afraid it had slid up into her brain. I was sent home with her to Mama but fortunately she sneezed, the pussy willow came out and we ran happily back to school.

That summer we all four visited the Taylors outside Arcola where Mama and Papa had met. It was a wonderful farm with a large house, many barns with big lofts, lots of children to play with and food which

I've never forgotten. Every afternoon at four o'clock we children ate outdoors hot graham biscuits with honey. It was the height of luxury. As I look back on this visit I realize that Mama and Papa had wanted once again to visit the family and the countryside where they had fallen in love and to have Phyllis and me along with them. We were like grandchildren in the home and it is still a delightful memory.

By 1909 Papa had discovered that there was not as much future as he had expected in Tilston and when his younger brother Ernie wrote to him from Lethbridge to come on a visit, Papa was only too happy to depart. When he returned, he sold the store in Tilston and made arrangements to buy property in Nobleford, Alberta, and to build and open a general store there. As usual Mama was shocked and unwilling, but followed along. Papa had brought Phyllis and me beautiful red shoes from Lethbridge; we found these moves exciting and could not understand Mama.

The "town" of Noble (later Nobleford), 1909

In Lethbridge we stayed a week with Uncle Ernie who was a real estate dealer living in a lovely modern house with a bathroom, toilet and hot and cold running water. It was the first such house I had seen and I was impressed. He took us all to a movie, my first. We sat on what I thought were kitchen chairs in a very bare room and the pictures jiggled. I was very disappointed in them. Then Uncle Ernie rented a car and drove us himself to Nobleford to the boarding house where we were to live until our own home would be ready. The countryside was very flat with almost no trees and I found it uninteresting after the Tilston district. The town was in its very infancy. The Noble family had a house and an office and owned large farms round about. The only other building was the new frame unpainted boarding house with two upstairs bedrooms which we rented. The landlady did all the work. She suffered terribly from eczema of the hands and this worried Mama who felt although we were paying for our board and room, it was cruel to expect this poor woman to wash dishes. I spent my days watching our store being built. I was fascinated to see the horses and workmen digging out the enormous cellar, the stonemasons building the foundation, the carpenters putting up the large one-storey building, the front half of which was to be the store and back half our living quarters. Papa was handy and knew something about all trades so gradually the building was well under way. However, winter arrived and Mama was bored with living in a boarding house. Papa was able to buy a large three-room tent in Lethbridge. This he put up near the store and there we spent the winter. The stove burned day and night. There were enormous snow banks that winter and we played happily with our sleighs. As spring advanced the building was finished and we moved in. Although still a child I had learned how to use a hammer and nails, how to mix mortar and lay bricks and all kinds of practical things. The workmen were all very good to me and kept me supplied with materials for building. I made myself a playhouse with all kinds of furniture and was very busy. Finally came the summer and the groceries, dry goods and hardware for the store arrived. I loved helping sort out everything. Papa had also received permission to have a post office so I learned to fill out money orders and all the simple things needed in connection with a country post office. Then we acquired a small telephone exchange. The farmers around telephoned in their orders and I became quite a capable little telephonist and helper.

There were no children of my age in the little town but there were several playmates for Phyllis. I was thus more or less driven to take refuge in books so I started to read everything in our library, at first secretly and then more openly. Papa and Mama had all the most famous English classics so I was very busy. A small cabin had been built on the grounds in order to store flour and cereals. It was not locked during the day and on warm days I used to sit on those cool sacks of grain and read in peace the books Mama and Papa thought were too old for me. Some of these I had to read bit by bit when Mama was out for walks and it was a nerve-wracking procedure because I had to sit on a window sill and keep one eye on the road outside in case Mama would appear. I found this situation very unfair because my parents were always reading either newspapers or books and my fate seemed to be to go to bed early. I remember reading "The Scarlet Letter" at this time without ever discovering what the title implied.

There was yet no school in the town and I had a lot of time on my hands. I had to do arithmetic every morning for my mother and history and geography every afternoon for Papa. He was not a pedagogue and I found geography boring. Mama was strict and a good teacher, but I thought she expected too much of me. One evening, when I had made several mistakes in my "three-line" problems, she gave me quite a scolding. I told her I had to go to the outdoor toilet and there I retired in a rage. It was about eight o'clock in the evening and I was longing for revenge. I decided to run away. After about 200 yards I regretted my decision and returned to our own yard, where I sat down on the grass in the dark. I thought it would do Mama good to have to hunt for me. Soon I heard voices calling but I did not answer. Gradually I heard many voices but no one found me until 10:30 and then it was Papa. He was gentle and understanding and did not scold me at all. He simply told Mama never to be so strict again with my arithmetic and she never was.

It was about that time that the railway from Lethbridge to Calgary was laid. It was an amazing sight. For weeks many workmen built the roadbed. then came the day when that imposing machine laid the rails on the ties and men drove in the spikes. I could hardly believe my eyes. One of the most remarkable features was the extent to which the workmen were drilled. At the sound of a gong they would stop work, take up positions like soldiers at equal distances from one another, draw down their trousers and make their evacuations, in the full sight of the people in the town. I was amazed. Other groups of workmen soon arrived and built a red frame station and from then on we were part of the world.

I had already transformed the box in which Mama's organ was always transported into a really charming playhouse. I used the cover as a roof which extended over to the outside wall of the store. I closed one opening with double canvas and used the other as a door. Then I built very nice furniture. Orange boxes with one end knocked out are quite acceptable arm chairs. Apple boxes placed with a little ingenuity in a group of four make a good table. There we played cards, mostly "authors" or parchesa, and were protected from the hot sun or the cold wind. Mama always let us have homemade bread and butter, marmalade and milk for our afternoon tea in the playhouse.

Papa had already prepared a very nice tennis court in our yard and I practised diligently with whomever would take me on. I soon became such a good player that Mama and Papa and all the other grown-ups were glad to have me as a partner. The problem for me, of course, was to get permission to stay up after dinner.

The business flourished from the beginning and Papa had a second floor built, and the family moved upstairs. He then sent for my first teacher, Nellie Medd, and she opened the first school in Nobleford. We were 10 children of all ages and our lessons began on shiny new school furniture in an office building across the street from our store. Gradually a very handsome school was built. I was more or less obliged to fit into a class with a girl of 15 and a boy of 13 although I was only 11. I did my best and in a year wrote the Grade VIII exams in Lethbridge and passed. My teacher who was remarkable in many ways and an old friend of Papa's was nevertheless very unjust to Phyllis. This made me unhappy because I could not understand it and could not feel really safe with her. Years later I heard from Phyllis the cause of the trouble. Nellie's fiancé, a young clergyman still at McGill, had praised Phyllis too much and had shown signs of interest in her.

The summer I passed into High School, Nellie took a six weeks' conducted tour in Europe and brought home countless small illustrated books showing the pictures and treasures in the continental galleries. Mama and she had always read the same books and now they studied these illustrations industriously. Not to be outdone, I borrowed them and learned the names of all the important pictures in the Pitti, Uffizi, Louvre and Munich galleries. I was fascinated by these pictures and made up my mind never to settle down until I had seen the originals.

A great part of the fields in and around Nobleford were still virgin grazing land. I remember I loved the lumber yard with the clean smell of lumber and sawdust and the protection from the ever-prevalent wind. Papa had brought out a childhood friend from Ontario to run this lumber yard and so I was felt to be in safe hands there. The first summer in Nobleford Phyllis and I had collected quantities of the buffalo skulls which lay in the fields. With these we plotted out houses on the grass, using the skulls for walls. We could change the position of the doors and windows and have a new house every day. The effect was very pretty but it did not keep out the wind. The next summer there were unbelievable quantities of mushrooms. I had never seen such large ones before. Many were as large as our dinner plates. Papa was an expert on mushrooms from his Ontario childhood so he inspected everything we picked and there were no accidents.

It was the fashion in those days to have satin cushions as decorative pieces on couches or sofas and these cushions were often decorated with bouquets of flowers painted in oil. Nellie Medd and Mama were experts at this hobby and I soon begged to learn. My results were sent at Xmas to my relatives far and wide. I remember distinctly a spray of apple blossoms on black satin. Mama and Nellie were also very energetic with their studies in French. They had keys and worked through their High School exercises diligently Other evenings when Papa was busy, they read aloud to each other. On such occasions, I sat on the floor in my nightie, inside my bedroom door and tried to hear every word. It was really hard work. "The Harvester" had just come out and I had quite a time following the romance through the door. We were never allowed up after eight o-clock and there were no exceptions.

About this time Mama discovered a small lump in one breast and went off to the Mayo Clinic. It turned out to be benign and she was at home again in 10 days. Phyllis and I did not understand the seriousness of the occasion at all. On the contrary, we found it great fun to keep house for Papa. I got out the cookbook and baked a cake and a custard pudding the first day. The cake was burned but the custard was perfect. Mama had never let me cook so this was a great adventure. I've been very interested in occasional cooking and in special recipes ever since.

A new teacher came to replace Nellie Medd at this time. She was a University graduate in mathematics from Nova Scotia and her name was Kathleen Forbes. I had never really understood mathematics. Mama had been too strict while teaching me and I had been able to pass the final examinations without really understanding. This teacher was a born pedagogue and within no time she had made everything clear, and wild horses couldn't have kept me away from the joy of solving arithmetical and geometrical problems inside and outside school. I was simply fascinated. This was the first time I remember experiencing a feeling of freedom in my life. I realized then that there existed a world of science that one could get into in time. I felt happy and uplifted. I passed into Grade X without any trouble.

---

[1] A prototype for Leone's birthday parties in Stockholm. Plus/minus 70 years later she was in the habit of inviting 24-30 guests for her birthday party.

Chapter 4   1912 -1915   Adolescence in Calgary

Just at this point we moved to Calgary where my Uncle Ernie already lived. Papa later said he moved this time to give us an opportunity to come to better schools but I presume it was his usual restlessness.[1] As soon as anything was going well, he loved to move and especially to be near his brothers. C.C.I. in Calgary was my first big school. There were 500 pupils, boys and girls, and I happened to be in the class of 45 girls in Grade X. I did not feel very comfortable at first. Most of them were three or four years older than I, which was quite a difference at that age. We had a different teacher for each subject which was most exciting, especially as they were almost all men. I was soon as happy as a child can be. The teachers were excellent and I loved them all dearly. At first I was very afraid that I did not know enough, but after a week or so when Mr. Lord praised my solutions in the geometry class, I was on my way. The only catastrophe I can remember was the biology teacher who was ugly, fat and odd, and who asked us suddenly one day (1913), "What is the difference between a girl and a boy baby?" The whole class was speechless. No one could say a word. Whereupon he said, "A boy has square shoulders and a girl sloping." The next day he was discovered to be a morphine addict and psychotic and we never saw him again. It was my second encounter in life with a mentally ill person.

By then I was very good in tennis and had won the Junior Tennis Singles Championship. The teachers as well as the students wanted to play with me and I spent all my spare time on the courts. I had not had any languages until I came to Calgary so I had a lot to catch up on. The German teacher, Mr. McKim gave me free lessons after school until I was on a level with the class. A college friend of Papa's happened to visit us for several months and he plugged me up on Latin every evening until I was actually ahead of my class. I was never able to take French in High School because I wanted Matriculation plus Grade XII and to get that I had to take physics and chemistry in the French hour.

In Grades XI and XII the classes were mixed and very stimulating. I was always the youngest in each class because at that time most students in Grade XII were from 18 to 21 while I was only 14 and finally 15. The

Grade XII year was a most happy one, although the boys all teased me as if I were a child. However, many played tennis with me and even the men teachers and boy graduates sought me out so although still rather shy, I was acquiring a little more security.

One of the most interesting boys in the class was Bill Jewitt. He was brilliant and dared to revolt against any teacher he did not approve of. I can still hear our literature professor saying, "Jewitt, go to the office," and Bill taking a full five minutes to get from his seat to the door.

The girl I found the most interesting in the class was Beatrice Timmins. She belonged to a very musical family where each member could play several instruments. She was completely natural and very pretty. She was also in my Sunday school class. This class met once a week in the Y.W.C.A. for baked bean dinners at 10 cents each after a swimming lesson in the pool.

The war broke out while we were in Grade XII and by spring most of the boys in the class and a lot of the teachers had enlisted. I felt as if life was passing me by. Some older girls I knew slightly enlisted to drive ambulances. I envied them tremendously but the minimum age for enlistment was 18 and I was only 15. [2] It seemed to me that life was very unjust. There was no future for me except to pass my Grade XII exams and to play tennis. At this point, however, a brilliant and handsome boy appeared at the tennis courts. He was English and at 18 was already taking his final law exams in R.B. Bennett's office. He was a top tennis player and a genius in many ways. He fell in love with me at once and invited me to play in a mixed doubles tournament with him. I was shy and quite overwhelmed when he invited me to ice cream sundaes after our evening tennis games. When we arrived at home in the evenings he charmed Mama immediately and they became the best of friends. They discussed books and politics in complete comfort while I sat listening. Very soon Percy (Broad) asked Mama if he could take me to a theatre matinée. Omar Khayyam was being given and Mama was so surprised that she said yes. It was my first date and I was anything but comfortable in the situation. I can only say that I survived. Percy was very little older in years but so much older in wisdom and experience. I had to be home by nine. Phyllis used to hide behind a tree in the front yard and call out loudly, "Mama, Leone is coming home with a boy." This nearly killed me. Then Percy came in with me to talk to Mama.

As soon as he took his final law exams he enlisted. Until he was killed in Belgium a year later he wrote to Mama and me every week. I felt terrible when he was killed and couldn't eat a morsel for several days. I called on his mother later and she gave me my photo which had been found in his pocket when he died.

LEONE   CALGARY 1916

During this same Grade XII year I made one of the major decisions of my life. Until then I had more or less accepted my father's religious views, although I had never been made to go to church or Sunday school or to be confirmed. However, Mama's skepticism must have been working within me. I wanted very much to have a white dress for graduation. I mentioned this to Mama but she paid little attention so I decided to turn to God. Until this time I was still saying my prayers in the evenings, but with some doubts and hesitations. I decided to test the whole matter seriously, so I made a major effort to follow all rules at school from Xmas to June, in the hope that my prayers would be answered. It was the first time I had ever asked for anything concrete for myself. Unfortunately I did not mention the matter to Mama but trusted in the Lord and the dress did not come. From that graduation day when I walked down the aisle in a dark dress, I have never spent a moment wondering about religion in any way. From then on I realized that I had to arrange things myself. I did not even tell Mama about my great disappointment but I never went to church or Sunday school again and have never missed them.[3]

During my Grade XII year I had become quite fluent in writing German and after hearing a classmate tell how she kept a diary in German in order to keep her mother in the dark, I decided to do the same and found it quite easy and amusing. The chief problem was to keep the matter a secret from Phyllis and Mama. I did my homework always at school after four o'clock and had almost nothing to do in this way at home, where I arrived just in time for dinner. In order to keep the diary book secret, I had to write in it after I was in bed.[4] I was still wearing black stockings, as was everyone else. These I laid on the floor to close the crack under the door which could tell Mama that my light was still on. Phyllis was another problem. She could come tearing into my room at any moment. Despite these difficulties I kept a German diary all the Grade XII year and was horrified not to be able to find the book (locked) when I hunted for it several years later at my parents' home.

While in Grade XII I had no concrete idea as to what I was going to do in the future. I intended to study and have a profession, but otherwise I scarcely thought about the matter. The really lucky boys and girls seemed to be those who could go off to the war. The rest of us unlucky ones were doomed to go to Normal School and be teachers and miss everything exciting in life. At this time a lovely girl, Mary Simons, came home from Queen's University and started to play tennis on the High School courts. I like her immediately. I thought her clothes were beautiful. She had the first really long skirts I had seen on young girls. Her best suit had a slit through which could be seen a cerise petticoat. She told me a lot about University life in the east and how exciting it was and she lent me Freud's "Interpretation of Dreams" which I devoured. From that day my life was changed. It awakened me and I saw that there was a future for me even if I could not get to the war. Mary has remained a dear and true friend all my life. She was half English and half French, very broad-minded and clever and has always been an inspiration to me. She also became very good friends with my mother.[5]

---

[1] Leone's father had been a partner in the store in Noble. His partner John Medd took over the Noble store (presumably buying Matthew's interest) and others the post office and telephone exchange. In Calgary he entered the employ of a goods wholesaler as a clerk. The two farms he inherited from his father ten years earlier were gone. He had failed in his theological and his law studies, and now in his career as a businessman. In this draft autobiography, written in 1969, Leone omits or minimizes her father's failures. Her 1969-1976 correspondence is more candid (see Chapter 21).

[2] WW1 began July 28, 1914. Leone turned 15 on January 19, 1915.

[3] For her university graduation Leone made her own white dress. Before meeting Folke Hellstedt in 1931, she had many "beaux", as she called them. At their first meeting Folke told her he was an atheist. In Leone's view this immediately qualified him as husband material.

[4] Writing in bed became a lifetime habit. Leone's daughter Mona told me that she never saw her mother write a letter; yet Leone's correspondence was voluminous. In many of the letters written to her Viennese friends she notes that she is writing while in bed.

[5] Leone's identification with her mother was such that a mutuality of affection between Mama and a friend of Leone's seemed important to a close relationship with that person for Leone. e.g. Percy and Mary.

Chapter 5   **1912-1915**

If civilization makes us neurotic, what is normality? Love and work was his (Freud's) simple answer; or to be more precise, in his own terminology, achievement and pleasure (Leistung and Genuss).[1]

I loved every day in high school, every subject, and almost all my teachers, unbeknown to them. All but one were men.[2]

At the age of 15 Leone was a psychological success. She had passed through infancy, childhood and puberty with an outstanding capacity for work which, combined with her high native intelligence, yielded exceptional performance. She derived pleasure from interpersonal relationships and was already displaying tolerance for the failings of a loved one, notably her father, which would characterize her later life in the form of gracious or forgiving responses to disappointment and even betrayal.

Leone's description of the family's circumstances in Noble and the move to Calgary is perhaps misleading. Consider the reality of living in a tent through an Alberta winter - which Leone said her mother preferred to living in the boarding house. How bad was the boarding house? I don't think her father owned a thriving business in Noble, as Leone indicated. It is more likely that he was given the onerous task of establishing it by his partner(s). In 1911, when it was up and running and living conditions in Noble became less primitive, John Medd operated the store and Matthew McGregor became an employee of Brumpton & Gaetz, a department store in Red Deer, 180 miles to the north.[3]

A grocery store was built and opened in 1909 by Matt McGregor from Carnduff, Saskatchewan where he had farmed from 1898 until 1907. Early in 1910, his former partner, John H. Medd, joined him, then the business was conducted under the name of "McGregor and Medd". Mr. and Mrs. McGregor, Leone and Phyllis lived in rooms at the rear of the store. McGregor also had a little Post Office in his store from which the mail was distributed. A short while later McGregor moved to Red Deer, the business was then taken over by John Medd, and the Post Office by F.W. Hunt.[4]

There was no church in Noble: *... services were held by Matt McGregor, who had partially completed ministerial studies before changing his occupation, in C.S. Noble's office until the school was built in 1910 or 1911.*[5]

The family was still resident in Noble and Matthew McGregor ostensibly still a partner in the store as late as June 6, 1911, when the information for the Fifth Census of Canada was recorded: in District 3, Macleod, Enumeration District 10, on page 6, in Township 18, Range 23, west of the 4th meridian; line 8 McGregor, Matthew born April, 1871, Presbyterian, General Merchant, employer; line 9 McGregor, Minnie born September 1872; line 10 McGregor, Clara Leone born January 1900; and line 11, Phyllis born March 1902.

Leone indicated that she entered high school in Calgary in September, 1912, and that her parents lived in Calgary while she was in high school. Probable confirmation for this was in *Henderson's Calgary City Directory*. It began listing Matthew McGregor in 1913, as an employee of "Territorial Inv Co". In 1914, 1915 and 1916 he was listed as a clerk with S G Freeze & Co. The family's address in Calgary changed three times during this period.[6]

Normally a child's upbringing would suffer from frequent changes of residence. Leone's mother and father were well educated, however, and provided a calm, scholarly home environment. Evenings were passed reading books from the local library. In high school Leone did her homework at school after classes, before she went home for dinner. Leone's mother had been a schoolteacher and Leone had the good luck to meet women who recognized and cultivated her prodigious talent. In the later (1977) autobiography that Leone contributed to *Women Physicians of the World*, she credited Kathleen Forbes, her teacher in Noble before Leone went to Calgary to attend high school: *She had an M.S. in mathematics, and within a very short time she had chased me through all the requirements for four years of high school. I was fascinated and realized that a new world had opened up to me.*[7]

Among her influences around this time Leone mentioned two women doctors and Sigmund Freud's *The Interpretation of Dreams*.[8]
  This was my first introduction to psychology, and another new world opened up for me, the world of the unconscious. This was only 1914, and I did not know that psychoanalysis could be a profession, or that the famous

analyst Ernest Jones was practising in Toronto. The book, however, gave me so many ideas that entirely changed my life.[9]

Why Was Leone Different?

Freud's ideas have changed many lives. In precisely what ways they changed Leone's will, alas, be forever conjecture. She died in 1977 and perhaps did not tell anyone directly, apart from her analyst, just how a book first published in 1900, the year of her birth, changed her life. Having read hundreds of pages of her correspondence, her autobiographies, everything that has been written about her, learned about her from acquaintances and her children, and having read *The Interpretation of Dreams* and other works by Freud many times, I feel qualified to speculate on what she meant by "...so many ideas that it entirely changed my life."

Most obvious in *The Interpretation of Dreams* is the enterprise of self-observation. Because unconscious activity is revealed to consciousness via dreams, the interpretation of dreams is a path to self-understanding; Freud called it the *via regis,* the royal road to the unconscious. Leone had embarked on a quest for self-understanding with Freud as her guide.

Not only Leone thought highly of *The Interpretation of Dreams;* Freud himself said it represented "the insight of a lifetime". Leone's adolescent apprehension agrees with that of the distinguished psychoanalyst Erik Erikson, who said the significance of this work was the discovery of the *unconscious,* or more properly the recognition of the importance of the unconscious. Freud said that conscious mental activity is a tiny part of what goes on in a human brain: *The unconscious is the larger circle which includes within itself the smaller circle of the conscious; everything conscious has its preliminary step in the unconscious, whereas the unconscious may stop with this step and still claim full value as a psychic activity. Properly speaking, the unconscious is the real psychic; its inner nature is just as unknown to us as the reality of the external world, and it is just as imperfectly reported to us through the data of consciousness as is the external world through the indications of our sensor organs.*[10] To many in the nineteenth century the idea was heretical; to scientists today, however,

Freud would seem, in the immortal words of Basil Fawlty, "a master of the bleedin' obvious." Of course our nervous systems are running all kinds of processes without our giving them conscious thought: respiration, digestion, homeostasis; and the thoughts and perceptions of the moment, those of which are conscious, are in the same brain that processed all our thoughts and perceptions in the past, obviously a much larger quantity. The unconscious is all these things and imponderably more.

Freud was a neurologist before he was a psychologist. In his time the study of brain-damaged patients indicated that regions of the brain had specialized functions. Two hundred years before Freud the "science" of phrenology made fanciful maps of cerebral functions. A hundred years after Freud science has correlated numerous behaviours with specific areas of the brain.

As an MD-psychoanalyst, Leone followed progress in neurology. For example, in a letter to her Viennese friends dated 27/9/75: *Papa had a 5-minute stroke at 71 - apparently in the substantia nigra - where Parkinsons is located. He then developed stiffness in the joints, etc. - not much tremor - but it was heartbreaking to observe.*

Eric Kandel, winner of the 2000 Nobel Prize in Physiology or Medicine, elaborates examples of brain/behaviour correlates and relates them to Freud's insights in his latest (2012) book, *The Age of Insight: the quest to Understand the Unconscious in Art, Mind and Brain from Vienna 1900 to the Present.* The role of the amygdala, an almond-shaped bit deep within the cerebral cortex,[11] is of special interest in understanding Leone's personality. It is involved in what Kandel calls a "theory of mind", an ability to imagine what someone else is thinking or feeling. Piaget and others have indicated that a minimum level of physical growth is necessary (ages 2-7 years) to begin acquiring this ability.

The ability to take the view of the other (without losing his own) and the corresponding social norm of logical consistency are acquired gradually, through repeated social interactions in which the child is compelled again and again to take account of the viewpoints of others. This social feedback is extremely important in developing the capacity to think about his own thinking, without which logic is impossible.[12]

A corollary is the inability of those who have amygdala-related brain damage or functional electrochemical impairment to formulate a theory of mind, to empathize. Kandel related in his books and in Charlie Rose PBS-

TV interviews many examples. Some individuals are much better than others at interpreting the facial expressions and body language of others; typically these people are less talented at mathematics, otherwise they would make formidable poker players. Leone was extremely good at mathematics; and she became a psychoanalyst, someone trained to observe and interpret others' behaviour. Was her pursuit of psychoanalysis a compensation for weakness in empathy? Or would she have made a formidable poker player?

THE HIERARCHY OF SYSTEMS in the brain that makes possible the theory of mind connects and interacts dynamically with the amygdala and parts of the prefrontal cortex. The amygdala, as we have seen, has multiple functions in emotion and orchestrates two separate emotional systems, positive and negative. The prefrontal cortex integrates the bodily reactions triggered by the amygdala and plays a large role in social cognition. Empathy, for example, is mediated by a region of the prefrontal cortex, as is triadic attention (the attention two people pay to each other and to a common task), which is required for collaborating on a shared goal.[13] An obvious example is psychoanalysis.

Leone was radically precocious. If her mother is to be believed about Leone's progress by age two, Leone's mental development occurred much earlier than normal. Accordingly she would have had a cumulative advantage throughout childhood in the formation of what Kandel calls a "theory of mind".

Neurologists have learned enough about the structure and functioning of the brain to have an appreciation of how little we know: *In some manner not yet properly understood, the mind and the brain are one thing.*[14] A century after Freud, despite enormous advances in technologies available for studying physical and chemical neurological activity, and the promise of more in the 21st century, we must still rely on reports from someone's consciousness for nearly all our information about his thought. Psychoanalysis seeks to reveal the unconscious of the analysand jointly to analyst and client. With the help of the analyst, the analysand can lift the lid of repression and shine a light into the unconscious.

The Power of the Unconscious

Encouraging women to benefit from the power of the unconscious is the theme of a book which was on the New York Times Best Seller List for 145 weeks: *Women Who Run With Wolves: Myths and Stories of the Wild Woman Archetype.* The author, Clarissa Pinkola Estés, PhD, is a Jungian psychoanalyst. She encourages the repressed modern woman to seek her atavistic she-wolf centre in order to become a fully functioning member of the pack: aggressive (able to assert herself and kill for food), yet cooperative and nurturing for the sake of her cubs and the future of her species.

When women re-surface from their naïveté, they draw with them and to themselves something unexplored. In this case the now wiser woman draws an internal masculine energy to her aid. In Jungian psychology, this element has been named animus; a partly mortal, partly instinctual, partly cultural element of a woman's psyche that shows up in fairy tales and in dream symbols as her son, husband, stranger and/or lover - possibly threatening, depending on her psychic circumstances of the moment. This psychic figure is particularly valuable because it is invested with qualities which are traditionally bred out of women, aggression being one of those most common.

And two paragraphs later,

The stronger and more vast the animus (think of animus as a bridge) the more able, easily and with style the woman manifests her ideas and her creative work in the outer world in a concrete way.[15]

Estés draws from ethnobiology and is a poet: she uses folk tales to demonstrate the common themes from women's collective unconscious; while the effect is attractive as literature, the message is not as clear as it is in the writing of her intellectual ancestor, Carl Jung.

In the middle of her life Leone changed direction. She abandoned the pathology laboratory, its microscopes, tissue samples and precision, for the vague and messy material of psychoanalysis. There were no training analysts in Stockholm where she lived with her husband. She travelled to Zürich, where she heard lectures from Carl Jung, began a training analysis and work in a hospital. Soon, however, in 1935, she returned to Stockholm, to undertake qualification for a Swedish medical licence, which she obtained in 1937. Eventually the flight of qualified psychoanalysts from Europe provided Leone with the opportunity of training in Stockholm. Did Leone cast off the fetters of conventional female repression (as Estés counsels) in mid-life, having been influenced by Jung, or had she already at age fourteen, on reading Freud, sought strength and insight from her unconscious, from self-analysis?

Outstanding artists before Freud sought inspiration from deep within - via dreams, meditation, religious ecstasy and the effects of drugs and alcohol on the self-censor. The list of artists seeking to benefit from psychoanalysis includes Thomas Mann,[16] Gustav Mahler,[17] George Gershwin,[18] Salvador Dali,[19] Jackson Pollock,[20] Hedy Lamarr, [21]Marilyn Monroe,[22] Oscar Levant, Marlon Brando, Stephen Spielberg, Woody Allen, Gene Wilder[23] and many others.

Leone knew she was different. Her capacity for learning was incomparably greater than that of her classmates. Her special aptitudes for mathematics and drawing were more characteristic of boys than girls. She wondered why.

[1] Fine, Reuben, *Narcissism, the Self, and Society*, Columbia University Press, New York, 1986, p. 128
[2] From Leone's six page autobiography in Hellstedt, Leone McGregor, *Women Physicians of the World: autobiographies of medical pioneers,* Hemisphere Pubishing Corporation, Washington & London, p. 201.
[3] Red Deer News, June 4, 1919, p. 8.
[4] *History of Nobleford,* publication of the local historical society, p.21.
[5] ibid, p.22.
[6] Henderson's Calgary City telephone directories, 1911-1916.
[7] op cit, Hellstedt, Leone McGregor, *Women Physicians of the World*, p. 200.
[8] Leone had studied German in high school, since this was the language of science at that time. Therefore she might have read the original *Die Traumdeutung,* Franz Deuticke, Leipzig & Vienna, 1900, 375 pages, or the revised and expanded second (1909, 389 pages) or third (1911, 418 pages) edition. More likely, she read the first translation into English by A.A. Brill, *The Interpretation of Dreams,* George Allen & Co., New York, The MacMillan Co., 1913, 510 pages.
[9] op cit, Hellstdt, Leone McGregor, *Women Physicians of the World.*
[10] Freud, S., translated by A.A. Brill, *The Interpretation of Dreams; The Illustrated Edition,* Sterling the Common Publishing Co. Inc., New York, 2010, p. 526 .
[11] Kandel, Eric R., *In Search of Memory: the Emergence of a New Science of Mind,* W.W. Norton & Company, New York, 2006, p. 45.

[12] Phillips, John L., *The Origins of Intellect: Piaget's Theory,* W.H. Freeman and Company, San Francisco, 1969, p. 63.

[13] Kandel, Eric R., *The Age of Insight: the Quest to Understand the Unconscious in Art, Mind and Brain from Vienna 1900 to the Present,* Random House, New York, 2012, p. 420.

[14] Plotkin, Henry, *The Imagined World Made Real: Towards a Natural Science of Culture*, Rutgers University Press, New Jersey, 2003, p. 163.

[15] Estés, Clarissa Pinkola, *Women Who Run With Wolves: Myths and Stories of the Wild Woman Archetype,* Ballantine Books, New York, 1992, p. 62.

[16] "Many of Freud's followers were more optimistic than their master. In the journal *Die Psychoanalytische Bewegung,* in 1929 the first paper was by Thomas Mann, then considered perhaps the world's leading literary figure." Fine, Reuben, *A History of Psychoanalysis,* Columbia University Press, New York, 1979, p. 451.

[17] Kennedy, Michael, *The Master Musicians: Mahler,* J.M. Dent & Sons, London, 1974, 2nd ed. 1990, pp 3, 71, 99; and Mahler, Alma, *Gustav Mahler: Memories and Letters,* translated by Basil Creighton, edited by Donald Mitchell and Knud Martner, The Viking Press, 1946, 4th edition Cardinal 1990, pages xvi, 175, 335.

[18] Roazen, Paul, *How Freud Worked: First-Hand Accounts of Patients,* Jason Aronson Inc., Northvale, New Jersey, 1995, p. 186.

[19] Dali, Salvador, *The Secret Life of Salvador Dali,* translated by Haakon M. Chevalier, originally published by the Dial Press in 1942, Dover Publications, New York, 1993 pp. 18, 167, 392, 397.

[20] Gedo, John E., *Portraits of the Artist,* The Guilford Press, New York, 1983, p. 24; and Hagman, George, *The Artist's Mind: a Psychoanalytic Perspective on Creativity, Modern Art and Modern Artists,* Routledge, New York, 2010, pp. 128-141.

[21] Rhodes, Richard, *Hedy's Folly: the Life and Breakthrough Inventions of Hedy Lamarr, the Most Beautiful Woman in the World,* Doubleday, Random House Inc., New York, 2011, p. 203.

[22] The Jewish and creative themes of psychoanalysis have naturally been expressed in Hollywood: *The other analysts I met in the Los Angeles area, with one exception, had no personal contact with Freud. But they provided me with valuable background material and helped forward my understanding of psychoanalysis. Some of these analysts were strikingly successful in terms of their having dealt with famous Hollywood producers, directors, actors and actresses. For example, psychoanalysis became so successful in America that Marilyn Monroe's New York analyst (she also had one in Los Angeles, and both were in regular contact with Anna Freud) was chosen by Jacqueline Kennedy as well.* op cit, Roazen, Paul, *How Freud Worked: First Hand Accounts of Patients,* p. 37.

[23] Wilder, Gene, *Kiss Me Like A Stranger: My Search For Love And Art,* St. Martins Press, New York, 2005, pp. 3, 23, 72, 134-136.

Chapter 6   1915-1919   The Road to Medical School

The August 14, 1914 edition of an Edmonton daily newspaper published the Alberta Department of Education list of those *...eligible for entrance to the first year of the University of Alberta in the faculty of arts.* Among the 35 names was "Leone McGregor, Calgary". At the age of 14 Leone could have gone to university; but her parents considered her too young, and anyway they hadn't the money for tuition and board.

Normal School and Teaching

Swalwell   Calgary   Camrose

Most of the girls in my Grade XII class went immediately to Normal School. I also applied but the principal, Dr. Coffin, simply laughed and said I was much too young. This was a terrible blow for there was nothing else in Calgary to do and I did not have money enough to go to Edmonton to the University. I went back to Grade XII and repeated until Xmas in order to put in time. A Scottish history teacher, Mr. Beveridge, who liked to play tennis with me, asked me why I had not applied for a University scholarship. It was the first time I had heard the word, and I had no idea how to go about the matter. It gave me some impetus, however, because in December, 1915 I presented myself once again to Dr. Coffin at the Normal School and asked him if I could begin in January, although I would not be 16 until January 19 and the minimum age was 18. He made an exception and I am eternally grateful to him. I loved Normal School. The teachers were excellent. I was in the class with the B.A.s and the Grade XIIs and had the good luck to sit behind my friend Mary Simons. It was a most inspiring six months. I worked hard, enjoyed my classmates, learned to dance and was assigned my first research thesis, "Children's Playgrounds". No one had ever taught me how to do a thesis, but as my parents had more or less lived in the Calgary Public Library I felt very much at home there and found out how to use it. This was the beginning of my interest in play as therapy for children. It was a completely new field to me and I read with fascination. The practice teaching was difficult, but interesting and as I have a natural pedagogic tendency, I had no

trouble. When the results came out at the end of the term, "I", the youngest, was at the top of the list. I was very surprised but this plus Mary's advice led me to apply for a school in the country near Swalwell and I was accepted, as I remember for $100 a month. Then first did I tell my parents. I was only 16 and they were shocked to death. Mama refused to consider the matter but Papa gave in and said I might try and that if I didn't like it, I should come home immediately and neither of them would criticize me. Then he took me downtown and bought me a trunk and a suitcase.

I was soon on the train to my first school, very frightened but brave and longing to be independent. I was met by a young, newly married couple who took me to live with them in their farm house about two miles from Simcoe School. Their house had one living room, a kitchen and two tiny bedrooms with a curtain over each door. They must have been as embarrassed as I was, if not more, but they needed the money. There was exactly enough room for a single bed, a chair and table with pitcher and wash basin in my room. I opened the window and went to bed feeling terribly lonely. The frogs croaked in a pond nearby and I thought they made a terrible noise. Suddenly the family cat, which I had not known existed, leaped through the window and landed directly on my chest. I screamed from fright. The next morning the neighbours' children came past and drove me to school. During those first weeks, it was Papa's attitude which gave me courage and helped me to endure the trials of teaching at 16 in a country school with 12 children of all ages, one of whom older and taller than I. I was terrified of this boy who simply sat and stared at me instead of doing his lessons. Neither did I know how to busy the children who were not having a lesson. I wrote in great alarm to two friends. One, a law student, sent me his country school time table which I immediately adopted and my life was saved. The other, a girl, wrote, "Just keep a stiff upper lip and all will be well." Those first two months seemed a lifetime to me.

In the meantime my landlady became pregnant and asked me to find another place to live.[1] This was very fortunate because a charming young American couple, both University graduates, invited me to live with them and gave me a horse and buggy or a riding horse, whichever I preferred. They had a big ranch with lots of cattle and they enjoyed life. Mrs. Claypool was only 26 but I regarded her as a middle-aged woman. She was a graduate in domestic science and I learned by observation many things which have been of use to me all my life. They had interesting friends who came for weekends and we often drove off to barn dances around the country.

I soon had the school children in good training and became very fond of them. In the middle of the term a letter came from Mama to tell me that Percy Broad had been killed in Belgium. She was very shocked and I was too. It was my first contact with death since my little brother had died. It was difficult to teach in those days. I told the children about it and they were sympathetic and helpful. At the end of the term, the inspector came and awarded us the first prize in Alberta for physical education. I had drilled them so that each child was able to conduct the class in Ling gymnastics. In addition the school received the first prize for general efficiency, and I was very happy. We celebrated the last day of the term by making fudge on the big heater in the middle of the room. Each child had arrived with sugar, cream, butter and nuts and we had a wonderful party.

I rode home to Claypool's having many barbed wire gates to open and a deep creek to ford, but feeling as if I had done a good job.

Perhaps Leone's father had not been doing a good job. At the age of 45, he was no longer a clerk at S G Freeze & Co. in Calgary. Leone indicated above that in the summer of 1916 the family had moved from Calgary to Red Deer. Papa was probably again working in the grocery department of Brumpton & Gaetz Limited, a department store. The first independent confirmation of Leone's recollection of the summer of 1916 is an article in the Red Deer News of December 27, 1916, in which Phyllis McGregor is listed as a player in the Methodist Sunday School Christmas Entertainment "Dialogue".

Mama and Phyllis were active in church - related programs. Phyllis excelled in athletics. She stood sixth in a high school grade IX class of 42 in the October, 1917 examinations.[2]

The Red Deer News of December 26, 1917 reported on page 8, "Miss Leone McGregor, who is teaching at Calgary, is home for the holidays".

Neither in her autobiography nor in her extensive correspondence does Leone have anything to say about her family in 1918-1919. In her album there is a studio photo of Leone labelled "Vancouver 1919" and this item in the Red Deer News of June 4, 1919: *Mr. McGregor, who has been residing at the coast for some time, returned last week to take charge of the grocery department of Brumpton & Gaetz. His many friends in Red Deer will be glad to see him back again.*

And at the bottom of a full page Brumpton & Gaetz advertisement in the Red Deer News, August 20, 1919: *OUR GROCERY DEPARTMENT has been thoroughly reorganized in the last few months and is being most efficiently administered by Mr. McGregor and Mr. Anthony, who will be delighted to meet their old friends and supply their needs in this department. Nothing but the best will find its way into our stock.*

Phyllis was a member of the Choral Society[3] and her musical talent found a limited outlet in the December 9 and 10, 1919 performances of the Lyric Theatre production of *A Nautical Knot: A Bright and Tuneful Operetta in Two Acts Presented by Thirty Young People of Red Deer.* Phyllis was in the chorus, listed on the playbill as one of the twelve "Townsfolk and Artists". A leading role, "Nance, a Fair Damsel", was played by Miss E. Brumpton. Piano accompaniment was provided by Miss L. Brumpton.

Leone's portrayal of her father as a political conservative and entrepreneur has thus far been questionable. It receives a fatal blow from this item in the Red Deer News, April 21, 1920, page 3:

RETAIL STORES EMPLOYEES ORGANIZE AT RED DEER

The retail stores employees formed an association at the Orange Hall on Friday night, and some 60 to 70 have given in their names as members of the organization. Mr. C. H. Snell was chosen President, Mr. M. McGregor secretary-treasurer and Messrs. Hamley, D.A. Smith, Harrison, Miss McIntyre, Mrs. Best, Miss McBride, executive. The half-holiday was also discussed, and a committee appointed to meet the Retail Merchants' Association.

At this time there was political turmoil in Canada following the success of the Bolshevik Revolution in Russia. The Winnipeg General Strike of May and June, 1919, which idled 30,000 workers including the public service, police and firemen, shut down the city and saw riots in the streets, had raised fears of a communist revolution in Canada. One of the labour leaders charged with sedition was a former Methodist minister, J. S. Wordsworth. In 1921 he was elected to Parliament in North Winnipeg and held that seat until 1942. The Canadian Communist Party was formed secretly in 1921, but its activities were monitored from the beginning by the Royal Canadian Mounted Police.

Mama was a supervisor of the Red Deer Girls Athletic Club,[4] an examiner for the Toronto Conservatory of Music[5] and active in Methodist church affairs: *Mrs. M. McGregor was the delegate from the Methodist church W.M.S. to the annual convention at Edmonton last week.* Red Deer News, June 16, 1920, page one.

Mama and Papa were leaders in the fight against the Demon Rum.[6] Alberta had a form of Prohibition, beginning in 1915. Public sale of alcohol was allowed only for medicinal, sacramental, manufacturing and scientific purposes. The public sale of 2.5% beer and the consumption of liquor at home was legal. Because use for medicinal purposes was allowed, pharmacists became de facto liquor vendors with a limit of 40 ounces per customer, per sale. There were loopholes, home distilleries and bootlegging.
   After police raided the sophisticated basement operation, with its 70 gallons of fine, finished Scotch whisky in March, 1923, its maker, George Packwood remarked: "Yes, I voted for prohibition and I'd vote for it again. I went broke farming." [7]

Nevertheless the McGregors fought the opponents of Prohibition. The Red Deer News of August 4, 1920 carried this headline on page three:

PROHIBITION CAMPAIGN

Officers and Committees are Elected

The Prohibition campaign committee met in the schoolroom of the Methodist church on Tuesday evening, July 27, to receive the reports of the striking committee. The following were present. Revs. Brown, Armstrong and Metcalf, Mr. and Mrs. J.J. Gaetz, Mr. and Mrs. McGregor, ... et al.

...

It was agreed to devote the open collection of the evening union service held in the Chautauqua tent to the Prohibition Campaign.

Mama was named to the Women's Committee and Papa to the Propaganda Committee and the Enumerating Committee. A province-wide plebiscite November 5, 1923 ended Prohibition in Alberta.

It is likely that Leone did not drink when she was a student. She could not afford it, for a start, while she was saving from a modest income for university tuition and board. In later life, in Europe and Sweden, where drinking was an integral part of civilized discourse, Leone did imbibe. She was never drunk, but her correspondence occasionally indicated regret for the quantity of champagne she had taken the previous evening.

Leone's holiday visits to her family were reported by the Red Deer News.[8]

My parents were now living in Red Deer and I took the train to them. While there on holiday, Dr. Coffin, the principal of the Calgary Normal School telephoned and asked me to supply in the practice school. This was a great honour as I was still only 16 and I was happy to accept. During this year I was fortunate in being allowed to live at the William Carsons' because I had gone to Normal School with Evelyn and the family liked me. Mrs. Carson was very interested in all social problems and would nowadays be called a liberal. She was opposed to war and dared to say so publicly which was very brave at that time. She was a remarkable, broad-minded woman and our dinner table conversations were always stimulating. Her second son was already at the front. I fell in love with her eldest son, Harold, but he was also soon off to the war in the air force. Very soon there were almost no boys in my age group in Calgary. I was sure life was passing me by; so I registered for an evening course in motor mechanics at the technical school with the vague hope that it might eventually help me to get to the front as an

ambulance driver. It was hard work to teach all day and go to school every evening, but I learned a lot that I was to need in the future.[9]

The following year I taught in the Camrose Practice School. It was no happy year. I had not lived in a small town since early childhood and had no idea as to what was expected of me, for instance, that it was absolutely necessary to go to church on Sundays and that as a Protestant, I ought not to associate with Catholics. I had made friends with the nicest girl in town, Lucia Adam, soon after my arrival in Camrose. The family was Belgian and Catholic and they spoke French at home. The mother was warm-hearted and hospitable. Their house was large and there were several cars. Three sons were still away at the war. There was a charming summer cottage in the country. Lucia was pretty, an expert shot, a good hockey player and full of fun. When her brothers returned from the war within a few months, I and another teacher, Jessie Chrystal, were naturally invited to meet them. The next Sunday morning during church hours, I was seen out walking with one of the brothers. Some Protestant reported this to the Principal of the Normal School and he sent for me and scolded me. It was a lesson for my life. I avoided all possible such criticism from that day and saved my money, but I was very unhappy in Camrose.

———————————————

Because Alberta's young men were away at war, schoolteachers were scarce. One room schools had been scattered over the thinly populated Canadian prairies to provide grades one through nine for the exploding population of immigrants and their children. Although underage and without any financial support from her parents, Leone was given the opportunity to earn and save enough for university tuition and board, and she seized it.

Leone's plans were influenced by her wish for a secure lifetime profession, by her confidence in her scholastic ability, especially in mathematics, and by several environmental factors. Her choice of medicine would not have been possible a generation earlier, or indeed in Alberta and in her circumstances, even one year earlier.

59

Alberta was just the place for an intelligent, energetic and ambitious woman. In Edmonton in 1912: Annie May Jackson became the first female police officer in Canada. In Edmonton in 1916: Emily Murphy became the first woman to be appointed a magistrate in the British Empire; and the Alberta Equal Suffrage Act gave women "absolute equality" with men in provincial and municipal affairs. In 1916 women could vote and run for office in all Alberta-based elections. Not until 1918 would the Canada Elections Act grant women over 21 the right to vote in federal elections. Even later, in 1920, women in the USA were enfranchised by the 19th Amendment to the Constitution.

Leone had seen Dr. Rosamund Leacock and Dr. Evelyn Windsor in Calgary. *From that moment on, I knew it was possible to be a young, beautiful, and clever woman and even to have men patients.*[10] Female physicians were rare, but not altogether absent from Canadian medicine. The first to receive a licence was Jenny Trout, a graduate of the Women's Medical College of Pennsylvania, registered with the College of Physicians and Surgeons of Ontario May 13, 1875.[11] Before the turn of the century some wives of clergymen, notably Methodists, took medical training in order to bolster their husbands' missions in China and India. The University of Toronto began accepting women as medical students in 1906.

In Alberta there were few women physicians. Dr. Elizabeth Scott Matheson was recognized by the government in 1901 as a district health officer along the North Saskatchewan River downstream from Edmonton, although the College of Physicians and Surgeons did not grant her a licence. No matter, she was too busy with hundreds of patients and her husband's mission to be concerned.[12]

The bounds of propriety were narrow in the first two decades of the century. Physicians must look at naked people; the idea of ladies viewing naked men was abhorrent. Social pressure guided early women doctors into gynaecology, radiology, anaesthesiology, pathology, teaching and research.

One of the ladies Leone had seen in Calgary, Dr. Frances Evelyn Windsor, in 1916 became the first woman to join the Canadian Medical Corps - with the aid of R.B. Bennett, MP, who was said to be infatuated with her. Dr. Windsor worked as an anaesthetist in England until her marriage to Edward Leacock (brother of Stephen Leacock, the Canadian economist and humourist), also a captain in British service, eventuated in a pregnancy.

Since pregnancy was not on the list of causes for medical discharge, Dr. Windsor Leacock had to take advantage of a mild case of pleurisy for this purpose. A few years after returning to Canada Dr. Windsor Leacock became Medical Superintendent of the Gleichen, Alberta, Blackfoot Indian Reserve. It was a relatively senior position for a woman at the time. And the Blackfoot men were said to be happier having a woman examining their women. Dr. Windsor Leacock was at Gleichen for 20 years.

It would be easy to idolize Dr. Rosamund Leacock - from the Calgary Herald of July 4, 1917:

Lady Motorist Makes a Record Run from Banff

Driving from Banff to Calgary in a Ford Runabout on two and a half gallons of gasoline in exactly four hours and ten minutes, Dr. Rosamund Leacock of this city believes that she has established the record run for the trip from this summer resort. There was one stop in Cochrane which took ten minutes, and allowing for this the journey was covered in four hours. Dr. Leacock, in company with Miss M. Muir of the Herald, left Banff at 2:45 p.m. and reached Calgary at 6:55 p.m. The road was in excellent condition and the young ladies drove for a record all the way.

And from the Calgary Herald of September 17, 1919:

Guests at Military Ball and Their Gowns
Dr. Rosamund Leacock, pink taffeta and chiffon ....

Prominent among early female doctors in Canada was Montreal's Maude Abbott. She was an outstanding scholar while an undergraduate at McGill University, but the McGill medical school would not admit her. She grudgingly studied medicine at Bishop's, and after initial rejection by Montreal hospitals and subsequent public outcry, was able to intern in Montreal. After three years abroad, studying and doing research, notably in Vienna, the world's centre for medical science in the 1890s, Dr. Abbott returned to Montreal and set up a medical practice treating women and children. Her brilliance and energy, however, led her into additional work as the curator of the McGill Medical Museum (1899) and further research.[13]

Maude Abbott received international recognition as the organizer and permanent secretary of the International Association of Medical Museums and as the author of the section on congenital heart disease in the most authoritative medical textbook of the day, *A System of Medicine* (American title, *Osler's Modern Medicine,* sixth edition, 1907), edited by Dr. William Osler since its first publication in 1892. Of Osler's 104 authors in the sixth edition, Dr. Maude Abbott was the only woman.[14]

William Osler figured prominently in Leone's education. He was born in southern Ontario and educated at the University of Toronto and McGill. At age 25 (in 1874) he became "Baby Professor" at the McGill Faculty of Medicine. He spent vacations in Berlin, Vienna and London studying medical techniques. He learned German, the language of advanced medicine at that time. Osler's outstanding energy and ability resulted in appointment as Professor of Theory and Practice of Medicine at the new and well-endowed Johns Hopkins University Medical School. In 1888 this was considered the most desirable medical appointment in North America.

William Osler was legendary among physicians and veterinarians for his powers of observation, insights and teaching ability. The study of his bedside manner and examination technique was the purpose of pilgrimages by students and physicians from around the world. Osler's motto was *Aequanimitas;* his conviction that a physician should be good-humoured but at the same time evince calm, authority and control, and that only men could bring this off, was widely shared by his contemporaries, and not only physicians. Female physicians, he said, could not gain the trust of men, women or children in the same way men could. He praised Maude Abbott's article on congenital heart disease as being the best thing written on the topic in English, and very likely the best in any language; but he believed that women's role in medicine should be confined to the subordinate one of nursing, or in "staff" functions like research or administration.

Extracurricular activities at the University of Alberta Faculty of Medicine included an Osler Club. Leone McGregor was its secretary. In this connection one can't help but notice Leone's fondness for her male teachers in high school and her esteem for Dr. Pope of the medical school faculty, whose description resonates with William Osler's. Leone's *Green and Gold* graduation photo caption says, "She worships the Pope", yet Dr. Pope declined to recommend her for a postgraduate fellowship, averring that he would not presume to direct a woman into a career in medicine.

In 1910 Maude Abbott became a Lecturer in Pathology at McGill, but it was 1917 before females were admitted to first year medicine at McGill.

Leone had difficulty deciding between architecture and medicine. In a letter written to a Viennese colleague in 1968, she recalled how she had spent the last two weeks before the application deadline agonizing over this decision. In other letters and in her autobiography, however, her direction into medicine seems firm. As a child she was intrigued by unsolved medical conditions, especially the curious sensations of cold in the left arm and hand of her sister Phyllis. At age 14 she read Freud's *The Interpretation of Dreams* and said that it changed her way of thinking forever. Psychosomatic illness is an important topic in this book. Impairment of limb functioning in the absence of organic cause was common among women, the term for the conversion of mental conflicts into physical symptoms , "conversion hysteria' or just "hysteria" having been derived from the ancients' idea of a wandering womb as a cause of illness.

In the period from the onset of the Great War until her application to medical school in 1919, Alberta/Canada/the western world was centrally concerned with medical problems: casualties from the war and the worldwide influenza epidemic. Women were breaking into the medical profession. In the light of such powerful contemporary influences, it seems that Leone was destined to be a physician.

Leone was affected by the fact that only two of the 24 students in her high school graduating class were boys; the rest had gone to fight for the British Empire in the Great War. Today it is difficult to imagine how deeply Albertans of that time were involved in the war. **Ten per cent of Alberta's total population** of 470,000, 2/3 of whom were farmers, enlisted in WW1 - 48,885 men and women, not including the many who enlisted in British units. Alberta provided 21 infantry battalions, four mounted regiments, three artillery brigades and a field ambulance unit. Of the 39,752 Albertans who fought in the Canadian Expeditionary Force in 1914-1918, 6,140 were killed.

When Leone was admitted to the first MD class in 1919, most of her ~120 fellow students were WW1 veterans. Three of the beginning students in this class were women.

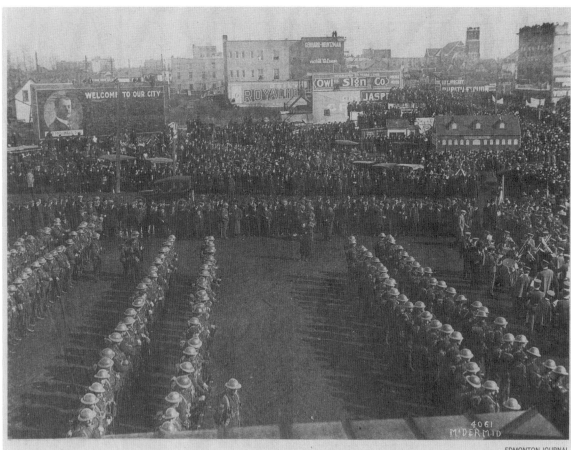

A local parade welcomes home Edmonton soldiers returning from the First World War on March 22, 1919.

March 22, 1919: soldiers welcomed home

DEB DITTRICK
Edmonton Journal

On this sunny spring day, 30,000 Edmontonians — half of the city's population — lined the streets of downtown to welcome home the 49th Battalion from the First World War.

Mayor Joseph Clarke declared this day a civic holiday so every citizen could take part in welcoming the heroes. The soldiers were travelling aboard two trains that had left Halifax five days earlier. The journey across the High Level Bridge came to an end at the Canadian Pacific Station on Jasper Avenue and 109th Street

Lt.-Gov. Dr. Robert G. Brett and Premier Charles Stewart were among the dignitaries greeting the troops. The soldiers then marched in battle order in a parade that ended at the legislature building.

Of the 4,050 men who served in the battalion, 977 were killed and another 2,282 were wounded.

From the Edmonton Journal, March 22, 2012

---

[1]   The Census of Canada and the Acme Historical Society disagree on Leone's residence in 1916, probably because the census was taken while Leone was still with the first couple. From the 1916 Census of Canada: *Leone McGregor, single age 16, home in 1916 Bow River Enumeration District 23, Bow River, Alberta, r29, t24, merid4, section?, LJD 2792, west of the Red Deer River, including the Village of Carbon, Occupation school teaching. Other household members Sheldon Brown 25 and Lesaie (Leslie?) Brown 21, Leone the lodger. All household members Methodist.* From *Acme Memories,* Acme Historical Society, 1979, p. 364: *Leone McGregor taught Simcoe School for two years 1914-1916* (sic). *She boarded with*

Mrs. Austin Claypool and rode the two and one-half miles to school. When the Kneehill Creek was in flood and impassable she stayed with Mrs. Charlie Wyndham.

[2] Red Deer News, November 21, 1917, p. 1.

[3] Red Deer News, March 2, 1921, p. 2.

[4] Red Deer News, January 14, 1920, p. 1.

[5] Red deer News, August 11, 1920, p. 1.

[6] *At the W.C.T.U. meeting, Friday, Mrs. McGregor will give a report of the Calgary convention.* Red Deer News, December 29, 1920, p. 1.

[7] Kaufman, Bill, *Calgary Sun,* February 3, 2012.

[8] December 29, 1920, p.1; March 30, 1921, p. 10.

[9] Leone drove from Minnesota through northern Ontario to Boston in 1929, probably in a Model T Ford. Another motoring adventure which would have certainly called for mechanical expertise - maintenance and possibly repair of her 1929 LaSalle Cabriolet - was a three month tour (in 1934 with two girl friends from Alberta) from Stockholm across Europe to Sicily, from Palermo to Tunis by boat, across North Africa on dusty desert roads, back to Spain by boat, a tour of the French Riviera, then by road back to Stockholm, still in her trusty V8 LaSalle.

[10] From Leone's six page autobiography in Hellstedt, Leone McGregor editor, *Women Physicians of the World*, p. 201.

[11] Hacker, Carlotta, *The Indomitable Lady Doctors,* Clark Irwin & Company Limited, Toronto, 1982, pp. 38-5.

[12] ibid, pp. 122-123.

[13] ibid, pp. 149-166.

[14] Bliss, Michael, *William Osler: A Life in Medicine,* Oxford University Press, New York, 1999, pp. 347-348.

Chapter 7   1919 - 1925   Medical School

University of Alberta   M.D.

I discovered that several people of my age, mostly teachers, were planning to start university in Edmonton in the fall of 1919. I was saving all I could of my salary so I sent in my application too. I studied the university calendar for weeks trying to decide what faculty to enrol in. My best subject had been mathematics so I considered architecture very seriously but as I knew of no woman architect I was afraid I might not be able to earn my living with such training. I discussed with my parents the various possibilities and when I told Mama I was leaning toward medicine she said, "But, my dear, it takes six whole years. Isn't that too long for you?" Anyone else I talked to said, "Why start medicine? You'll be married in a couple of years." As for myself, I only knew that I wanted to have a profession which I could enjoy pursuing all my life. It never entered my head that I might not marry. I had always been romantically in love with some boy or some man teacher and I couldn't imagine life otherwise. There had always been some nice boy pursuing me. Mama had gone to Normal School and had been a teacher. She had always been popular with men and she married, so I expected to follow in her footsteps. Finally, and it seemed as if by chance, I thought of my cousin Isabella Teskey Ayer who was studying medicine at Toronto and of Doctors Windsor and Leacock, the two beautiful women I had often seen practising medicine successfully in Calgary. I knew that they had both been very successful and had been happy in their work. Anyway I signed up for medicine.

That summer, in order to get still more money in my savings account, I taught for six weeks near Rocky Mountain House and lived with a Danish family in a log house which seemed to me to be full of bed bugs. They swept them up each morning in the dust pan. I survived, but it was trying. The four legs of my bed were placed in tin cans filled with coal-oil. The first week I looked as if I had measles, but I gradually became immune.

LEONE   VANCOUVER 1919

At last, at the end of August in 1919 I arrived in Edmonton and settled down in my room in that lovely girls' dormitory called Pembina Hall. It seemed like paradise to me after living in other people's homes all my life. I'll never forget the wonderful feeling of independence I experienced that day. Several Calgary schoolmates were on the same corridor and everyone was excited and friendly. That first day I paid my board and room and tuition fees for the year. There was little left over, but I was thrilled with all the possibilities.

This first year class in medicine turned out to be composed of over 100 boys, mostly returned soldiers and a very few girls. These ex-soldiers were of course about four or five years older than I. They had been in Europe or elsewhere for almost five years and they were gay and grown up. I felt very shy but admired them very much. The ones I immediately selected as the most attractive were Jack Fyfe, Gordon Douglas and Johnny Walker and time proved that they were all unusually gifted. We were soon all listening to Dr. Lehmann's chemistry lectures, conducted in the European manner with a foreign accent and great fatherly charm. I was so terrified by the gaps in my knowledge of chemistry that I got to work immediately. The boys in the class were all very nice to me and so were all the teachers. There was no favouritism for boys whatever. All the teachers in the preclinical years were excellent. We were the first students in the world to see the effect of insulin (in a rabbit) demonstrated in the classroom by Dr. Collip and about a year later parathyroid which he also isolated.

I enjoyed the dormitory and social life immensely. There was always an informal dinner in the boys' dormitory every Saturday night from seven to 10 p.m. These evenings were very exciting because they gave us an opportunity to meet boys from other faculties. After these dances we usually had small eating parties in the dormitory. It was the custom for parents from out of town to send us roast chicken, turkey or even game. We had electric toasters where we made wonderful hot sandwiches. Some girls always had percolators and could make coffee.

I had a dark brown tailored suit with a large beaver collar, a brown winter coat, a more or less sailor type of brown velour hat, several skirts and georgette blouses (through which the lace on our camisoles was clearly visible), some pastel pullovers which I knitted myself, one blue georgette evening dress and a pretty grey silk afternoon dress, the latter two having been made for me by a very good dressmaker in Red Deer. Ready made dresses had not yet arrived in Alberta.

All university girls went bareheaded to lectures or to the tuck shop no matter how cold the weather. This was a new custom and indicated that we were university girls. I had very thick naturally curly hair which I steamed every morning and I did not mind the winter cold on my head. The boys we were "going with" were usually from Athabasca Hall. They called for us at 10 p.m. A little maid in a black dress and white apron knocked on our doors and announced them. We descended and departed with them for the tuck shop. There a cup of coffee plus a bun cost us 10 cents each. A few really rich boys and girls ordered ham and eggs for 25 cents. We girls had always to sign out in a book and to sign in again before eleven. This seemed to us very cruel. Another injustice which provoked us all was that the maids in Athabasca made the boys' beds and tidied their rooms while we had to do our own, although we paid the same price as the boys. Neither did the boys have to sign in and out. Their dormitories were never locked. Ours always were. Boys could smoke in their rooms and girls could not. I did not smoke and did not even want to, but I found the principle unjust. I presume all these rules have long ago disappeared but I well remember what a nuisance they were and how we envied the girls who lived in town with their parents. The Dean of Women, who ruled with a rod of iron and lived in Pembina, was Miss Florence Dodd. She was from the east and determined to make us all observe eastern customs. She did not approve of even one goodnight kiss, so there were spotlights trained on all the outer doors. Neither did she think it correct if a boy took a girl's arm as was the custom when out walking.

I was actually terribly busy with my courses. Breakfast was at 7:30, lectures began every day at 8:00 and continued until 5:00 or 6:00 even on Saturdays. I had to do my laundry on Sundays instead of being able to sleep in as I longed to do and as most of my friends could because they sent their laundry home. All the girls I knew were studying in other faculties and had a good deal of spare time. I had almost no spending money so I never once went to a movie while at university. I saw a few theatre plays as there was a good stock company and also some operettas when I was invited by my boy friends, but most of the students in those days had very little money so these luxuries were rare.

Nevertheless, as I look back on those years in Pembina, I still think of them as very close to paradise, despite Miss Dodd and her rules and the shortage of spending money.

I had learned to play hockey in Camrose but the other girls who played at the university were better skaters than I so I had to be goalie which I detested and was not particularly good at. However, I made the team. Then I was chosen to be in the year play which the medical students put on and we had great fun during the preparations and the final evening, despite the fact that I have no talent as an actress. However, Gordon Douglas from my class and Douglas Emery from the third year were also in the play and I liked them so much that it all seemed like a grand adventure. I went to the first big formal university dance with Roland Michener who was graduating in law. He was handsome and charming and the Rhodes scholar-to-be, so I was very thrilled.[1] I was invited to all the dances that first year, my program was always full far ahead and I was doing splendidly in my courses. The professors were all wonderful to me and I was very, very happy.

When the Xmas examination results came out in the newspapers I was the most surprised person in the world to see my name listed first in almost all the courses. From that time on I never worried any more about whether I could study or not.

The next summer I was able to get a summer school not far from Camrose, where I lived with a very simple Norwegian family and nearly died of loneliness. In the middle of the summer I had my tonsils out for the second time in my life. I remember coming out of the anaesthetic in that little hospital and hearing my own voice repeating like a child, "Mama, Mama, Mama". I came back to Edmonton two weeks late in the term in order to have more money to put me through the second year. I didn't have any spending money at all nor any new clothes and I couldn't even buy myself a chocolate bar at the tuck shop. However, I was happy. The clothes problem for girls had not really arrived at this epoch. As I remember it, the first ready-made dress I saw was about 1921. Some of the arts girls had spent the summer motoring in the States and had bought ready-made there. We others were lost in admiration. Wilda Blow wrote me from the states to send her $25 and she would buy me a beaded georgette dress. I did not dare spend so much money on clothes so I did not send it. Until then we had all worn skirts and blouses or knitted sweaters in pretty colours. In my second year I took my grey silk dress, dyed the skirt black, put a black velvet border around the bottom of it and a black sequin bodice at the top. The dying was done in an aluminium pot on a little electric stove in my room in the dormitory. We all thought the result was marvellous. Several of the arts girls were getting very clever at sewing and were able to make pretty dresses during the summer months and even during the term. I many times wished I had taken arts first before beginning medicine, partly because I always wanted to know more about history, philosophy and art, and partly because I would have liked to have more free time to get to know students in other faculties. For instance, it seemed to me that the most interesting boys were often in the faculty of law.

That second summer I taught school near Hanna. The family I lived with was very nice and I was not at all lonely. I was lent a beautiful riding horse and a pharmacy student from Edmonton, working in a drug store in Hanna, took me to all the country barn dances. The local doctor lent him one of his cars on such occasions and we felt very elegant. To the doctor's and my horror, it turned out that although of good family, he was asocial and had forged his father's name on cheques and was not allowed to return to the university. He was the first such person I had ever encountered.

The third year in medicine was undoubtedly the most stimulating, but it was also sad as the most mature and cultivated boys in our class were to leave for McGill or Toronto in the fall. The Dominion Government had decided that all returned soldiers would be allowed to graduate a year ahead of the rest of us. The soldiers were to be transferred for their fourth and fifth years for condensed courses in the eastern universities. It did not seem fair to us who were left over that we should be made to study one year longer for the same exam. They had, of course, lost many years at the war but our fate was also hard to accept. My best beau this year was Johnny Walker. He had been on Dr. Ower's staff on the west front and could run a bacteriology laboratory all by himself. He plugged me up on bacteriology which was a blessing for me and brought me into the Johnnie Ower family where I have stayed ever since. I did not like either bacteriology or pathology but the Owers were such nice people. It was in this third year that Dr. Pope came as professor in medicine and really inspired us all. I thought he was the most fascinating and cultivated man I had ever seen and I more or less worshipped him as well as his subject. I read Osler's medicine from cover to cover in order to be able to answer his questions. No other professor in my six years of medicine made such an impression on me. His lectures were masterpieces, his clinic was well run and he was not only a physician, he was also a good amateur portrait painter and, as far as I could observe, led a happy and interesting life. During the second and third years of medicine we had one other outstanding teacher, a Mr. McPhee in normal and abnormal psychology. He had been analyzed in Scotland and was well acquainted with psychoanalytic theories. From then on I knew that I would always be interested in mental problems. However, I had no idea of how to go about getting to be a psychiatrist. He did not tell us and perhaps did not know that Ernest Jones was practising in Toronto at this time. I worked hard at these courses and got the top marks as well as in internal medicine. I spent not a second considering what field I would eventually land in, because my major current problem was always how I could earn enough money for the next year.

That next summer I taught at Hythe in the Grande Prairie district. I almost died of loneliness, and it was only Johnnie's letters which kept me going. I saved every cent and returned to Edmonton as usual three weeks late in order to have more money. I had slept all summer in the parlor of a large log house which faced a valley with an Indian encampment. I could look out from my bed through the open door, down to the camp fires and dancing which went on each evening. The Indians sold us moose meat and berries and my landlady paid by sewing for them on her sewing machine. Rats were numerous and gnawed at the feet of my wooden bed posts, nearly frightening me to death. The mosquitoes were frightful. I slept under netting and rode to school with newspapers inside my stockings and a big straw hat with mosquito netting tied around my neck. I thought the summer would never end.

The fourth, fifth and sixth years of medicine were very tame after the loss of our interesting classmates. However, we worked away and I presume acquired the usual amount of knowledge. At least my exam results seemed to show this. The greatest change in my life during these years was that I was selected with a few other girls in 1922 to be trained to be a Chautauqua director. This was most fortunate because I turned out to be very successful at getting contracts signed and even at getting lost contracts and at being in charge of Chautauqua programs. The work was strenuous but fascinating and as most of the circuit was manned by Americans, I came in contact with a new group of young people whom I liked very much. My circuit supervisor was Mary Chorn from Kansas City and she is still one of my closest friends. My life has been very much influenced by Mary. We have not been able to meet very often but we still seem to have the same ideas about almost everything. She has kept on with her education and has held important posts all her life. She and her brilliant husband, Leland Hazard, are now both to be given doctorates at the University of Pittsburgh. I have always regarded her as a rock of safety and understanding. These American girls on Chautauqua and the boys (the tent men) were less shy and more enterprising than Canadians and we had a lot to learn from them. The other blessing for me was that the pay was good and I at last had almost enough money saved each summer to carry me through the winter. I did not need to teach any more and this new work gave me a chance to travel a little and to see at least the west of Canada. I learned to introduce speakers and to talk freely to large audiences, which has been a great help to me.

It seems incredible to look back and realize that I had no plans and no idea what I would do after graduation. I apparently expected a job to drop upon me from heaven and it did. About one month before graduation Dr. Ower asked me if I would take an internship in pathology as soon as I had my degree. I was delighted to have a job although I knew little pathology and was not at all interested in the subject. I had, however, the gumption to know that it was the best possible basis for other medical fields. In addition, my boy friend, Bill Genereux had still one year to go to graduation and I was glad to be in Edmonton near him. I worked very hard all that spring to get good final marks and to my joy succeeded. I won the Moshier Memorial Medal and the Fellowship in Internal Medicine. Dr. Ower asked me whether Mama was coming to my graduation and when I said no, he insisted upon advancing me the money to invite her. Phyllis had just graduated from the Calgary General Hospital without any of us present. She had won the gold medal but none of us could afford to be there which was very sad.[2] Mama came for my graduation and lived in the dormitory with me. The graduation day was beautiful. I had made a lovely white dress trimmed with lace and I had bobbed my hair. The bathtub was filled with wonderful roses from Johnnie and Bill and

73

others, and I was very happy. The graduation ceremony was elegant and dignified. Mama was proud of me and I hoped Dr. Pope was also.

LEONE   GRADUATION IN MEDICINE   EDMONTON 1925

In regard to my hair: I had not been allowed to bob it before graduation. At that time hospitals did not allow nurses or girl medical students to have short hair as it was regarded as unhygienic. Most of the arts students already had short hair so I was one of the very last to be bobbed. I had natural curls, so it was no trouble and I regarded the bobbing as evidence of freedom from stupid rules. I even felt tempted to smoke "a" cigarette but decided that was expensive in the long run and a bit dumb. So I didn't even try smoking until five years later, on the boat on my way to Europe.

During that winter Phyllis became engaged to Charles Bouck, one of the leading surgeons in Calgary and they decided to be married in Edmonton so that I could be present. I helped her buy her trousseau while she stayed in the dormitory with me. After the wedding dinner in the Macdonald Hotel they left for the coast on their honeymoon. It seems incredible but I don't think either one of us ever discussed the fact of marriage for even a minute. He was a splendid, gifted, well-to-do man and they were in love and that was all there was to the matter.

I soon learned a lot of pathology and was able to run the surgical diagnostic part really efficiently. I don't think any woman M.D. in Alberta had done an autopsy at that time and I didn't even want to. Instead I started reading the medical literature in the library to see what else I could learn. I hit upon Florence Sabin's work with blood cells only by chance and found it fascinating I fixed up a warm cupboard with a microscope inside and began to study living cells. I needed help and direction but there was none available. However, one day I brought Dr. Shaner down to look at my living cells taking up dyes and he encouraged me. I realized, however, that I needed graduate training and I was beginning to think that I would prefer research work to the care of patients. I asked Dr. Pope one day what he thought about a career in medicine for a woman and mentioned that I wanted to get started in some field where I could continue all my life even after marriage. He was kind and charming but of another generation so he told me that he did not think a career after marriage was worth the struggle. This remark by the professor I had most admired was a great disappointment to me. Until then I had believed every word he uttered. I still admired him but I felt disoriented. Within a few months, however, I got up my courage and asked for an appointment with Dr. Tory, the president of the university. I explained to him that I had to have more training in order to do research. He was perfectly understanding and promised to think the matter over. About two weeks later I received a telegram from Dr. Bell, the head of the department of pathology at the University of Minnesota, offering me a three-year fellowship at 75, 100 and 125 dollars a month. I had never heard of Dr. Bell nor of the University of Minnesota but I accepted at once. It turned out that Dr. Tory had given the valedictory address for the graduate school in Minneapolis and had asked the Dean if he had anything to offer me.

---

[1] Roland Michener was born in Lacombe, Alberta in April, 1900. He played with the Oxford Ice Hockey Club and earned two degrees from Oxford. He practised law in Toronto, was elected to the provincial legislature and became a member of Parliament, but is remembered best for his majestic impartiality and good taste in his roles as Speaker of the House, Ambassador to India and Governor General of Canada (1967-1974). In retirement he remained Chancellor of Queen's University and lived in Toronto, where Leone visited him (and his wife), still friends 50 years after their date.

[2] To be unable to attend their daughter's graduation in medicine, Papa and Mama must have been poor indeed. They lived in Red Deer, equidistant from Edmonton and Calgary, less than 100 miles from the University of Alberta, with good rail service available in 1925. Return bus fare from Red Deer to Edmonton or Calgary today is about $50, or two hours' worth of today's wages for a senior grocery clerk, a job equivalent to that of Leone's father.

Chapter 8   1919 - 1925   How Medical School Was Realized

To improve the golden moment of opportunity, and catch the good that is within our reach, is the great art of life.   Samuel Johnson

Leone's career was time/place specific: it could not have happened at any other time in any other place. A girl from a family whose sole provider was a grocery clerk could not have become a medical doctor at any time prior to the first quarter of the 20th century.

Alberta and the times provided the opportunity. Leone's intelligence, determination and hard work enabled her to seize it. This chapter concerns the societal developments that made a medical career for a woman possible, and the circumstances which determined Leone's career path.

Medicine Becomes a Legitimate Profession for a Woman

Leone's Alberta of 1919 was a European civilization superimposed on the sparse and faded landscape of native Indian cultures.

In 2029, or perhaps a year or two later, most Canadians will be of Asian origin, demographers tell us. But in 1919 there was little of the Asian in Leone's intellectual heritage. Students at the University of Alberta learned that for the arts and sciences they were about to acquire they should thank the ancient Babylonians, Greeks, Romans, the monks of the Dark Ages, the Europeans of the Renaissance and their descendants in North America. The art of medicine in this multi-millennial tradition was generally the preserve of men.

From time to time notable women practitioners of medicine appeared. Circa 2700 BC in Egypt there was a female physician, Merit Ptah.[1] In classical Greece, 4th century BC, Agnodice cut her hair and dressed in men's clothing in order to attend classes for would-be physicians. When discovered, she was saved from punishment by influential women, who were later instrumental in having the law changed so that women could practise medicine.

The medical profession, according to the elder Pliny, was a Greek art which was seldom practised by Romans. Julius Caesar, by giving civic rights to physicians from Egypt and Hellenic lands, while he raised the status of the medical calling, also stimulated the immigration of foreign practitioners. The rank and fortune attained by the court physicians of the early Caesars, Antonius Musa, the Stertinii, and others, which almost rivalled the medical successes of our own day, seemed to offer a splendid prize. Yet the profession was generally in low repute. It was long recruited from the ranks of old slaves, and men of the meanest callings. Carpenters and smiths and undertakers flocked into it, often with only a training of six months. ...we are bound to conclude that the profession held a very different place in public esteem from that which it enjoys and deserves in our own time.²

During Europe's "Dark Ages", 500 - 1000 AD, literacy was largely confined to the clergy.   To distinguish themselves from ordinary folk and thus help render plausibility to their status as arbiters of grace - with the power to hear confession of sins and grant absolution - priests were supposed to abjure the worldly.   Bodily concerns such as injuries, disease and healing were distractions from communication with God.   The net effect was to leave the healing arts largely in the hands of the least educated and least ethical.

The prejudice against the practice of physic as incompatible with the purity of an ecclesiastic was widespread and long-lived, as chronicled in the canons of numerous councils prohibiting it.   ... but it was not always so. In 998 Theodatus, a monk of Corvey, received the bishopric of Prague from Otho III, as a reward for curing Boleslas I, Duke of Bohemia, of paralysis, by means of a bath of wine, herbs, spices, and three living black puppies four weeks old ....³

The movement toward worldly priests was arrested during the papacy of Gregory VII through his vigorous enforcement of sacerdotal celibacy. In 1074 he began pressing bishops to abandon their wives, concubines and children on pain of dismissal and even excommunication.

The priest must be a man set apart from his fellows, consecrated to the one holy purpose, reverenced by the world as being superior to human passions and frailties, devoted, soul and body, to the interests of the Church, and distracted by no temporal cares and anxieties....⁴

Many clergy rebelled, claiming that celibacy was unnatural ("If God had wanted me to be celibate, He wouldn't have ...."). Gregory was overthrown, but after a few years of turmoil his successors were able to convince the hierarchy of the benefits of sacerdotal celibacy. Among these was restraint of the tendency of bishops to pass their property along to their sons instead of the church. Here and there in Christendom clergy continued to violate the canons against marriage and licentiousness despite advice from Rome that sacraments administered by these priests were invalid, and despite some excommunications of priests and bishops.[5]

During the Middle Ages in Europe there were sporadic initiatives by religious orders to train their members in the healing arts. Some nunneries were known for their care of the sick. A midwifery guild survived in Germany for centuries.

Arabs and Jews brought medical knowledge to southern Italy. Notably, translations of Arabic into Latin in 1070-1095 at the monastery of Monte Cassino facilitated improved practice of medicine in the city of Salerno, 120 km to the south. Salernitan medicine was disseminated throughout Europe by the *Trotula,* a set of treatises in Latin, compiled around 1200, on *The Conditions of Women, Treatments for Women* and *Women's Cosmetics.* Partly because "Trota" and its diminutive, "Trotula", are women's names, it has been maintained that the editor/contributing author of the *Trotula* was a woman.[6] Recent scholarship has not succeeded in answering the question of who edited the *Trotula,* but many of its eclectic sources have been identified.[7]

The limits of oral tradition in medicine are obvious. The sheer quantity of knowledge, even in the middle ages, implied recording and conveyance in writing. In Christian society literacy was uncommon outside the priesthood. Among the Jews, however, the advantages of reading and writing were highly valued.

Until the fifteenth century the Jews were perhaps the most literate of peoples, despite all the disabilities which they endured. Nearly every male child could read and write and the proportion of truly educated was commendable. Boys began their study of the Bible almost as soon as they could speak and then went forward, without a qualm, into the intricacies of the Talmud. All types studied, even business men and labourers, for study was a mode of worship. Every fairly cultured home had its library of Hebrew books; certainly a Bible and a "Shas", a set of the Talmud.[8]

The advantages that Jewish scholarship had for medicine in Europe were attenuated by social restrictions imposed by Catholic majorities. Jews were confined to certain occupations and often could not own property outside the ghetto.[9] Social contact was discouraged. Excesses occurred: the persecution of Jews in England in the century before the expulsion in 1290 could have been a model for Nazi Germany - confiscation of property, prejudicial treatment by courts, mass executions.[10]

After 1290 medicine in England suffered by the absence of Jews and their scholarship. A small colony persisted in Oxford for a few generations, but significant repopulation of Anglo-Jewry would not occur until after 1655 when it became legal. In the meantime there was secret tolerance for Jewish physicians imported by royalty and nobility, desperate to procure superior medical skill for treatment of their loved ones. In 1586 a Portugese Jew, Roderigo Lopez, was appointed chief physician to Queen Elizabeth, who was reported to be overly interested in, and tolerant of Jews.[11]

English Jews inevitably came under pressure to convert to Christianity. Many did not, however, preferring exile to apostasy. Some of those who left found pockets of tolerance in Europe, where the benefits of learning were wanted. Of course the Catholic aversion to usury and the prohibition against Jews participating in the mainstream feudal system of agriculture and guilds had resulted in Jewish expertise and power in finance.[12] Sovereigns and aristocrats relied on Jewish financiers for their wars and capital projects. Less well known but significant for their survival was the presence of Jews where scholarship was important: besides medicine, the art/science of navigation made possible the lucrative spice trade, the plundering of the Americas, and it conferred advantage in war. Ships of all nations carried Jewish navigators, interpreters and doctors.

In the series of discoveries by which the sixteenth century is marked, Jews took a not inconsiderable part. A Jew, Jehuda Cresques, was the director of Prince Henry the Navigator's School of Navigation at Sagres. Another, Abraham Zacuto, compiled the astronomical tables that were constantly used by Columbus, and which, on one occasion, saved the life of the navigator. Columbus also on his first voyage to America had a Jew as an interpreter. The money that enabled him to make his first voyage was lent by a Jew, Luis de Santangel. His map was drawn by Ribes, the "Map Jew"; his ship's doctor was Bernal, also a Jew; his superintendent, Rodrigo

Sanchez the Jew. The Jewish sailor Rodrigo de Triana was the first to see land, and the interpreter, Luis de Torres, the first to set foot on shore.[13]

With the invention of the printing press and the spread of secular education, knowledge of medical arts became widespread and increments accumulated in libraries - that is, above and beyond oral traditions.

Female doctors were still unthinkable. Margaret Jones, a midwife and practitioner of medicine, was the first person to be executed for witchcraft in the Massachusetts Bay Colony, June 15, 1648.[14]

Replacing the Medicine Man: the Rise of Medical Science, 1800-1900

The beginning of the end of absolute male dominance in medicine was the development of science which occurred in the 18th century. When doctors began to qualify for their profession by reason of objective knowledge, and this knowledge was valid, that is it produced better results, then the ancient authority of the *medicine man/witch doctor* which was based on masculine strength and dominance, became available to the well-informed practitioner of either sex. Still, there was inertia: at about the time Leone was considering career options, the famous Canadian medical school teacher William Osler told an audience at the London (England) School of Medicine for Women that women responded to the calm authority of a distinguished man and did not trust female physicians:

...which made their aptitude for work on diseases of women and children difficult to apply. He recommended that women get good advice from experienced female doctors before going into general practice, and that they consider such alternatives as medical missions in India and institutional staff work.

Osler told the medical women that there were excellent openings for their sex in laboratory work and in studies related to scientific medicine.[15]

Recognition of the cause of disease (aetiology), is crucial to control (prevention and cure). The germ theory of illness was not held generally prior to 1800. A few *philosophers* had speculated that the phenomenon of contagion was caused by tiny animals, invisible to the naked eye, reproducing in the human body and traveling from one body to another. Nearly all *physicians* held other theories.[16]

Among the early dissidents was Alexander Gordon, a practitioner in Aberdeen, Scotland. In 1795 he published *A Treatise on the Epidemic Puerperal Fever* in which he used statistics, autopsy reports and his clinical experience to formulate a theory:

   That the cause of this disease was a specific contagion, or infection, I have unquestionable proof ... (It) was not owing to a noxious constitution of the atmosphere...for, if it had been owing to that cause, it would have seized women in a more promiscuous and indiscriminate manner. But this disease seized such women only, as were visited, or delivered, by a practitioner, or taken care of by a nurse, who had previously attended patients affected with that disease .... The infection was as readily communicated as that of the small-pox, or measles, and operated more speedily than any other infection, with which I am acquainted....It is a disagreeable declaration for me to mention, that I myself was the means of carrying the infection to a great number of women.[17]

Gordon's tactless attacks on his fellow physicians and midwives resulted in ostracism. He was driven out of Aberdeen, joined the Navy and died of tuberculosis at age 47. His entreaties for sanitation measures were ignored, as were those of isolated physicians in Europe and the United States, [18] and childbed fever continued to be epidemic.

The highest mortality rates from childbed fever were in the large general hospitals being built in major cities. In Paris and Vienna the hospitals attached to medical schools offered free childbirth care. Women unable to afford the cost of a doctor or midwife coming to their home were admitted to crowded, filthy wards where they might be placed in a bed which still contained afterbirth from the previous occupant. Professors and students commonly went from dissection of corpses to examinations or deliveries, and from one examination to another - without washing their hands. Under these conditions the incidence of puerperal fever was much higher in hospitals than in private homes. Systematic study of this phenomenon was undertaken in Vienna by the Hungarian-born physician, Ignàc Semmelweis.

In 1860 Semmelweis published his conclusions in *Der Aetiologie, der Begriff, and die Prophylexis des Kindbettfiebers.* By presenting factual results from thousands of cases and interpreting these in the light of various explanatory theories, Semmelweis was able to discard theories which did not agree with the facts, to choose a theory which best fit the facts, and to devise experiments which could confirm or deny the theory (scientific method). Through suitable experiments, notably having those physicians or midwives involved clean themselves and the patient's surroundings between deliveries, Semmelweis was able to show distinctly lower rates of childbed fever.[19]

> *In order that these measures will be observed everywhere, medical personnel must be made to swear an oath and in the official instructions given when they receive their diplomas that they will conscientiously do all that is required by these prophylactic measures. ... Instead of losing 1 patient for every 3 or 4 admitted, those who observe these measures may lose as few as 1 in 400 - certainly less than 1 in 100.*[20]

In 1860 the young English surgeon Joseph Lister (1827-1912), having spent 20 years in Edinburgh studying medicine and experimenting (with the help of his wife) on animals and patients, received admission to the Royal Society and appointment to a senior hospital post in Glasgow. The death rate following surgery in British hospitals was greater than 10%, mostly from sepsis, or "hospital disease." Amputation was particularly dangerous, and undertaken only when the patient would surely die otherwise.

> *In British hospitals the death rate following amputation fluctuated between 25% and 50%. ... The average at Edinburgh Infirmary was about 43% and at Glasgow, 39.1%, in 1865.*[21]

When a colleague referred Lister to the work of Louis Pasteur, in 1865, Lister took advantage of his upper class education, which included French language, to find in Pasteur's papers the clues to mysteries encountered in his surgical practice. Lister recognized that micro-organisms like the ones that soured milk [22] and fermented wine [23] could grow in wounds unprotected by a coating of skin; moreover, he tested and developed chemicals and methods for antisepsis. Lister and Pasteur corresponded.[24] Lister's prodigious energy [25] and long life resulted in a massive, universally recognized contribution to medical science.

Replacing the Medicine Man: Women Follow Science

The scientific revolution in medicine had the effect of destroying old ideas and creating places for new ones. Cracks appeared in ancient social structures, including the system of male privilege in medicine. A big step for women's entry into the profession was the founding of the Female Medical College of Pennsylvania in 1850. Canadian women enrolled.

The phenomenon of Florence Nightingale was timely:

But the Crimean War (1854-1856) *had one serious and beneficent consequence, the institution of nursing as a profession for trained women of a better type than Mrs. Gamp. The astonishing personal success of Florence Nightingale lay in the forcing of her modern methods of hospital management on the Crimean Army authorities, who in all else were so antiquated: they would not even make a railway for the few miles from Balaclava port to the siege lines before Sebastopol, till compelled by public at home, stirred up by the press and its first 'War Correspondents'.*

The idea of nursing as a serious profession, thus advertised by the sensations of the Crimean War, spread fast in civil life and soon made a new era in public health and medical practice. Moreover the idea of training women to professions, due to Florence Nightingale's initiative, invaded other spheres of life besides nursing. The ideals of Scott and Byron had demanded that a lady should prove her ladyhood by the beauty of idleness and by touching dependence upon her male protectors. But in the last half of Victoria's reign a very different idea began to gain ground, namely that upper and middle class women, more particularly the unmarried, should be trained to support themselves and to be of some use to the world.[26]

The power balances among nation-states were affected by differential population growth. Advances in British scientific medicine led to a doubling of its population, and consequent ability to strengthen the Empire.

This unprecedented increase, the herald of great changes in the life of our island, was not caused by immigration: the entry of cheap Irish labour which now first became a feature of our social and economic life, was counterbalanced numerically by English emigration overseas. The advance in population represented a rather larger birth-rate and a very much reduced death-rate. The survival of many more infants and the prolongation of the average life of adults marks off modern times from the past, and this great change began in the Eighteenth Century. It was due mainly to improved medical service.[27]

"May your tribe increase." Those charged with implementing this ancient salutation - kings, dictators, government ministers, archbishops, et al brought support to scientific medicine.

In 1870 a class for the medical education of women was offered at the Sorbonne, Paris.

Alexander Borodin was instrumental in founding a medical college for women in St. Petersburg in 1872. Borodin was the illegitimate son of a Georgian prince. As was the custom in feudal Russia, he was given the name of one of the prince's serfs, a man named Porfiry Borodin. When the boy showed intellectual promise and a gift for music, his mother, then married to a retired army doctor, was able to arrange for a good education in their home. Alexander learned several languages, earned a doctor of medicine degree, became a professor of biochemistry and a notable musician despite music being merely a hobby.[28] Some of his compositions are popular with symphony orchestras today: for example, from his opera *Prince Igor* the Polovtsian Dances and the refrain popularly known as *Stranger in Paradise.* Borodin's wife, a musician, was an advocate of women's rights and undoubtedly an influence in those achievements Borodin considered his most important, the education of young men and women and the founding of the School of Medicine for Women in St. Petersburg.[29] Russia led in the training of female physicians.

In Canada Jennie Trout became the first woman licensed to practise medicine - in 1875.

In 1883 the Women's Medical College affiliated with Queen's University, Kingston, Ontario. It was disbanded in 1906 when the University of Toronto medical school began admitting women.

The well-endowed and prestigious Johns Hopkins Medical College began admitting women, some Canadian, in 1893.[30]

The history of the movement for introducing women into the full practice of the medical profession is one of the most interesting of modern times. This movement has already achieved much, and far more than is often supposed.

Yet the interest lies even less in what has been so far achieved than in the opposition which has been encountered; in the nature of this opposition, in the pretexts on which it has been sustained, and in the reasonings, more or less disingenuous, by which it has claimed its justification. The history, therefore, is a record not more of fact than of opinion. And the opinions expressed have often been so grave and solid in appearance, yet proved so frivolous and empty in view of the subsequent event, that their history is not unworthy of careful consideration among that of other solemn follies of mankind.[31]

For newly minted M.D.s in 1908, miscellaneous advice was dispensed in the popular *Book on **The Physician Himself** and things that concern **His Reputation and Success*** by D. W. Cathell, M.D., ***The Twentieth Century Edition** Revised and Enlarged by the Author and His Son William T. Cathell, A.M., M.D., Baltimore, Maryland.*[32] Nowhere in these 411 pages is there an admission that the new physician might be a woman.

In the period 1800-1900 medicine in Europe and North America progressed from an art practised by men, many of whom were unqualified, to a profession which admitted only those with scientific education and ostensibly good character.   Nearly all doctors were men.   By 1900 the dominance of science in medicine, properly, had been accomplished; but equality for women would be the work of the next century.

Although the establishment of women's colleges of medicine in the second half of the nineteenth century permitted the entry of women into the profession, it also had the effect of distinguishing male from female practitioners in terms of the quality of their education. Women's schools generally had lower entrance requirements, inferior instruction and lower graduation requirements.[33]   There were female doctors, and prudish Victorian women were thankful for that, but it was generally understood that they weren't as well qualified as male doctors.

Demonstrable equality awaited coeducation. Only when men and women worked side by side with the same resources (professors, laboratories, cadavers, hospital rounds, examinations) could unequivocal comparison become possible.   Sporadic attempts at medical coeducation were made, some resulting in resignations of faculty, rebellion of students [34] and even street riots.[35] The first durable application of the idea came at the University of Zürich, where one of the Russian radical "women of the sixties",

Nadezhda Suslova, was admitted in 1864 and graduated in 1867. Following sharp questioning by skeptical faculty:

...Professor Rose congratulated her on her performance and lauded the experiment in women's education. Her thesis, said Rose, proved the aptitude of women for scientific work better than any theoretical discussion of the woman question. "Soon," he said, "we are coming to the end of slavery for women, and soon we will have the practical emancipation of women in every country and with it the right to work." It was the first medical degree awarded to a modern woman in a recognized university of high academic standards. "I am the first," wrote Suslova, "but not the last. After me will come thousands."

Word of Suslova's success sped across Europe and America.[36]

Following Zürich, medical schools in Lausanne, Berne and Paris began admitting women alongside men - with gratifying results.

A Swiss woman, Marie Heim-Vögtlin, became the first woman to practice medicine in Switzerland (1875). Moreover, she and her husband are credited with innovating a form of marriage a century ahead of its time - in which the profession of each is equally important.[37] Marie Heim-Vögtlin's story is linked to Nadezhda Suslova's more than superficially. The irreligious university student Marie was stimulated by earnest theological debates with her cousin Fritz Erismann, fell in love, and they were engaged in 1866.[38] While at the University of Zürich medical school with Nadezhda Suslova, Fritz fell under her spell and was converted to radical socialism. Fritz abandoned Marie to marry Nadezhda. He moved to St. Petersburg with her, where he lived until his death in 1915.[39] Leone enjoyed reading a biography of Marie Heim-Vögtlin and recommended it be placed in the archives of the Medical Women's International Association.[40]

Nadezhda Suslova   **Marie Heim-Vögtlin**

The spread of medical co-education in the first decade of the twentieth
century allowed women to compete on a more or less equal basis with men,
and thus to demonstrate the amenability of modern medicine to practice by
women: for example, the Universities of Vienna, Berlin, the Sorbonne,
Stockholm's Karolinska Institut and the University of Toronto. During
WW1 London medical schools began admitting women to fill the gaps left
by men gone to war, and to care for those returning. McGill University
medical school went co-ed in 1917. Harvard in 1945.[41]

The scientific revolution in medicine produced new knowledge at an
accelerated rate. Physicians were obliged to continue their educations
throughout their working lives in order to remain competent.   The power of
science was everywhere evident in new technologies - automobiles,
airplanes, electric light, telephones, weapons of war. Acceptance of new
ideas became routine. Scientists were honoured regardless of sex: Madame
Curie was awarded two Nobel prizes, in 1903 and 1911.[42] Doors were
opening and women were going through them.

Medical Science Comes to Alberta

The earliest doctors in Canada were in the service of the Hudson's Bay Company. In the 1820s in Alberta's first settlement, Fort Wedderburn (later Fort Chipewyan), Dr. William Todd was both factor and surgeon.

After the fur trade in northern Alberta came cattle ranching in southern Alberta. Many of the pioneers were from England. Some were doctors. They brought English institutions with them. Pincher Creek boasted the second polo club in America. A *Hunt Club* was established in Pincher Creek in 1883; unfortunately coyotes proved too much for the imported English foxhounds. [43]

Major population influx awaited the Canadian Pacific Railway, which reached Calgary in August, 1883.

When Calgary sought nursing assistance for its first General Hospital, Miss Birtles of Medicine Hat responded and gives many interesting reminiscenses (sic) of her pioneering there. Previous to her arrival, a small house on the Bow River had been used as a hospital with Mrs. N. Hoade in charge. The building had a door punctured by bullets and a few years previously had been used for immoral purposes. It was arranged to hold eight patients.[44]

Alberta was seen by many of Canada's distinguished physicians when the Canadian Medical Association held its annual meeting in Banff in 1889. When Alberta became a province in 1905, the University of Alberta was created by an act of the first session of its first legislative assembly. The Alberta Medical Association was formed in 1906.

When the Faculty of Medicine at the University of Alberta was founded in 1913, the profession was in its modern form. Since the revised Medical Profession Act of 1906, doctors wishing to practice in Alberta, excepting those previously registered in the North West Territories, were required to take the provincial licensing examination and apply for membership in the College of Physicians and Surgeons of Alberta (CPSA).[45] In 1912 the College asked the University of Alberta to examine candidates for practise in Alberta. The new Faculty would have to prove itself before it could graduate Doctors of Medicine. From 1913 until 1919 students pursued three year bachelor's degrees at the University of Alberta, then went to McGill or Toronto to seek MDs.

Grants from the Rockefeller Foundation enabled university president Henry Marshall Tory to start on a Medical Building and the Faculty to hire new professors. The first MD class was admitted September, 1919.

Leone Chooses Medical School

In the summer of 1919 (at nineteen years of age) I sent for the University of Alberta[46] catalog and studied the contents, looking for the professions where excellence in mathematics would be a help. Only medicine and architecture seemed suitable. I did not know of any woman architect, and as I quite clearly wanted a profession where I could earn my living all my life, I came to the conclusion that I definitely should choose medicine. I filled out two application forms, one for architecture and one for medicine, and after two weeks of hesitation sent off the latter.

We were 125 students in the first year in medicine, all but 3 being returned soldiers, who were four or five years older and far more mature than we 3 girls. From the first day, I decided to work very hard. There were dances on Saturday evenings and now and then a real formal. Between times there were walks on the campus and along the river. Despite all the romance, I concentrated so seriously that, to my utter surprise, when the Christmas term marks came out in the newspapers I had the highest marks in every subject.[47]

In 1919 two medical topics were prominent in Alberta newspapers: the contemporary influenza epidemic and the treatment of casualties of the Great War. Especially controversial was the treatment of psychological casualties. The number of these from the 1914-1918 war was unprecedented; major conflicts like the American Civil War and the Boer War had produced hardly any by comparison. Thousands of soldiers on both sides were appearing in field hospitals with no physical injury, unable to fight because of paralysis of limbs, inability to speak, see or hear commands, and exhibiting symptoms such as trembling and tachycardia (excessively rapid heart beat). One early explanation for the unprecedented number of these cases - in previous wars these men had been executed for cowardice, not sent to a safe, comfortable hospital well away from any combat zone. It soon became apparent, however, that this war and these soldiers were different.

Owing chiefly to the fact that these conditions were not fully recognized in the beginning, many cases were evacuated to England which would not otherwise have been, and the depletion of manpower in the front line from this cause became a very serious item. Some confusion was, I think, also caused by Major Mott, who showed that in soldiers killed as result of explosions without showing external wounds, minute hemorrhages and multiple cell changes in the nervous system showed the effects of concussion and that the cause of death was in the nervous system. This condition, which was really shell concussion, was very soon confused with the clinical condition which received the apt term of "shell-shock", but which on closer examination was shown to be rather a physiological or psychological condition without any organic anatomical lesions.[48]

Later in the war physicians were cautioned to avoid the use of the term "shell-shock". Recommended was "Not Yet Diagnosed - Nervous" (NYDN); thousands were thus returned to hospitals in England and eventually to Canada. Other terms used were: battle exhaustion, war neurosis, neurasthenia, hysteria. Physicians did not know enough about the phenomenon to give it a name. A further suggestion of the state of clinical psychology at the time was that the doctors involved did not have a universally recognized name for themselves: "psychiatrist" was used, but "alienist" still had currency.

The Great War was distinguished from previous wars by the participation of millions of conscripts. Professional soldiers, mercenaries and volunteers constituted the forces in earlier wars. The vast majority of the victims of war neuroses were from the ranks; officers were much less represented. Postwar analyses indicated that screening for personal or family history of mental illness or low intelligence would have been beneficial. The soldier unable to function, for whatever reason, was a danger to his comrades and a burden to the service.

The bulk of soldiers presenting a psychic disturbance have been observed to be individuals of mediocre mentality and have thus engaged, prior to their military careers in occupations requiring little skill.[49]

While Leone was at medical school thousands more veterans presented symptoms of what today is called "post-traumatic stress syndrome". Because these men were more or less unable to take care of themselves, the question of who should be responsible for their care was a leading public policy issue.

Coming as they did to me at least eight years after the armistice, they afforded an interesting opportunity of studying the persistence of post-war neuroses, and I was able to form certain conclusions as to the prolonged effects, sociological and physical, of war suffering upon the civilian soldier. At the very outset it was impossible not to be impressed by the fact that fully 80 per cent of the cases that came under survey were unskilled men of the labourer type with no trade to their hands.[50]

The lack of knowledge and logic evident in the debates among medical men would have dismayed a bright medical student. Physicians admitted that they could not reliably distinguish between cowardice/malingering and mental illness. "Predisposition" was generally agreed to be by far the biggest cause of war neuroses. The army's failure to reject those with "predispositions" was adduced as a reason for the government to pension psychiatric casualties; at the same time those opposed to paying drew attention to the fact that the "predispositions" in question were largely those which would have anyway prevented the individuals concerned from earning a good income in the normal course of civilian life. The same facts, perhaps tenuous, even when accepted by both sides, resulted in contrary views regarding the responsibility of the individual.

Despite her abiding interest in psychology, Leone steered a course through medical school away from psychiatry and into the harder medical sciences. By so doing she was able to demonstrate her academic superiority in no uncertain terms. Articles in *The Gateway*, the campus newspaper, indicated that she was the unquestioned leader of her class.

LEONE UNIVERSITY OF ALBERTA EDMONTON 1923

University of Alberta Hockey Team 1921, Leone in goal

Leone recalled her time in Alberta's Faculty of Medicine:

Our teachers were phenomenal. Dr. Egerton Pope, the professor of internal medicine, was my ideal as a person, a doctor, and a chief.[51] The leader in abnormal psychology, Mr. McPhee, gave brilliant lectures. The anatomy courses were also a joy for me, partly because of my ability to reproduce in drawing anything I saw.

Finally when we graduated, in 1925, my mother and Dr. Pope were in the audience. I had won the Gold Medal for the highest average percentage in all the subjects during the six years, as well as the fellowship in anatomy and the fellowship in internal medicine.

Actually, my only difficulty in my medical-school years was earning enough money to pay the high tuition and my room and board. There existed no monetary scholarships or fellowships. We always had a three-month summer holiday, and fortunately, I got a job every summer as a director with the Dominion Chautauqua Company at a very high salary.[52]

Chautauqua Summers Enabled University Winters

Chautauqua was a traveling tent show. It began as a Methodist summer school on the shore of Lake Chautauqua in New York State in 1874. Academic and religious instruction were offered at first, then uplifting lectures, then music and entertainment. Its popularity spread through the United States. Widely separated communities with populations too small to support orchestras or colleges welcomed the annual summer visit of the brown tents and the attractive young men and women of a Chautauqua troupe.

 Despite the economic hardship of the Great War, the first Chautauqua office in Canada was established in Calgary, in 1917. Personnel from Portland and Calgary sold and organized tours beginning in Portland that year. The first Canadian Chautauqua contract was signed in Lethbridge. Lectures and entertainments with Canadian emphasis were programmed. By year-end more than 100 towns in western Canada had experienced Chautauqua.

Chautauqua directors earned $40 - $45 per week, double the average income of men and triple the average income of women.[53] Nola Crites, the first Chautauqua manager in Canada, thought they were worth it.

Canadian Chautauquas, chiefly through Nola's advocacy, adopted a policy of hiring mainly women for the responsible position of superintendent. She preferred having women act in this capacity as she found them more conscientious, more persistent in rebooking, and more determined to do well.

...From the sheltered and carefully ordered life from a middle or upper middle class home, the type from which most of these young women came, a girl was quite suddenly precipitated into a position which required her to undertake many unusual and unconventional responsibilities.

...going alone into strange cities, towns or isolated settlements, introducing herself to strange men, men who were committee members and upstanding community leaders. She would also have to influence these men to act in such a way as to make the forthcoming Chautauqua a success. She had to cope with many responsibilities herself to ensure the same end, and finally she had to persuade the townspeople to sign a contract for the succeeding year.

...In an era of protective and restrictive parental authority, these women were permitted to step into a business territory which, with a few outstanding exceptions, had hitherto been untrod by feminine feet. They could do so because of the image of propriety and extreme respectability that Chautauqua projected. As times advanced in the twenties and the flapper flourished, this type of work requiring self-confidence and entailing high adventure, constituted a perfect avenue for the self expression young women were demanding.

The selection of these women was made very carefully. Nola considered such attributes as general attitude and interest; ability in scholastic and other fields, with evidence of initiative, self confidence and skill in communication; and appearance, manners and deportment. These young women within a few weeks would be representing Dominion/Canadian Chautauquas to thousands of people. In addition to being capable and resourceful, they had to be dignified and gracious, and their behaviour had to be socially acceptable at all times. Nola received help from the deans of women at the various universities.[54]

Tent man Hugh Saunderson and director Leone McGregor, 1924

en Chautauqua 1924

Leone enjoyed show biz during her Chautauqua summers.

Extracurricular

Notwithstanding her resolve to concentrate on studies, and her evident success academically, Leone's undergraduate activities were wide-ranging.

As a schoolteacher in the summers of 1920-21-22 and as a Chautauqua director in the summers of 1923 and 1924, she was able to meet her need to earn enough for tuition, board and room. During school terms she played goal on the university women's hockey team, she was secretary of the Faculty of Medicine's Osler Society and in her last year was vice-president of the Students' Union.

Leone pioneered as the first woman in the University of Alberta Faculty of Medicine. Her outstanding success in competition with men reinforced the case for women doctors. Today 60% of the Faculty's students are women.

---

[1] Pomeroy, Sarah B., *Women's History and Ancient History*, University of North Carolina Press, Chapel Hill, NC, 1991.

[2] Dill, Samuel, *Roman Society from Nero to Marcus Aurelius*, MacMillan & Company, Ltd., London, 1905, p.92.

[3] Lea, Henry Charles, *History of Sacerdotal Celibacy in the Christian Church*, University Books Inc., USA, revised fourth edition, 1966 (first edition published in Philadelphia, 1867), pages 184-185.

[4] ibid, p. 182.

[5] ibid. p. 189, p. 428.

[6] O'Dowd, Michael J., *The History of Medications for Women: Materia medica woman*, The Parthenon Publishing Group, New York and London, 2001, p. 123.

[7] *The Trotula: An English Translation of the Medieval Compendium of Women's Medicine*, edited and translated by Monica H. Green, University of Pennsylvania Press, Philadelphia, 2001.

[8] Sachar, Abraham Leon, *A History of the Jews*, Alfred A. Knopf Inc., 1930, 3rd edition 1948, p. 259.

[9] Grunwald, Max, *History of Jews In Vienna*, The Jewish Publication Society of America, Philadelphia, 1936, pages 10-12, 93, 306-311, 483-484.

[10] Hyamson, Albert M., *A History of the Jews in England, With Portraits and Maps*, published for the Jewish Historical Society of England by Chatto & Winds, London, 1908. pp. 87-97.

[11] ibid. p.134-144.

[12] Grunwald, Max, op cit pages 9-16.

[13] ibid, p. 141.

[14] Morton, Morton, *A Woman Surgeon: The Life and Work of Rosalie Slaughter Morton*, Frederick A. Stokes Company, New York, 1937, p. 23.

[15] Bliss, Michael, *William Osler: A Life in Medicine,* Oxford University Press, 1999, p. 354. In a letter to her Vienna MWIA colleagues and friends Martha and Hertha ("Dear Girls"), dated April 9, 1974, Leone regrets the difficulty being experienced in choosing a treasurer for the Medical Women's International Association: *It is no use selecting someone who lives according to the status quo. That means we will just slowly die out - which I think would be sad - and a horrible proof of the lack of trust between women which causes the men in turn to distrust us.*

[16] Nuland, Sherman B., *The Doctor's Plague: Germs, Childbed Fever, and the Strange Story of Ignàc Semmelweis,* W.W. Norton & Company, New York, 2003, p. 57-62.

[17] cited in Nuland, ibid., p. 46-47.

[18] Dormandy, Thomas, *Moments of Truth: Four Creators of Modern Medicine,* John Wiley & Sons Ltd., Chichester, England, pp.163-175.

[19] ibid, p. 194.

[20] Semmelweis, Ignaz, *The Etiology, Concept, and Prophylaxis of Childbed Fever*, Translated and Edited, with an Introduction, by K. Codell Carter, The University of Wisconsin Press, Madison, 1983, p.167.

[21] Fisher, Richard B., *Joseph Lister 1827-1912: the great surgeon who pioneered antiseptics and revolutionized 19th-century medicine,* MacDonald and Jane's, London, 1977, p.124.

[22] ibid, pp. 235-237.

[23] ibid, p.133.

[24] ibid, pl 203.

[25] ibid, Fisher. *With Mrs. Lister in almost constant attendance and assisted by almost anyone else who happened to be in the house, including the servants, he worked with single-minded intensity. Lectures had to be given and patients cared for, but otherwise his life for the next decade focused through a microscope. He began work at 7.00 and occasionally at 4.30 in the morning. At Leytonstone, on Boxing Day, 1871, Arthur Lister noted the time of an observation as 0.30 a.m. On occasion entries would be made in the Commonplace Books at intervals of from five to fifteen seconds for periods of an hour or more. Lister often remained at his microscope from early evening, immediately after dinner, until well past midnight, his wife with him to note down his observations. No one who has not peered through a microscope for three or four hours under electric light, let alone gas light, can imagine how tiring such work can be.* p. 197

[26] Trevelyan, G.M., O.M., *English Social History: a Survey of Six Centuries, Chaucer to Queen Victoria,* Longmans Green and Co., New York, 1942, p. 548-549.

[27] ibid., p. 341.

[28] *"Zu ihrer Kunst kommen dieser Musiker vielfach als Dilettanten, sozusagen nebenberuflich."* from p.362 in Bauer, Rudolf, *Das Konzert,* Deutsche-Buch Gemeinschaft, Darmstadt, 1955.

[29] *The Five: Nikolai Rimsky-Korsakov, Modest Mossorgsky, Alexander Borodin, Mily Balakirev, Cesar Cui, Tschaikowsky and the Five,* Wiki Series, Memphis, 2011, 9. 1-4 and *The My Hero Project: Alexander Borodin* on www.myhero.com.

[30] Bonner, Thomas Neville, *To the Ends of the Earth: Women's Search for Education in Medicine,* Harvard University Press, Cambridge, 1992, p.75.

[31] Jacobi, Mary Putnam, MD, *Woman's Work in America,* Holt & Co., New York, 1891

[32] F.A. Davis Company, Philadelphia, 1908, 411 pages.

[33] Bonner, Thomas Neville, *To The Ends of the Earth: Women's Search for Education in Medicine,* Harvard University Press, 1995, pp. 13, 37, 115, 121.

[34] *At Harvard, Harriet Hunt, who had been practicing medicine in Boston without formal training for a dozen years, almost gained entry to the famous medical school in 1859 before being told that "the faculty feared the students would leave Harvard and go to Yale upon the advent of a woman student."* Ibid, p.7.

[35] ibid, pp. 125-29.

[36] ibid, p. 37.

[37] *Auf der Grundlage einer grossen gegenseitigen Liebe hatten Marie und Albert Heim ihre Ehe erbaut. Beide Gatten leisteten in ihren Berufen Hervorragendes und waren der Ansicht, dass ihre verschiedene berufliche Arbeit ihnen auf geistigen Gebiet mehr gegenseitege Förderung zu geben Vermöchte als eine ganz gleiche Tätigkeit.* from Siebel, Johanna, *Das Leben von Frau Dr. Marie Heim-Vögtlin, der ersten Schweizer Ärztin 1845-1916,* Rascher & Cie., A.-G., Verlag, Zürich, Leipzig and Stuttgart, 1919, p. 115.

[38] ibid, p. 23.

[39] Müller, Verena E., *Marie Heim-Vögtlin - die erste Schweizer Ärztin (1845-1916): Ein leben zwischen Tradition und Aufbruch,* hier + jetzt, Verlag für Kultur und Geschichte GmbH, Baden, 2007, esp p. 41-48.

[40] letter of 20/7/73 to "Dear Girls" in Vienna, p. 3.

[41] More, Ellen S., *Restoring the Balance: Women Physicians and the Profession of Medicine, 1850-1995*, Harvard University Press, Cambridge, 1999, p. 232 .

[42] Curie, Eve, *Madame Curie: A Biography*, Doubleday, Doran & Company, Inc., 1937, DaCapo Press Edition 2001.

[43] Jamieson, Heber C., *Early Medicine in Alberta: The First Seventy-Five Years,* The Douglas Printing Company, Ltd., 1947, p. 37.

[44] ibid, p. 33.

[45] Lampard, Robert, MD, *Alberta's Medical History: "Young and Lusty and Full of Life"*, Robert Lampard, MD, 2008, p. 6.

[46] Leone did not have enough money to consider any school other than the University of Alberta.

[47] Hellstedt, Leone McGregor, editor, *Women Physicians of the World: autobiographies of medical pioneers,* Hemisphere Publishing Corporation, Washington, 1978, pages 201-202.

[48] Russel, Colin, *The Management of Psycho-neuroses in the Canadian Army,* Journal of Abnormal Psychology 14 No. 1-2 (April-June 1919), p. 27-33, cited in Copp, Terry and Humphries, Mark Osborne, *Combat Stress in the 20th Century: the Commonwealth Perspective,* Canadian Defence Academy Press, 2010, p.22.

[49] Dover, H., *Medical Board Work on Psychiatric Cases,* Canadian Medical Association Journal, 10, no. 6, (June 1920), p. 543-547, in Copp, Terry and Humphreys, Mark Osborne, *Combat Stress in the 20th Century: the Commonwealth Perspective,* Canadian Defence Academy Press, 2010, p.97.

[50] Coplans, Eric, *Some Observations on Neurasthenia and Shell-Shock,* Lancet, 31 October 1931, 960, from Copp, Terry and Humphreys, Mark Osborne, ibid.

[51] *Dr. Egerton L. Pope, a totally different type of person, was appointed full-time head of the department of medicine and medical director of student medical services. Also a McGill graduate, Pope took postgraduate training in London, and then practised in Winnipeg and taught at the Manitoba medical college. He was a unique character, always flawlessly dressed in a cutaway coat, pin-striped trousers and spats, an upturned stiff collar, and highly polished shoes. He carried a cane or an umbrella and wore a top hat. His own chauffeur drove him to class in a large limousine, accompanied by a small poodle dog. His manner was dignified and courtly, and he spoke with perfect diction. Artistic by nature, he painted and did needlepoint. He was also a Greek scholar and frequently quoted from mythology. He based his lectures on William Osler's 'The Principles and Practice of Medicine', first published in 1892, but personalized them with his own aphorisms.* Corbet, Elise A., *Frontiers of Medicine: A History of Medical Education and Research at the University of Alberta,* University of Alberta Press, Edmonton, 1990, pp. 32-33.

[52] ibid, Hellstedt ed., p. 202. According to the records I was able to find, Leone worked only the summers of 1923 and 1924 as a Chautauqua director. The *Red Deer News* of October 12, 1921 carried the following on page one: *Miss L. McGregor, who has been teaching near Hanna during the summer, is visiting her parents, Mr. and Mrs. M. McGregor, for a few days before resuming her studies at Alberta University.* Apparently Leone did not work as a Chautauqua director every summer of medical school, as she indicated in her six page published autobiography.

[53] Rashid, Abdul, *Seven Decades of Wage Changes,* Perspectives on Labour and Income, Census of Canada, Summer 1993, (Vol 5, No.2), Article 1, Table 1.

[54] Jameson, Sheilagh S., *Chautauqua in Canada,* Glenbow-Alberta Institute, 1979.

LEONE   AFTER GRADUATION   EDMONTON 1925

Chapter 9   1925-1929

When Leone graduated in May, 1925, her future was uncertain. Fortunately she was able to get an internship at the University of Alberta Hospital, despite the practice of the time which distinctly favoured men over women.

About one month before graduation we were told that there were no internships available anywhere in Canada. The professor of pathology, however, offered me a position that I accepted, and I thus learned the basics of practical medicine that year.[1]

Elise Corbet helped us to understand the times and the curious relationship between Leone and the professor of medicine, Dr. Edgerton Pope. Referring to an article in the University of Alberta student newspaper, *The Gateway,* of 15 May, 1925, Corbet wrote:

The first class graduated in 1925. There were eleven new M.D.s., "ten sturdy men and one enchanting woman," according to Pope. It was a momentous occasion, and no one was prouder than President Tory. The occasion was celebrated with a banquet at the Macdonald Hotel. Members of the faculty were present, of course, and many prominent members of the profession. It was an all-male affair, though, so the "enchanting woman" could not attend, even though she had won the Moshier Memorial Award as the top student of her class. Dr. Pope gave the toast to the graduates and asked that they "remain in this great dominion and help its reconstruction." [2]

Leone was the gold medalist. She had won the merit-based fellowships in anatomy and internal medicine. She was prominent in extracurricular activities and acknowledged by her classmates as their leader. The lingering dominance of the Medicine Man, however, disqualified her from being present at the traditional ceremony where these honours were conferred.

The depression was on its way in Canada, and I did not know what to do. A surprise came from heaven in the form of a telegram from the professor of pathology at the University of Minnesota in the United States, Dr. Elexis Bell, who offered me a three-year fellowship to work for my Ph.D. Although I would never have chosen pathology, I was definitely more interested in research than in taking care of patients.[3]

The U of A pathology professor was Dr. Ower. Leone was a favourite student, one of those with whom he kept in touch for many years after graduation.[4] Dr. Ower had written Leone letters of recommendation and otherwise supported her pursuit of post-graduate studies.

Leone Worshipped the (Dr.) Pope

Leone revered Dr. Pope, professor of medicine, and he recognized Leone as the best of his students. He told *The Gateway* at graduation that the first class was composed of "ten sturdy men and one enchanting woman." The caption under her graduation photo in the *Green and Gold,* the university yearbook, says that Leone "worshipped the Pope."

Leone with patient sketched by Dr. Pope in 1925

Leone, in her MWIA autobiography, 1978:
   Our teachers were phenomenal. Dr. Egerton Pope, the professor of internal medicine, was my ideal as a person, a doctor, and a chief.

... Finally, when we graduated, in 1925, my mother and Dr. Pope were in the audience. I had won the gold medal for the highest average percentage in all subjects during the six years, as well as the fellowship in anatomy and the fellowship in internal medicine. [5]

Dr. Pope declined to recommend Leone for graduate school. He said he "...would not presume to direct a woman in a career in medicine." With becoming grace, Leone simply observed that he was of another generation.

Edgerton [6] Llewellyn Pope, BA (Queen's), MD (McGill), FRCP (London), FRCP (C.), Professor of Medicine, came to the University of Alberta in 1923 from a practice in Winnipeg and a teaching post at the University of Manitoba. He admired William Osler and based his lectures on Osler's *The Principles and Practice of Medicine.*

Dr. Egerton L. Pope ... was a unique character, always flawlessly dressed in a cutaway coat, pin-striped trousers and spats, an upturned stiff collar, and highly polished shoes. He carried a cane or an umbrella and wore a top hat. His hair was well brushed and glossy (the students strongly suspected it was dyed), and he wore a pince-nez, attached by a long ribbon to his jacket. His own chauffeur drove him to class in a large limousine, accompanied by a small poodle dog. His manner was dignified and courtly, and he spoke with perfect diction. He was also a Greek scholar and frequently quoted from mythology. [7]

Dr. Pope advocated frequent examination of medical students.[8] He wanted to see high standards maintained. In his dress, comportment and work he excelled. Leone emulated Pope in her way. She was fashion conscious and meticulous about her clothes, and favoured more formal dress and dignified behaviour. Like Dr. Pope (and her mother), Leone abhorred unplanned pregnancies.

The Sexual Sterilization Act was assented to at the 1928 session of the Legislature. This was the first such Act in the British Empire. A Eugenics Board was appointed composed of one medical practitioner selected by the council of the College of Physicians and Surgeons, another by the University Senate and in addition there are two lay members. By this Act, mental defectives and mental patients, "if the danger of procreation with its attendant risk of multiplication of the evil of transmission of the disability to progeny" was evident, could be sterilized. ... The first board was composed of Dr. Edgerton L. Pope, Professor of Medicine; Professor John Malcolm MacEachran (sic), *of the Department of Philosophy; Dr. George Mason, of Calgary, and Mrs. J. W. Field, of Edmonton.*[9]

Alberta Sexual Sterilization Board, 1936
(L-R) Dr. George Mason, Mrs. Jean Field, John MacEachern, Ph.D., Dr. Egerton Pope

University of Minnesota   M.Sc.   Ph.D.

Within a few months I was on a train to Minneapolis and Dr. Bell, one of the most fortunate accidents of my life. He was about 50 years old, a brilliant researcher and teacher, very international and with no ideas that girls could not have a career. He was from Missouri and had done his graduate work in Germany. He had a marvellously organized department with many research projects all more or less dealing with kidney disease so he suggested that I join in on one of these and that I take Dr. Downey's hematology courses for a minor, thus developing my own little effort from Alberta. My diagnostic ability with surgical specimens, which I had learned from Dr. Ower, was a great help to me in the beginning. Dr. Bell showed us all his most difficult slides every day and none of the other "fellows" (we were five) had had the training I had had in Alberta. Each "fellow" had a class of medical students to teach microscopic pathology and I had no trouble there either. Dr. Bell wanted me to work out some new technique to take blood pressure in rabbits which I was able to do and I received my Masters Degree for my paper on this plus the hematology courses. Then I was put to work on my Ph.D. problem, a study of the histological changes in kidneys in health and disease, especially in essential hypertension. I slaved away for two more years under daily encouragement from Dr. Bell. The experimental efforts to produce high blood pressure in rabbits did not succeed despite many different approaches. As I look back on it, I should have had more surgical training. I needed colloidal chemistry, however, and all my extra time was spent on that. I also had to do a great many autopsies. I managed to endure this part of the work for the sake of the extra money I earned. Actually Dr. Bell had a right to the money but he always gave it to us "fellows". He was a wise and generous man and a magnificent teacher.[10]

I finally got my thesis together and submitted it. The day for the oral examination by 10 professors was set. I was not worried about my own work but I was nervous about questions in related fields. I survived the ordeal which took place in a terrible heat wave in June 1929. A few weeks later came the graduation ceremony in the stadium. I had expected this to be at least as exciting as my graduation in medicine. However, a thunderstorm came up and the President suddenly announced that all degrees were granted. The names were not even read and the crowd dispersed. I was very disappointed but received my Ph.D.[11]

In spite of the ideal working situation in the Pathology Department with such a wonderful chief and the feeling that I was learning more every day, I did not like living in Minneapolis itself. The residential districts with beautiful homes where I was now and then invited were delightful. I was continually taken out by most interesting young men and imagined myself in love with them one after another. Yet I remained a foreigner in that city. I was at home in the medical school and in the dormitory but nowhere else and I had no desire whatever to remain there longer than the length of my three-year fellowship. When it was time for me to leave I had no regrets. I did not at all realize that I would never find another Dr. Bell in the world.

I had, however, met in his department several very interesting young men who have remained my friends for life, chiefly Arthur Hertig, who became Professor at Harvard Medical School, and Charlie Slocum, internist at the Mayo Clinic. Arthur had already spent a couple of years in Peking in research with his elder brother, a Professor of Entomology at Harvard. Having seen much of Asia and of Europe he had wider interests and experiences than most of his classmates. I also found two lovely girls who have been my faithful friends all these years. Muriel Lauer was doing social studies and was the first person I had met who could talk freely about anything. She lived in the same dormitory and there we discovered another congenial soul, a Chinese girl getting her Ph.D. in botany. Muriel had run away from home to marry and was divorced. She earned her expenses by writing magazine serials. She was brilliant in every way. The family was very musical and her favourite aunt was a star at the Metropolitan. This aunt later sent for her to study music. However, Muriel returned to social studies, took her Masters degree and worked in New York until she met the man she married. We are always in letter contact with one another. Grace, the Chinese girl, was a few years older than us. She was the 13th girl in her family and had been given away by her mother to the first mission school for girls in China (Rulison Girls' School). This was not for economic reasons. The father was Post Master in Kiukiang, a city of three million, but he did not want any more girls. The head mistress, an American woman missionary, became interested in the clever child and sent her off later to Nanking University where she was one of the first four girls to graduate. She was then granted a mission fellowship and came to the States to get her Ph.D. on a study of algae. We three girls from so different environments were like sisters and will always remain so. Our discussions about life in general and for girls in particular were most exciting. Muriel believed in birth control and sterilization and did not hesitate to say so. Grace said she would never marry as no woman in China could be happy for the next hundred years. Her three Nanking University classmates had all married prominent Chinese (with Ph.D.s from the States) and their letters to her in English were read aloud to us. We were so amazed to find that these girls had exactly the same ideas as we had.

During four months in Minnesota I was invited to share an apartment with Carol Fisher, a Ph.D. in zoology from Yale. She had grown up in Cologne and was very international. We were the same age and congenial and could have very gay dinner parties with our various men friends. Unfortunately she developed an acute T.B. and had to retire to a sanitarium in the east for a couple of years.

One of my important memories from Minneapolis is the time Phyllis wrote that she was expecting her first baby. I was thrilled to death and ready to tell everyone the great news. To my surprise I found that most people were embarrassed to hear such a matter mentioned so openly.[12] This was very strange to me. However, Marilyn was born and I bought her a little white embroidery dress for $25, which was more than I could afford but I had such pleasure picking it out.

Arthur Hettig 1928
Prof Path Harvard

Minneapolis 1928

Carol Mallory
Me 1928

Grace Woo
Ph.D. in Botany
Minneapolis 1929

Some Notes Regarding Minnesota

While disillusioned with Dr. Pope, who would not recommend her for graduate school, Leone found the perfect mentor at the University of Minnesota in the person of Dr. Elexis T. Bell. He was supportive, an excellent teacher and a master of his discipline. Bell's *Text Book of Pathology* was widely used in teaching both medicine and veterinary medicine. In the seventh edition (1952, 1,008 pages) there appears a drawing done by Leone, from the *American Journal of Pathology,* **6, 1930,** p. 347 (Structure of Glomeruli).

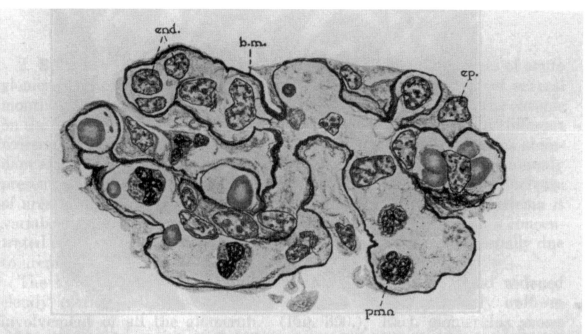

FIG. 388.—Subclinical glomerulonephritis. A few glomerular capillaries showing mild acute glomerulonephritis; from a patient dead of puerperal sepsis. The kidneys showed cloudy swelling. *b.m.*, Basement membrane; *end.*, endothelial cells; *ep.*, epithelial cell; *pmn.*, polymorphonuclear leukocyte. Drawing.

Leone admitted to a talent for drawing: *The anatomy courses were also a joy for me, partly because of my ability to reproduce in drawing anything I saw.*[13] Unfortunately I was not able to find examples of Leone's drawing. Cultivation of this talent could have been in imitation of her hero, Dr. Pope. When I visited Leone's daughter Mona in Stockholm, I hoped to see sketches or drawings by Leone, if not those done recreationally, at least some from her anatomy classes. Mona surprised me by saying that she had never seen her mother drawing.

Leone taught microscopic pathology to medical students, did her M.Sc. thesis on a new technique for taking blood pressure of rabbits and a Ph.D. on histological changes in kidneys. She wrote up work and saw it published in professional journals and cited in other text-books.[14] Her Ph.D. thesis of 1929 was cited in medical literature into the 1970s.[15]

[1] Hellstedt, Leone McGregor, *Women Physicians of the World: autobiographies of medical pioneers,* Hemisphere Publishing Corporation, Washington and London, 1978, p. 202.

[2] Corbet, Elise A., *Frontiers of Medicine: A History of Medical Education and Research at the University of Alberta,* University of Alberta Press, 1990, p. 38.

[3] op cit Hellstedt, p. 202.

[4] telephone conversation with Dr. Robert Lampard, March 14, 2011.

[5] op cit, Hellstedt, p. 202.

[6] Of the dozens of references I have seen to Dr. Pope, the authors are divided about evenly between "Edgerton" and "Egerton"... regarding the spelling of his first name it is 60/40 and pick 'em.

[7] Op cit, Corbet, Elise A., p. 33.

[8] Pope, Egerton L., *The Examination of Medical Students,* Canadian Med AJ, October, 1933, pp. 427-428.

[9] Jamieson, Heber c., *Early Medicine in Alberta,* Canadian Medical Association, Albert Division, 1947, p. 80.

[10] My brother-in-law, Ole Nielsen, did a Ph.D. in veterinary pathology at the University of Minnesota and was a beneficiary of the legacy of E.T. Bell. A standard resource in Ole's work was Bell's *Text Book of Pathology,* Lea & Febiger, Philadelphia, Seventh Edition, 1952, 1,008 pages.

[11] From the University of Minnesota Archives under "Doctors of Philosophy": *Leone McGregor M.D. '25 University of Alberta M.S. '27 University of Minnesota Major, Pathology Minor, Zoology and Bacteriology Thesis, The Finer Histology of the Normal Glomerulus and the Changes that Occur in Glomerulonephritis Major Adviser, Dr. E.T. Bell.*

[12] Reminiscent of Leone's daughter Mona's observation that Leone was much more outgoing and candid than Swedish women, who were often shocked and dismayed by Leone.

[13] op cit, Hellstedt, p. 202.

[14] Boyd, William, *A Text-Book of Pathology: An Introduction to Medicine*, Lea & Febiger, Philadelphia, 1955. Recommended for *Additional Reading* under *Glomerulonephritis* is *McGregor: Am J Path, 1929, 5, 559.*

[15] *Am J Pathol 1975 August: 80(2): 227-234,* "Age-related incidence of sclerotic glomeruli in human kidneys", C. Kaplan, B. Pasternack, H. Shah, and G. Gallo; *Can Med Assoc J. 1957 October 1; 77(7): 679-686,* Matthew J. G. Lynch, "Some Observations on Glomerular Vascular Architecture"; *Am J Pathol. 1958 August; 34(4): 685-715,* "Histologic Studies of Kidney Biopsy Specimens from Patients with Hypertension", Sheldon C. Sommer, Arnold S. Relman, and Reginald H. Smithwick..

Chapter 10   **1929 - 1931**

<u>Boston City Hospital and Harvard Medical School</u>

Dr. Bell had recommended me for a National Research Fellowship to continue my work under Dr. Mallory at the Boston City Hospital and I had been accepted. So off I went to Boston, luckily by car, motoring through Ontario where I had not been since four years of age. I found the landscape beautiful but the unpainted farm houses and barns were depressing to look at in 1929. Minnesota had been much more prosperous looking. In Toronto I drove around to look at the Normal School where Mama had studied and I took a snapshot for her. I wanted very much to visit Belleville (Papa's birthplace) and York (Mama's) but I had neither time nor money. I was amazed to see that eastern Canadians on an average were not as tall as Minnesotans or western Canadians. The drive down through New England was a dream of beauty and the suburbs of Boston were charming. The lovely big frame houses with trees, space and gardens made me feel immediately that I would never want to leave this city.

I went at once to see Dr. Mallory at the Boston City Hospital. I remember so well that I wore a large black felt hat, slightly dropping, and a mauve linen dress and felt very chic. Dr. Mallory was charming and very helpful. He had arranged for me to have a room at the Stuart Club on Fenway. The girls there were all students of some sort and very nice. However, there was no laundry and there were very few bathrooms. I had a small room on a tiny court and had to queue to get washed or to bath. Also I had to fetch a key from the matron if I wanted to be out after eight and to sign my destination. The food was good and I was so happy to be in Boston and in Dr. Mallory's well run laboratory with clever colleagues that I stood the Stuart Club until Xmas. After Xmas three of us got a furnished flat nearby. Alice was the chief secretary of a big chain store organization and "Trackie" Halpenny was an Irish M.D. studying brain tumour diagnosis with Harvey Cushing. We had a negro woman who cleaned our flat once a week. In between we had parties and kept things going very comfortably. I was the only one who could cook so I often felt a bit imposed upon but our two rooms, dinette, kitchen and bathroom were such luxury after the Stuart Club that I did not complain.

At the hospital everything was interesting. Being a woman I was not allowed to eat in the M.D. dining room, which Dr. Mallory regretted but could not help, so I had to lunch with the technicians. Most of those girls were clever but had not studied medicine as they would have been perfectly capable of doing and there was always a certain amount of envy in the air. My men colleagues were after all potential husbands so the girls did their slides first. However, the work in every other way was very agreeable. I continued my studies on kidney disease and learned a great deal from Dr. Mallory about liver conditions and pathology in general. His younger son Kenneth worked at a desk beside me and we soon became close friends. In the beginning I had tried to take a street car to the hospital in the morning but after three or four attempts I found I was not brave enough. The hospital lay in the negro district and the street car was filled with negro men who did not look friendly. I was terrified so I decided to walk to work along the Fenway boulevard, actually a beautiful winding path along the water. This was also impossible as white men in large cars drove slowly along beside me, begging me to accept a lift. It was still more terrifying. So when Kenneth and I became friends, he fetched me every morning and brought me home at five in his car. I was really relieved and thrilled. On Sundays Dr. Mallory always invited his older son Tracy with his wife Edith and Kenneth and me to dinner with wonderful food. Edith was a Ph.D. in psychology, teaching at Wellesley and a beauty as well as a fascinating woman. Kenneth and Tracy were on the quiet side so Edith and I were the life of these parties. It was a lovely atmosphere of unspoiled, modest, clever people and I was very happy there and at peace with the world.

Dr. Mallory had been somewhat skeptical about girls in medicine and had never accepted one as a "fellow" before me. However, he soon announced to all that I was the most cheerful person he had ever had in his laboratory and from then on I had every help I needed. Curiously enough, Dr. Ower had been trained by Dr. Mallory before the first world war so I had heard much about him. The other "fellows" were all interesting. Tom Spies later became famous in medicine. Arthur Hertig was finishing his medical education at Harvard and we met often. [1]

The whole year in Boston was most exhilarating and rewarding and I met many interesting people. Helen Taussig worked for a few weeks in our lab. At a party for foreign "fellows" I met Andrea Andreen, divorced from The Svedberg, the Nobel Prize winner. She was beautiful, about 43 years old and doing research in chemistry at Harvard. She was the first feminist that I had ever met. She told us all about the Swedish Match King, Kreuger, of whom none of us had ever heard. She believed him to be a genius at that date. She was violently opposed to capital punishment, which had already been abolished in Sweden. These were all new subjects for me as I paid no attention whatever to politics.

Arthur Hertig
Prof. Path Harvard
1929

By Xmas of that year Dr. Mallory asked me if I would like to work under Dr. Flexner the following year at the Rockefeller Institute in New York. Dr. Flexner had asked him to recommend an assistant and Dr. Mallory had chosen me. I was quite overwhelmed. A telegram from Dr. Flexner arrived and I went down to New York to meet him. When he asked me what I wanted to do in the future, I said "research", but that I very much wanted a year in Europe in some laboratory before settling down in the States. He understood and advised me to get my fellowship renewed for the year in Europe and then to come and see him when I returned. At that time in 1929 it really was exciting to be considered for such a post in the Rockefeller Institute. However, I had been wanting to see Europe since I was eight years old and I also wanted to work in the laboratory of either Aschoff or Fahr as they were the top pathologists in Europe in my field. I wrote to Dr. Fahr in Hamburg and was accepted. My fellowship was renewed and Kenneth Mallory was also coming a little later to Hamburg so everything seemed perfect. The month before I left Boston I was offered an assistant professorship in pathology in the University of Boston. I had been lecturing to the students there all winter and had apparently succeeded.

I left Boston on a Hamburg-American Line boat which let me off in Galway, Ireland, where I met Trackie again. We spent two weeks touring Ireland and then took a three weeks Cooks' tour of the Continent. She, however, had developed a severe depression, not having dared to break off her engagement to a man she found she did not want to marry. I knew little about depressions and was amazed to find that this otherwise jolly girl was a terrible travelling companion and could scarcely get herself out of bed before noon each day. We saw the Rhine and Paris, Lucerne, etc. but under a dreadful cloud which even the men I had picked up on a boat could not disperse.

The "Fellows"

Eppendorfer Krankenhaus, Hamburg

Finally I arrived in Hamburg in beautiful weather and was met by my Alberta friends Max and Jerry Palmer. He was the Assistant Canadian Trade Commissioner. If I had thought Boston lovely I found Hamburg still more of a paradise. Max and Jerry shared my attitude. They introduced me to all their colleagues in the foreign service and I was at parties everywhere. I was soon invited to dinner by the Friends of the U.S. in Germany where I met Erich Warburg who introduced me to all his German friends and especially to Wolfgang Rittmeister with whom I started to go around.

Jerry helped me to find a room in a very nice Jewish widow's home. One of her daughters was an M.D. and Frau Friedheim became a real mother to me for that year. [2] The Pathology Institute was a new building in the beautiful park grounds of an old pavilion hospital. Theodore Fahr was a fascinating lecturer and a father for the whole department. He could speak no English and I could only read German so we could not talk together. Nevertheless he had a cocktail party in his home for me and the German "fellows". I went to his lectures every day, studied German diligently, kept up with the laboratory routine but was unable to get going on a research project of any real account. I operated twice a week on animals with the Professor of Surgery and learned a lot but could not express myself in German and none of the senior men could talk English at that time. It took me a whole year to learn to talk despite much help from the three nicest German "fellows", Hans Heinrich, Klaus Hoffman and Fred Pfander. Fred had studied medicine for a year in England and had been engaged to a Scottish girl whom he still loved dearly. He knew by experience how difficult it is to talk fluently in a foreign language so he always spoke German to me and let me answer in English until I dared to start in German. He and Hans Heinrich used to try to make me tell them in German each morning what I had done the evening before. Thanks to them and their generosity on this point, I gradually got up my courage and could begin to talk with Germans. Fred was well educated in historical and cultural fields and he took me to see many beautiful places. I spent an unforgettable weekend with his family in Halberstadt. He is now Professor in Bremen and our families visit each other. Klaus Hoffman and his cousin, the publisher of the Hamburger Fremdenblatt,[3] drove me out on Sunday trips all over the lovely countryside around Hamburg. They were interested in all historical sites and I learned a lot from them. It was such fun to eat lunch in one country inn, drink afternoon coffee in another village and then come back to Hamburg to a splashy formal dinner in Dr. Krumbhaus's flat with interesting guests from the publishing and theatre world.[4]

I had never before been exposed to so many interesting groups of people. I had my hospital friends who took me out to the lovely coffee houses of the countryside. I had Max and Jerry who introduced me to the diplomatic crowd. I had my landlady, Frau Friedheim, who invited me to all her parties so that I met many interesting Jews. Lastly, I had Wolfgang Rittmeister who fascinated me more than any man I had ever met. He had a brother who was a psychoanalyst.[5] He lived with his father in a charming villa and I was invited to all their dinners and musical evenings as well as to Erich Warburg's who was his best friend. Wolfgang and Erich had both lived in the States for several years and we had lots of fun together except when sailing. I did not enjoy sailing because I always froze. I only went along to be with Wolfgang. He was unhappy in his work as he was supposed to take over his father's import and export business which did not interest him. He would have preferred to have studied medicine like his brother. The economic depression was in full swing in Hamburg and he saw bad times ahead. I was full of enthusiasm and optimistic and that is perhaps what drew us together. I loved Hamburg, my work and the hospital, the life and my friends and felt as if I never wanted to leave. I could not understand how anyone could be pessimistic about the future.[6]

At Xmas Wilda Blow from Calgary invited me down to Milan. She was studying to be an opera singer. We had been friends in High School and in University. She lived with an Italian family in a flat so cold that we stayed in our beds each day until noon. The rest of the day we did sightseeing. She was fluent in Italian and most of her friends were Italians. Luckily, however, one of them spoke quite good German and to my surprise I began to speak German fairly well. We spent the Xmas days in a lovely hotel in San Remo but I was happy to get back to cosy Hamburg, my hospital work and my friends.

I was beginning to realize that I would be unable to finish a scientific paper of value during my one-year fellowship. The language handicaps were too great. I could not discuss the problems with my professor or colleagues, nor could they with me. From this experience I became convinced that fellowships in a foreign country should never be for only one year as it takes a whole year to understand the different conditions and to overcome the language handicap. Nowadays this is a more minor problem, but in 1930 no one in the hospital was able to discuss scientific problems in English, nor could I in German.

After Xmas Kenneth Mallory also came to Professor Fahr and we went to lectures together, struggled with our German, watched autopsies, read Aschoff's text book and in our free hours saw a great deal of the countryside. Dr. Fahr always left the institute for the day at two o'clock and we could all leave soon after if our work was done.

In January I was invited by Andrea Andreen, whom I had met in Boston, to come to a meeting of the Swedish Women's Medical Club and to stay with her for a few days. The program was to be an interview with me about conditions for medical women in Canada. Actually I had been gone four years and in addition was a complete innocent in regard to interview technique. The women colleagues were all much older than I, very feministic and very nationalistic. I tried to answer their questions truthfully and was amazed to hear their conclusion (that Swedish medical women had a better economic and legal position than Canadian). I found the Swedish people reserved and in the three days in Stockholm I was continually perplexed over the difficulty of crossing a street. Not until I returned to Hamburg did anyone tell me that Sweden had left-hand traffic.[7]

---

[1] Arthur Hertig also became famous in medicine. His pioneering work at Harvard included a substantial contribution to development of "the pill" for birth control. Hertig is a common Ashkenazy Jewish name. Although Arthur was not prominent in synagogue or Jewish organizations, he was probably of Jewish heritage. Leone remained in contact with Arthur Hertig and managed to visit him and his family in Boston in the 1960s and 1970s.

[2] Leone does not mention the wartime fates of her Jewish "mother" Frau Friedheim and family, if indeed she knew. Leone visited her Hamburg friends occasionally until her death in 1977.

[3] The Hamburger Fremdenblatt was an innovative illustrated newspaper. It was expropriated by the Nazis in 1936 and did not survive the war.

[4] Goodbye Carnduff. Here Leone is suggesting that she was acquainted with many Jews, denizens of "the publishing and theatre world" in Hamburg and Berlin in 1930.

[5] John Rittmeister became head of the clinical department of the Berlin psychiatric organization that essentially replaced the psychoanalytically-oriented Deutsche Psychoanalytische Gesellschaft (DPG), antithetical to the Nazis largely because Freud was Jewish. A masked form of psychoanalysis continued to be practised and taught in the Deutsches Institut für Psychologische Forschung und Psychotherapie. The DPG was voluntarily disbanded in 1938, by which time nearly all its members, most of whom were Jewish, had left Germany. John Rittmeister was executed in May, 1943 for his subversive left wing politics and contact with a Russian organization.

[6] Well informed Germans were aware of the social upheaval occurring at the time. Leone's optimism and naiveté recalls themes in the popular musicals *Cabaret* and *The Sound of Music*.

[7] It is strange that someone accustomed to driving would not have noticed immediately that Swedes then drove on the left. Leone had seen this phenomenon before in Ireland.

LEONE   HAMBURG 1931

Chapter 11   1931-1932

Marriage to Folke Hellstedt

The day I returned to Hamburg was a most momentous one in my life. I was invited to the Dana Wilgresses to a big dinner. Dana was the Canadian Trade Commissioner. After the dinner, where most of the guests were dressed for a masquerade, we all went to the Cosmopolitan Club to dance. At the dinner I met Folke Hellstedt, [1] who took me home from the party and whom I married about six months later. He was an economist and director of a large iron works [2] near Hamburg which was owned by the Swedish Alfa Laval Company. To my surprise, I heard that de Laval had been a Swede [3] and that all those cream separators I had seen in my childhood were the result of one of his inventions and that the head office of de Laval was in Stockholm. Folke had lived on all the continents of the world. He spoke fluent English and was tall and handsome. I remember thinking that first evening while still at the party, "That is the type of man I want to marry." This surprised me because I had thought myself completely wrapped up in Wolfgang. I was very impressed by him and still more when I discovered that first evening that he was an atheist. My only disappointment was when I asked him where he would best like to live and he answered Stockholm. I could not imagine that anyone who had seen the whole world would still choose his home town. He had grown up in a large family and was in favour of education and professions for women. He was one of the few nonmedical admirers I had had and I found it very refreshing to be off medical subjects. I even thought it would be inspiring to learn something about political economy. Folke had a beautiful flat furnished in perfect taste with antiques and oriental rugs. He had an excellent housekeeper so I was often invited to dinner. He had a car and chauffeur so we were able to get about in great comfort.

From Xmas to June I went out with all these interesting men, medical and nonmedical. I liked so much Folke's way of knowing what he wanted and going after it. He gave me the feeling that I would be protected, helped and loved all my life, and he understood and he approved of my desire to study, work and have a job.

In June we became engaged. Like so many women and men before me, once I became engaged I suddenly realized that I was taking a very serious step. Kenneth and Wolfgang both became depressed which saddened me. Suddenly Carol Fisher arrived to visit me. She and Kenneth got on famously and soon fell in love. Curiously enough, it was a great surprise to me that he could comfort himself so quickly. He and Carol wanted to motor in Italy and as I was not to be married until September, we three drove in Kenneth's car on a month's holiday. Carol and I studied our Baedeckers and decided from day to day the destination and the sights we wanted to see. It was a marvellous trip. We got as far south as Florence before we turned back to Hamburg. There Folke was waiting for me. We were married late in September and I moved into his beautiful flat. I knew that we would be moving to Stockholm in four months so I quit my hospital work (my fellowship was over) and spent my days with Jerry Palmer at auctions. The depression had caused many families to sell their possessions. This was of course tragic but I was able to get some very lovely things we needed for our home at a very reasonable price.[4] I also took an excellent course on antique furniture and glass at the museum. Kenneth and Carol were

married in our home in Hamburg in October and left for Vienna for a year.

Leone   and   Folke   Newlyweds

On September 28, 1931, Leone and Folke were married. From her 1978 autobiography: *We married at the end of my fellowship year, and I moved into his beautiful, large flat. Four months later, he was made vice-president of Alfa Laval, and we moved to Stockholm, where his head office was. This was 1932.*[5]

Having spent nearly all of 1930 and 1931 in Hamburg, Leone had seen economic travail and political strife expressed in strikes and violence in the streets, if not directly, then certainly via the newspapers. Until the winter of 1931-1932, local and regional politics were characterized by a mixture of Communists, Social Democrats, National Socialist German Workers Party (Nationalsozialistische Deutsche Arbeiterpartei = NSDAP = Nazi party) and armed clashes in the streets between goon factions of these political parties. Riots were quelled by the police, usually after numerous serious injuries, and sometimes deaths. The turning point seems to have come in January of 1931, when the Nazis were voted a majority on the Bergedorf town council [6] and the Communists suffered a defeat in the streets at the hands of Nazis and police. During that winter of 1931-1932 unemployment reached unprecedented levels and a desperate electorate made the NSDAP the strongest party in Hamburg (April, 1932).[7] Having gained power, the Nazis used it to terrorize and remove opposition. Elected members having "un-German spirit" (Communists) were removed from the town council.

Bergedorfer Eisenwerk was one of the three major industries of Lohbrügge, a district of Bergedorf, a suburb of Hamburg. "Eisenwerk" was founded in 1859 and became a daughter of Alfa Laval via share purchases between 1907 and 1914. It was already an old company and a vital source of municipal tax revenue when victimized by a Communist-organized strike October 24, 1923. Bergedorf could ill afford the Communist mission of anarchy, the overthrow of existing governmental conditions which Marx said would, by degrees, inevitably bring socialist paradise.[8] In addition to the humiliation of defeat in WW1, the Treaty of Versailles required Germans to pay enormous reparations. The burghers of Bergedorf wished to work together to recover their economic security and their honour; they had had enough of insecurity and chaos; Hitler's appeal, aimed precisely at these sentiments, resulted in Bergedorf becoming an early NSDAP conquest.

Donald Hellstedt, Leone's son, told me that his father's promotion to Stockholm head office was at least partly due to the influence of Jacob Wallenberg of the prominent Swedish banking family. Jacob was a classmate of Folke's in Sweden's elite naval officer training school before WW1. They trained on the same sailing ship. Jacob had joined the parent Separator AB board of directors in 1931.

The Hellstedts moved to Stockholm, but Folke remained the representative of the parent company on the Bergedorfer Eisenwerk board of directors. It is not far from Hamburg to Stockholm. Both cities, however, were a world away from the sod houses of the Canadian prairie, its muddy roads over vast distances, primitive settlements and culturally infantile cities.

From the tumult of Hamburg Leone had escaped to Stockholm: quiet, orderly, with paved streets and indoor plumbing. She lived in a large and luxurious apartment and had an "excellent housekeeper". With "a husband in a top position" [9] she could afford to attend concerts and the opera. In the 1931 season the Stockholm Opera presented Jussi Björling, considered by some experts to be the best tenor ever, in *William Tell* and *The Barber of Seville*; in 1932, Leone heard Björling in *Rigoletto* and *The Elixir of Love*; in 1933, that epic voice in *La Traviata, Romeo and Juliet* and *Tosca*. By then an opera lover could have died happy. But 1933 was just the beginning of a great adventure for Leone, as it was indeed for civilization.

[1] Donald tells us that his father had been invited to a dinner at the Canadian Trade Commissioner's and had arrived a bit late. *He had been told that "a Canadian woman doctor, a Rockefeller scholar", would be among the guests. When he entered the room he saw a group of gentlemen surrounding a sofa, where apparently a lady guest was sitting and lively entertaining the group in English. So, he decided to find out what created such an interest and walked over to the sofa ...."*

[2] Bergedorfer Eisenwerk.

[3] From the official company history, *Alfa-Laval 100 Years: The Growth of a Global Enterprise,* Alfa Laval AB, 1983, we learn that: *It was 1867 when de Laval began his studies at Uppsala University and made friends with a couple of young men who started reading for the same difficult mining engineering degree at the same time. One was Oscar Lamm Jr., who came from a respected Jewish family in Stockholm that had very good connections both in Sweden and abroad.* (p. 8)

... in February, 1878, the partnership was formed. Gustaf de Laval put up his invention and Oscar Lamm 4,000 kronor - the profits of the business were to be shared equally. (p. 9)

[4] Contrast this with university when she could not afford to buy a chocolate bar at the tuck shop.

[5] Hellstedt, Leone McGregor, in *Women Physicians of the World,* editor L.M. Hellstedt, Hemisphere Publishing Corporation, Washington, 1978, p. 203. Leone and Folke moved to Stockholm in January, 1932.

[6] Denkhaus, Markus, *Der Kampf der Republikgegner in Bergedorf gegen die Werte der Weimarer Republik* in *Bergedorf in Gleichschrift: Ein Hamburger Stadtteil im Dritten Reich,* Kultur & Geschichtskontor, Hamburg, 1995, p. 18.

[7] ibid, p. 22.

[8] *Whenever a certain stage of maturity has been reached, the specific historical form is discarded and makes way for a higher one. The moment of arrival of such a crisis is disclosed by the depth and breadth attained by the contradictions and antagonisms between the distribution relations, and thus the specific historical form of their corresponding production relations, on the one hand, and the productive forces, the production powers and the development of their agencies, on the other hand. A conflict then ensues between the material development of production and its social form.* Marx, Karl, edited by F. Engels, *Capital: a Critique of Political Economy, Book III, The Process of Capitalist Production as a Whole,* Foreign Languages Publishing House, Moscow, 1959, p. 861.

[9] op cit Hellstedt, *Women Physicians of the World,* p. 203.

Folke Hellstedt circa 1910

Chapter 12   1932 - 1933

<u>Stockholm</u>

I had all my life thought it would be wonderful to have a long holiday but before those four months were up I was looking forward to getting back to my work in a hospital or laboratory in Sweden. So when we got settled in Stockholm in a still larger flat, also with a perfect maid who planned the meals and arranged everything for us, I started to look around for work.

In Germany no one questions the validity or quality of foreign medical degrees so I was quite unprepared to discover that Swedes did not accept on equality any other medical education. North American or British medical degrees were regarded on a par with a chiropractic exam. This was the greatest shock of my life and caused me much unhappiness. I was, however, allowed to do volunteer work on research projects. There was as yet no team work, and experimental pathology did not exist. The professor of pathology, Folke Henschen, was charming but kept any interesting research material for himself. This was a tremendous contrast to the method of my previous chiefs. There were no "fellows" in the pathology department. It was quite a devastating experience. After six months [1] I managed to extricate myself, moved over to the Radiumhemmet and did some work on tumours. However, I had been so accustomed to inspiring professors and cooperative colleagues that I found it dreary working away alone at a microscope on a relatively dry project. I gradually saw that during my lifetime, pathology here would never be on the level it was in the States or Germany, so I looked around for another field. I had always really wanted to be in psychiatry or psychoanalysis and had landed in pathology by accident. Now in Stockholm where pathology seemed to be such a dry, hopeless field, I decided to switch over. But first of all I wanted to know more about how I could have been so naive as to land in such a complicated life situation.

A woman married in a foreign country finds herself in a strange world and one that she has never anticipated. If her husband is 10 years older, as mine was, she is at once surrounded by his friends and their wives, all much older than herself. At the epoch in which I arrived in Sweden, so-called "family" girls rarely studied at universities. They usually married after high school. They had never been exposed to dormitory life and were on the whole rather suspicious of each other and especially of girls with a profession. In addition, by the time I came here, they all had children of up to 10 years of age and were fully occupied with their social duties (dinners, etc.), the selection of clothes and the bringing up of their children. I had nothing to talk to them about. Our lives had been too different. [2] I had spent 10 years in hospitals chiefly with men while they had been carrying on as housewives with one man and several children. I was used to a gay and easy comradeship with men but I quickly learned to be more reserved in order not to make enemies of any wives. I pondered and pondered on how to solve my situation. Mama had always taught me to look first for the fault in oneself in all emergencies. This attitude I now know was far overdone in her case and was not good for me. [3] However, as I had always had an interest in psychic processes, I decided to go in analysis in Switzerland where I knew through a German friend [4] that there were many excellent analysts. I thought surely an analyst could help me to solve this problem of how to make a happy and useful life in a foreign country despite the difficulty in making deeper contacts with reserved people like the Swedes. As I look back now, I realize that this must have worried Folke too. He had lived all over the world but as a bachelor and with easy superficial contacts. He was an economist and not used to bothering about psychic processes. He had married the girl he loved and had come home to Stockholm to a big job which fully occupied his time. He then had to discover that she found Swedes boring, and that she could not accept the superficiality of the human contacts. We met everyone of importance because of his old friendships and of his work. We were invited to hundreds of dinners in beautiful homes and we gave countless dinners. [5] It seemed to me that real conversation did not exist. Each person was in possession of at most five conversational "gramophone records" which he or she struggled to get a chance to play during the evening. The main subjects for the records were: (1) how Stockholm is the most beautiful city in the world and has no slums; (2) how stupid Anglo-Saxons are at learning foreign languages; (3) how naive and childish Americans are; (4) how Americans have no culture; and (5) how much better the schools, universities and doctors are in Sweden than in any other place in the world. In 1930 when I arrived here no one had heard of Canada so I soon felt responsible for the whole American continent and obliged to defend it.

Having lived in the States and in Germany very happily, I was totally unprepared for this type of aggressive conversation. Neither did I know or even suspect that each nation has its own permitted and accepted forms of aggression and that on the whole it is a completely different problem to live married and unmarried in a foreign country. It took me many years to learn these things and then be able to let the rain run off my shoulders. [6]

Anyway, with Folke's help and blessings, I spent several months in Zürich chiefly going in analysis with Professor Gustaf Bally, listening to Jung's lectures to the medical students and observing in the neurology and psychiatric clinics. At the present moment, it seems incredible that I did not choose Vienna and Freud. The reason was that I did not know a soul in Vienna.[7] The months in Zürich were most satisfying. Folke was in South America on business so he did not need me. My resentment toward the Swedes became somewhat milder when I discovered that the Swiss also considered their medical education the best in the world.

Zürich is such a lovely city and I had an introduction to one of the nicest old families belonging to a young married woman named Ilda Schindler. She had three children and was studying medicine. Our friendship ever since has been very valuable to me. Her childhood friend, Suzanne Öhmann, had married a Swede and lived in Stockholm so we also became friends. The analysis was of course only initiated but I came home determined to take a Swedish medical degree to get rid of the disgrace of only having a Canadian M.D. and an American Ph.D. This was more easily said than done. As I did not have a Swedish matriculation (a holy status symbol in this country), I could not enter the University without special permission. No one had ever heard of the University of Alberta so I had to get a copy of my matriculation marks and a statement from the British Ambassador here that the University really existed. As he had never heard of the University either, he refused to give me a statement. At that time Canadians were British subjects and Canada had no government representatives here. [8] I had automatically lost my British passport when I married a foreigner. Finally the University authorities here made a great exception and gave me a large document signed by Gustav V, and with a large seal, where it states that they accept my Ph.D. instead of a Swedish matriculation and they allow me two years of medical studies in exchange for my M.D. As far as I know, only one other foreigner had ever tried to enter the medical school here. I had to spend one whole month in the medical laboratory doing routine urinalysis and faeces examinations. The whole experience was humiliating but I survived. No one, not even the doctors, could understand why a woman married to a man in a high position with a good income would want to work. Finally I got my Swedish medical licence in 1937.

During the first five summers of my marriage Folke and I always took our holidays in the summer and by car. We drove down through Sweden, Denmark, Germany, Austria, Switzerland, Italy and France every summer. [9]

In those days there was no traffic. We never needed to order hotel rooms ahead and motoring was a real delight. I was always devouring Baedeckers and looking for historic sights. Folke was more entranced by the landscape. I loved to go into every famous old church, not to pray, but to gaze at the sculpture and architecture. He disliked churches intensely, and almost always sat outside in the car and waited.

One summer when Folke had to go to Hungary on business, we drove down in our LaSalle Cabriolet. I had not been there before and was thrilled with the distances, the spaces, the size of the fruit and vegetables, the beauty and gaiety everywhere. Hungary is the only country which has ever reminded me of Canada. With a Baedecker and a Magyar taxi driver with whom I could not converse, I managed to see all the sights of Budapest while Folke worked.

We then drove around the country and off to a golf hotel on the Wörther See where we had reserved rooms. [10] It turned out to be perfect. Before leaving Budapest I had packed and sent all our evening clothes by train to Stockholm. To our surprise this little golf hotel turned out to be very elegant with evening clothes for every dinner. Alfonso XIII was staying there and several English socialites. There were court curtseys before and after each meal. The first evening Folke told me not to look around but that Alfonso was staring at me. Before we left the dining room he came over to our table and invited us to have coffee and cognac with him in the salon. I had always imagined from the newspapers that he must be a dreadful person. To my amazement he was charming, very intelligent and interested in everything. This was during the civil war in Spain, after he had left the country and was living in Rome and separated from his wife. Each evening General Franco or his aide telephoned from Spain. That first evening Alfonso called me "Leone", saying, "You allow me, Mr. Hellstedt?" He had interested himself in the olive oil industry in Spain and knew all about the Alfa Laval centrifuges used to purify the oil. He had taken a serious part in the planning of the new medical school in Madrid. His mother, a German princess, had founded the first nursing school in Spain. The tragedy of haemophilia in his children had led him to read everything written on the subject. In short, there was nothing human which did not concern him. He and I played golf every day for three weeks while Folke played with his aide, I think the Duke of Toledo. During these golf games Alfonso and I discussed everything on the face of the earth and became very great friends. Folke liked him very much [11] and as we drove off at six a.m. one morning, Alfonso was down in front of the hotel to say goodbye, to kiss my hand and to send his best regards to my

mother. It had not mattered one bit that I had only kept two short woollen dresses, one pink and one pale blue, to go to dinner in.

---

[1] After the first half of 1932, she moved to the Radiumhemmet.

[2] What Freud called "housewives' psychosis" - intellectual deprivation from exclusively infantile contact .

[3] Strong superego productive of neurosis.

[4] Probably John Rittmeister.

[5] Contradicted later in letters.

[6] Mona confirmed that Leone did not fit in with most Swedish women. She was more outgoing and outspoken, she spoke Swedish with a strong accent and had a taste for the less traditional, e.g. she shocked everyone when she painted her fingernails, followed the latest Paris/London clothing fashions and used pink instead of white tablecloths.

[7] John Rittmeister, Wolfgang's brother, was hearing Jung's lectures and working in the same clinic then.

[8] Canada began issuing its own passports in 1947.

[9] Leone and Folke were fully aware of what was going on in Germany. The autobahns were an impressive testament to the Germans from a motorist's point of view.

[10] The Wörthersee is a large lake in southern Austria. From the golf resort it is 350 km northeast to Vienna and 250 km southwest to Venice.

[11] Leone's son Donald told me that the only evidence of jealousy on the part of his father occurred with respect to Leone's friendship with Alfonso, while at the same time Folke liked and respected Alfonso.

Chapter 13   **1933 - 1934**

In December of 1933 Leone visited London and the home of her friends from the University of Alberta, Jean and Matthew Halton.   Matthew was a foreign correspondent for *The Toronto Star*. He took the opportunity of her visit to interview Leone for his employer. The following article appeared on page one of the December 20, 1933 issue of *The Toronto Star.*

BANANA FLY TESTS REVEAL

Brilliant Girl Graduate of University of Alberta Tells

STUDYING   CANCER

By   M. H. Halton

London, Dec. 2. --- Take the banana fly, "Experiments with the banana fly," said the beautiful and brilliant Canadian girl who was the first woman to graduate in medicine from the University of Alberta and one of the few women to get her name on the register of fame called "American Men of Science," have shown beyond the remotest possibility of mistake that it is impossible for parents to determine or control the sex of their unborn children."

"That", I said to the beautiful and brilliant Canadian girl, whose name was Dr.Leone MacGregor (sic), and is now Dr. Leone Hellstadt (sic), "that is a forthright statement."

"The banana fly," retorted the lady, "is a forthright animal. It multiplies so quickly that is is practically a grandfather before it's born."

"Did you say forthright or birthright?" "Forthright," said Dr. Hellstadt, who also possesses that characteristic; and I asked her what even the

magnificent philoprogenitive record of the banana fly had to do with controlling sex.

"Nothing to do with controlling sex," she replied, "but a great deal to do with not controlling sex;" and she proceeded with the story that will blast the hopes of so many young parents who are determined that their first child shall be named after daddy -- will prove. In fact, that we are such stuff as dreams are made of, and all our life is rounded with the permutations and combinations which cause this chromosome or that to unite with that chromosome or this.

Considering all that she has achieved, Dr. Leone Hellstadt is audaciously young as well as audaciously good looking. She was through high school when she was 14; graduated from the University of Alberta in medicine, the toast of the university; won a fellowship from Alberta to Minneapolis, and from Minneapolis to Harvard, and then a Rockefeller Foundation scholarship to Hamburg, where she made a brilliant success. Two years ago she married a Swedish engineer (sic) of outstanding reputation and went to live in Stockholm, where she is now doing research work in the famous Radiumhemmet of that city, said to be the largest radiological facility extant.

Must   Study   Characteristics

Well, about the banana fly and sex control, which is agitating the hearths of more than one son-less royal family today, "Before one could say whether or not it was possible for parents to decide the sex of their children," said Dr. Hellstadt, leaning eager, radiant and charming before my fireplace, "one had to know a great deal about what characteristics, if any, are transferred from father to son; and as it is obviously impossible to get conclusive results from the study of one or two generations, it was necessary to experiment with some creature whose span of life was shorter than man's."

So they -- being chiefly the Dr. Morgan who is this year's winner of the Nobel Prize in medicine -- took the banana fly. For the banana fly, said Dr. Hellstadt, is exceedingly and multifariously prolific, and that's a marvel of understatement. The banana fly, indeed, reproduces itself one thousand times in half the time it takes for a current of electricity to go three times around The Star Building -- or something equally amazing.

Determines   Various   Features

Which brings us to chromosomes, which are the next link in the chain of this strange eventful history. Chromosomes are the doodads in the growing cell of the unborn banana fly -- as well as in those animals allegedly are higher in the scale of life -- which unite with each other to form the various mature characteristics.

"For example," said Dr. Hellstadt: "The union of two particular chromosomes determines that the hair of the infant shall be red, the union of two others that the eyes shall be blue, the union of another pair that the sex shall be male, and so on."

Far away in the abysmal darkness I saw a faint gleam of light. I began, in fact, to understand. The various characteristics, including sex, depend on which particular chromosomes unite.

"Do you see?" said the charming lady. I saw and she proceeded, "The point now is, why do certain chromosomes instead of others unite in the individual cases? Is there some reason for it? Is it the result of certain inherited characteristics and can it, therefore, be controlled? Or is it all an accident?"

She was asking me? I suggested that life is nothing but a magic show, around which we phantom shadows come and go, and that, therefore, it was an accident.

Matter   of   Chance

"Right," said Leone, and we returned to the banana fly. The magnificent prolification of the banana fly, she said, enables the scientists to study, before his own eyes, almost uncounted generations of the splendid creature; "and it has been found," she concluded exultantly, "that it is the purest chance which chromosome unites with which."

And therefore, obviously, it is the purest chance which makes your new baby a boy or a girl. The chromosomes make their choice; nor all your dieting nor wit shall lure them back to cancel half a line.

"Isn't it possible that some day doctors will learn how to control this chance meeting of the chromosomes?" I asked with sudden rising hope; but Dr. Hellstadt said, in effect, that it was not in the realm of practical realities; she begged me to imagine the difficulties; I gave up; and we came after a while to cancer.

"The cancer scientists I know are specializing on the origins of the malady," said Dr. Hellstadt. "The cause of it has so far proved hopelessly baffling, but origin is a different thing."

This didn't seem right, because many people have gone round all their lives thinking the origin of a thing is the same as the cause; that cause, in short, is the origin. But that's one on them.

Seek   Origin   First

Cause, said the lady, is a much deeper thing than origin, and so they are letting cause ride for a while and concentrating on origin.

"Cause, for example," she said, "may have something to do with heredity and heaven knows how many other things. But if you can find the origin of particular cancers you will have gone far towards determining their causes."

Fair enough, I granted, and how were you going to find the origin?

"By experimenting with various irritants," said the lady -- after stopping long enough to engage in an argument with someone on her other side about the new Germany, of which Dr. Hellstadt is, to put it mildly, enamored. "It was known that, given certain other tendencies, possibly hereditary, there are habits which are often known to result in cancer -- such as carrying a pipe one side of the mouth, or chewing the betel nut."

I sighed with relief; I hardly ever chew the betel nut.

Cancer   in   Rabbits'   Ears

"It has been discovered," said Leone, sparkling her beautiful eyes with enthusiasm, "that some animals, the rabbit for one, develop cancer when their ears are painted regularly with a certain material."

"I don't blame them a bit," I said. "And from this process," she continued, "it is hoped very soon to learn more about cancer than we have ever known before."

"And this certain material, what is this certain material?" I asked. And that, apparently, is a secret. "But listen," said Leone, "if you get a cable

from me one of these days saying come to Stockholm at once, come at once. It will be the biggest scoop you ever got."

"Gee, will I have time to wire the office?"

"Don't wire anybody. Come at once." So if one of these days you don't hear from this reporter, you will know I'm painting rabbits' ears with a certain material on the shores of the Baltic Sea.

1933 - Two Albertans Abroad

Matthew Halton and Leone were two young Albertans with similar backgrounds: raised in Alberta, educated following the Great War at the University of Alberta, friends and exposed to the new Germany run by Adolf Hitler. By the end of 1933 Halton was an outspoken critic of Hitler and an advocate of Winston Churchill. In the foregoing article from December, 1933, he parenthetically observed that Leone was greatly enamored of the new Germany. Both travelled in Germany in 1933 and were close to the following events.

January 31: Adolf Hitler was proclaimed *Reichskanzler* of Germany.

February 28: Following the Reichstag fire, prison without trial was legalized throughout Germany. In the next two months the SA [1] and SS [2] imprisoned 25,000 Communists and other political dissidents. Many more went underground or left Germany.

March 8: *Machtergreifung* [3]

April 1: nationwide boycott of Jewish businesses

April 7: all Jews removed from public office [4]

April 11: law passed defining who is a Jew [5]

April 25: law passed against an excessive number of foreign students in German universities; Jews considered foreign

April 26: Nazi Gestapo [6] assumes power as the secret police of Germany

May 14: in Hamburg, a burning of books with "un-German spirit"

May 16: President Roosevelt asks for disarmament of members of the
League of Nations

October 26: Germany leaves the League of Nations

October 30: all important positions in the Hansestadt are in Nazi hands

November 12: 95% of delegates vote in favour of the Nazis becoming the
only political party in the Reichstag

How could Leone be enamored of the new Germany? She must have been
appalled at the treatment of her Jewish friends. On the other hand, she saw
emergence from economic depression, in Germany and in her adopted
Sweden. Her husband was chairman of Bergedorfer Eisenwerk and it had
shown its first profit in years. Germany was Sweden's biggest cultural
influence and trading partner. Rising morale and prosperity in Germany had
the same effects in Sweden. Indifferent to politics, Leone was surrounded
by Swedes enthusiastic about the new Germany. For a time in December,
1933, at least, it seems that Leone's opinion agreed with the majority of
Swedes and Germans who freely elected their governments at that time - a
phenomenon difficult to understand today.

Among those who were forced to flee their native Germany was a man who
knew Hitler personally and had opposed him as the leader of a democratic
organization at the University of Munich in the early 1920s. Writing in
1944, Konrad Heiden considered the events of 1933 to be a triumph of the
mass over the individual.

*The omnipresence of society, which embraces the individual in every State
form, began to grow noisy. Hitler liked to maintain that his State was the
best democracy; "an ennobled form of democracy", as Goebbels some
months later declared to newspapermen at the meeting of the League of
Nations; only that we do not "obscure the will of the people streaming
upward or render it infertile by parliamentary intercalculations." There
was more truth in this lie than the speakers themselves believed. For it is
not the force of armies, police, judges, but the so-called "will of the people"*

that almost imperceptibly, but most effectively, tyrannizes the will of the individual; caught in the popular will or the social mood, the individual is carried upwards by the mounting flood or drawn down by the receding wave - this is human nature and cannot be prevented by the most excellent State.[7]

Swedes in the upper class circles in which Leone moved were especially enthusiastic about the new Germany.

The power of accomplished facts called forth reluctant admiration; the worship of bigness, even when it is hostile, degenerated, in the Germany of 1933 into an ugly fanaticism and servility.[8]

In 1933 Swedish admiration for German culture - music, philosophy, literature, science and technology - was reflected in German language study being compulsory in Swedish secondary schools.

The new Germany's radical anti-Semitism was not a cause for widespread alarm in 1933. Jews were not welcome in Sweden. Limits on immigration of Jews into Sweden were strict, as they were in many countries, including the USA, Canada and Britain.

Sweden passed a fully developed law against unrestricted immigration in 1927, and renewed it essentially unchanged in 1932. This law formed the juridical basis for the country's response to the plight of many Jews seeking refuge in the late 1930s. The U.S. and Britain passed similar laws after Sweden. In all three countries these laws were aimed primarily against unwanted Jewish immigration. The dilemma for the democracies only deepened when the Nazis began forcing Jews to emigrate in ever greater numbers.[9]

More important to Sweden than the cultural and economic advantages conveyed by the new Germany, Hitler promised that a strong Germany would be a "bulwark against Communism". [10]

Sleeping With the Russian Bear: Russian Invasion the Swedish Nightmare

Sweden and Russia are close neighbours and ancient enemies.

In the time of the Vikings, these blond giants from the North in their multi-oared seagoing boats were universally feared. Around the year 1,000 AD, however, they experienced a series of defeats in war, beginning what for Sweden amounted to a 900-year losing streak. Russia's proximity implied territorial conflict - *The Great Northern War* of 1700-1721 exhausted Sweden. It would never regain its former glory as a world power. Sweden again fought wars with Russia in 1741-1743, 1788-1790 and 1808-1809. Fortunately for Sweden, Russia's vast size implied numerous neighbouring states; squabbles resulted in wars and uprisings which required Russian military attention throughout the 19th century. Napoleon had to be dealt with. Several wars were fought with Turkey. The Boxer Rebellion forced Russia to send 180,000 soldiers to Manchuria to protect its interests, notably the railroads. Japan and Russia fought the first major war of the 20th century in 1904-1905. Finland and the Baltic states were also helpful to Sweden as buffers against Russian aggression.[11]

Alliances by royal marriage had tended to stabilize the relationships of the Scandinavian countries, Europe and Russia during the 19th century. Close relatives of the Swedish royal family were slaughtered by the Bolsheviks in 1919. The accession of Joseph Stalin to Premier in 1929 heralded a new era of unprecedented terror.

Iosif Vissarionovich Djugashvili was born in a small town in Georgia December 21, 1879.

The boy grew up in a violent and bitter household. He was beaten by both parents, for Ekaterina was also something of a thrashing mother. It is clear that he underwent an early and intense hardening, quite sufficient to inaugurate the hatred of any authority other than his own that would mark him to his death. Physical factors contributed to his sense of resentment and inferiority. The young Stalin was ugly: his eyes were set unpleasantly close together, his face was pitted by smallpox and, above all, he was short. He never grew beyond five feet four inches. Moreover, he was handicapped: a childhood accident had brought a stiffening of the left elbow, the result of blood poisoning. He was also deformed: the second and third toes of the left foot were joined, a conspicuous handicap in a world in which children played barefoot. Stalin may not have been a hunchback, but he had enough physical shortcomings to give him the bitter drive of a Shakespearean bastard.[12]

There is no evidence that Stalin ever loved anyone. In years to come he would refer to his mother in appalling terms - for example, as 'that old whore'. At the height of his purges, Stalin decided that she needed a bodyguard and had Beria arrange one. It says much for her view of her son that when the guards arrived she fainted, assuming that they had come to arrest her. Stalin did not attend her funeral, and although she died a devout Christian, he did not permit a cross to be placed upon her grave.[13]

Young Djugashvili was a good student, sent to divinity school by his mother because the road to the priesthood was the only chance for a peasant lad to get an education. On leaving school he made his living by armed robbery, which resulted in several opportunities to resume his education by reading books in his cell during prison terms in Siberia.

Iosif Djugashvili's first wife died soon after giving birth to a son, Jakov, in 1908. Thereafter Iosif called himself Joseph Stalin, echoing the name of "Lenin" and the Russian word for steel, "stal".

After the success of the Bolsheviks against the Tsarist forces, Stalin rose quickly through the party ranks. By the mid-1920s ruthless tactics had made him a party leader and candidate to replace Lenin as head of state. By making a show of philosophical allegiance to Marx and Lenin, he was successful in Politburo campaigning.[14] In 1927, as de facto leader of the Communist Party, he assumed enough power to implement more openly his policy of exiling and murdering political rivals.[15] Stalin's hatred of Jews struck a sympathetic note in the anti-Semitic Soviet states. The masses did not object to persecution of the Jew Trotsky and the many other Jews in the Communist Party hierarchy, or Stalin's replacement of Lenin, whose mother was Jewish. Stalin's contempt for women, beginning with his mother and continuing with his second wife (also his secretary and the mother of two of his children) was perhaps less well known.[16] His reign of terror lasted until his death in 1953.

Stalin killed millions more people than Hitler; by 1933 he had already killed more of his own people than the entire population of Sweden.[17] Moreover, while Hitler was just getting started in 1933, Stalin's Russia was already notorious. Viewed from Sweden, it was terrifying - a traditional enemy with a huge population of armed barbarians ruled by a psychopathic murderer.

The Great Depression had eroded confidence in capitalism. Worldwide fear of Communism was at a peak. 1932 had brought news of a serious Communist challenge to the leaders of China. A terrorist who called himself Mao Tse Tung was succeeding in converting communities to Communism and using them to fight the corrupt Nationalist regime of Chiang Kai Shek. Mao followed Stalin's strategy of energetically discovering who disagreed with him, then killing them, plus their friends and neighbours for good measure. As a mass murderer he was in time able to surpass both Hitler and Stalin.[18]

While they admired and relied upon Germany, Swedes feared Russia.

Apolitical in a politically turbulent time and place

It isn't surprising that Leone was seeking a cause for and therefore a cure for cancer. She had never feared to be first. Nor is the familiar, jocular tone - Matthew, Jean and Leone were friends who had escaped their origins in rural Alberta for notable places in advanced civilization, an experience which, understandably, could make them at times giddy. Surprising, even shocking, to readers two or three generations later, is the offhand revelation that Leone was greatly enamored of the new Germany.[19]

In December of 1933 the superficial news from Germany was good: order had come out of chaos with suppression of the Communists; prosperity was emerging from severe economic depression; Germany was lifting neighbouring economies like Sweden's and Britain's. Leone's husband's business interests were thriving. Conservatives in Europe and Scandinavia, the upper classes, were pleased.

The deeper, darker story was known to Matthew Halton. He had travelled extensively in Germany that year, interviewing people from every walk of life: housewives, prison guards, prisoners, philosophers, administrators, farmers, students, teachers, in offices and in pubs, political losers and political winners - including Herman Göring. Halton was a liberal, agnostic advocate of the underdog. Although the Nazi party called itself "socialist", he knew better. He recognized the alliance that Hitler had formed with the industrialists and the old military upper class, and he feared the emergence of the war-loving German collective unconscious.

In 1932-1934 Leone was a member of the Swedish upper class. Her husband was a well-bred gentleman, educated at the best Swedish schools; he had represented Sweden in the Olympic Games (high jump, London, 1908, at the age of 17); he was fluent in several languages and a senior executive of a multi-national corporation with headquarters in Stockholm. Although Leone had travelled extensively in Germany, she had no interest in politics. Unlike Matthew, whose earlier inclination and then occupation were centrally concerned with international politics, Leone was otherwise occupied: with medicine, science, and the cultural and aesthetic advantages of her new situation (married, rich) over her old (single, poor). Although her vast correspondence forty years later, as the president-elect, president and past president of the Medical Women's International Association was full of MWIA politics, in these hundreds of letters Leone only once evinced the slightest interest in the politics of countries - when the Olof Palme influence resulted in the nationalization of Swedish medicine in 1975 and doctors became employees of the Swedish government.

Leone became Swedish. Matthew Halton lived his working life abroad, but was always conspicuously Canadian. He is buried where he was born, Pincher Creek, Alberta. Leone is buried in Eskilstuna, Sweden, beside her husband.

Matthew Halton ca. 1943

[1] *Sturmabteilung* - "storm troop" or "assault detachment", the "brown shirts". Originally formed in 1921 as a para-military organization to support the Nazi party. Unemployed men were attracted. By 1930 membership approached 100,000. In May, 1933, the army agreed to cooperate in training 250,000 SA members per year for eventual entry into regular military service. By the terms of the Versailles Treaty the German army was still limited to 100,000 men. Weale, Adrian, *The SS: A New History,* Abacus of Little, Brown Book Group, London, 2012, p. 89.

[2] *Schutzstaffeln* - "security staff" or "protection squads". Formed in 1925 to protect Hitler and his closest Nazi colleagues, the SS was originally a small, elite group who swore personal allegiance to Hitler. Tall, blond men who looked good in the tailored black uniforms were originally favoured. When Heinrich Himmler assumed leadership in January, 1929, the SS had only 280 subscription-paying members. His loyalty to Hitler, energy and organizational skill brought vastly increased membership despite competition from the SA. Hitler's ascension to Reichskanzler brought a wave of volunteers ("March Violets" in Nazi

slang): from January to May of 1933 membership doubled from 50,000 to 100,000; by June 1934 the SS doubled again, to 200,000. ibid, Weale, pp. 47, 50, 94.

[3] *Machtergreifung* - "seizure of power". Refers to the assumption of extraordinary powers by Hitler, especially following the Reichstag fire in February, 1933 (which was blamed on a Communist conspiracy which merited forceful, previously illegal countermeasures).

[4] While visiting Stockholm in August, 2012, I indulged my addiction to antiquarian book stores. A beautiful leather bound copy of Macaulay speeches caught my eye. Macaulay was a hero of Winston Churchill's and Churchill a hero of mine. I took it from the shelf and opened it in the middle, to the beginning of a speech by Lord Macaulay to the British House of Commons on April 17, 1833 concerning the "Disabilities of the Jews". Macaulay argued for the right of Jews to become eligible for election to public office in Britain. The knowledge that Hitler had taken this right from German Jews exactly 100 years later, almost to the day, and the force and eloquence with which Macaulay described a position consistent with the British democratic tradition (for which thousands of Albertans fought and died) caused my knees to buckle. I had to sit down to read further. A glance at the price of the book brought me back to reality - like many goods in Sweden it was about three times what it would have been in the USA and double what it would have been in Canada - in the Swedish democratic tradition.

[5] Degrees of Jewishness were defined by the number of Jews among parents, grandparents and great grandparents. Allowances were made for converts to Christianity and for those who won military medals fighting for Germany in the Great War. Notwithstanding, during WW2 Herman Göring proclaimed, "I shall decide who is a Jew."

[6] *Geheime Staatspolizeiamt* - "secret state police office".

[7] Heiden, Konrad, *Der Fuehrer: Hitler's Rise to Power*, Richard Clary & Company, Ltd., Bungay, Suffolk 1944, p. 445.

[8] ibid, p. 446.

[9] Levine, Paul A., *From Indifference to Activism: Swedish Diplomacy and the Holocaust: 1938-1944*, Doctoral Dissertation, Uppsala University, 1996, p. 29.

[10] Aselius, Gunnar, *Chapter 1: Sweden and Nazi Germany,* pp. 51-58, in *Sweden's Relations With Nazism, Nazi Germany and the Holocaust,* editors Stig Ekman and Klas Amark, Almquist & Wiksell International, Stockholm, 2003.

[11] Koblik, Steven, editor, *Sweden's Development from Poverty to Affluence, 1750-1970*, University of Minnesota Press, 1975.

[12] De Jonge, Alex, *Stalin and the Shaping of the Soviet Union*, William Collins & Sons Co. Ltd., 1986, Fontana Paperbacks, 1987, p. 24.

[13] ibid, p. 24.

[14] Tucker, Robert C., *Stalin as Revolutionary 1879-1929: A Study in History and Personality*, W.W. Norton & Company, New York, 1974, pp. 292-330.

[15] op cit De Jonge, Alex, p. 227.

[16] ibid, *...he hated intellectual women, referring to them as "herrings with ideas",* p. 144.

[17] ibid, De Jonge. Russia had seven million casualties in the Great War. In 1918 Stalin lost all 60,000 men under his command, then sought to have those who survived or escaped from the enemy executed as traitors. (pp. 126-128) The imposition of the Marxist ideal of government by the dictatorship of an urban, industrialized proletariat on what was essentially a feudal system caused massive dislocations, economic inefficiencies and societal disorganization. The literacy rate in the Soviet Union at the time of the revolution was 30%, the same as it was in revolutionary France in 1789. Confiscation of the agricultural output of 100 million peasants for the benefit of the ideal of an urban proletariat resulted in several national famines during which millions starved to death and cannibalism was common.

[18] Fairbank, John King, *China: A New History*, The Belknap Press of Harvard University Press, Cambridge and London, 1992, pp. 350-425 and Grenville, J.A.S., *A History of the World in the Twentieth Century,* The Belknap Press of Harvard University Press, 1994, pp. 636-641.

[19] In Leone's correspondence with her Medical Women's International Association friends in Vienna, Martha Kyrle and Hertha Dax, 1968-1976, she mentioned several times fear and loathing of books written by journalists. Perhaps this casual observation by Matthew Halton in December of 1933 caused some of her misgivings.

Chapter 14   1934

In the spring of 1934 I had planned with a Canadian university friend, Jean Halton, who was living with her husband Matt in London, that we would do a trip in my car, our chief aim being to see North Africa. Neither of us told our husbands in detail as they would have been worried to death about our safety. At that time no woman drove a car in Sicily or North Africa, except in Tangier. Jean invited her sister Kathleen to accompany us and I invited Mama and Phyllis. We planned and planned, but unfortunately my father was ill and Mama could not leave him. I was so sorry because she knew so well all the historical background of the places we intended to visit. Phyllis also decided not to come and I was very disappointed. However, Jean, Kathleen and I made a three months' trip which could not have been improved upon. I had already seen a lot of the continent with Folke so I took them first to all the places I loved and then we proceeded to central and southern Italy which I did not know.

The weather was perfect and after an unforgettable day in Perugia, which at that time was a quiet little village, we drove one morning to Assisi in our open cabriolet. An open Alfa Romeo with three handsome young Italians passed us on the winding country road. They waved their berets and we waved gaily back. There was no traffic. One saw cars only in the cities.

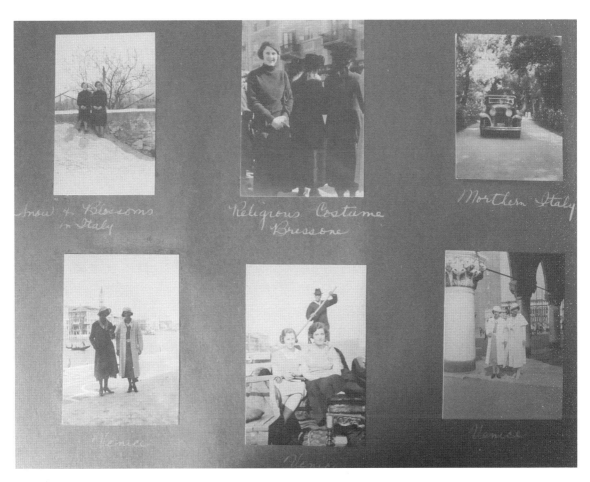

Snow & Blossoms in Italy

Religious Costume Bressone

Northern Italy

Venice

Venice

Venice

Perugia

In Assisi in the basement of the church we again encountered these young men all studying the famous frescoes. They invited us to lunch and showed us Assisi. In Rome that night they arrived with a gramophone and champagne and took us out on the Appian Way where we danced in the moonlight on the flagstones of one of the tombs. Our language difficulties were immense. None of them could speak English. One was a lawyer, one an agriculturist and one a historian, all with doctorates. The agriculturist could talk a little German, so he devoted himself to me. The other four struggled in French. Altogether it was a very amusing experience. We continued south to Naples, Capri and through perfumed lemon groves to Sicily. Everywhere the country people clapped their hands and called out "Bravo!" to see girls driving a car. We drove all over Sicily simply entranced by the sights and especially by the Grecian temples outside Agrigento. They were so beautiful that many years later the Acropolis was a disappointment to me. We studied our Baedeckers and Fletcher's Architecture diligently along the whole journey. Wherever possible we stayed in German pensions and were well taken care of. [1]

Finally we took the car on a boat to Tunis from Palermo and began to feel really adventurous. A young French medical student on the boat forced us to be vaccinated for smallpox although our passports showed that it already had been done. All passengers were lined up and the same needle used for all. I was terrified but we had no choice. We arrived safely in Tunis and were soon fascinated by a strange world. When I saw the few pillar remnants of Carthage I could hardly believe my eyes. The Punic wars had interested me more than any part of history.

From Tunis we drove south as far as was allowed in those days. There were no north and south roads, only sandy paths and lots of creeks to ford by car. [2] The Atlas Mountains and passes were frightening, especially as they were a surprise to us. The east and west roads all over the northern coast were paved and excellent except in Spanish Morocco. We saw only Arabs on camels who ran beside us screaming "argent" until we were frightened. In Constantine the wild street boys climbed all over the car while we drove and we could only get them off by whacking their hands with tools from the tool box.

Atlas Mountains & El Kantara

El Kantara Gorge

El Kantara Oas[is]

The Gorge El Kantara

Arab Village

Arab Village
El Kantara

Arab Village

In the oasis of Bon Saada we rode on camels and went to the night clubs where men were dressed as girls and danced and sang for us.

Finally we drove all one night and day on a path where we did not meet a single car or European. We had a large tin of gasoline and a big can of water with us. The sunrise was heavenly.

Heading west at dawn in the desert

The Grand Mosque

We saw beautiful tiny white mosques out in the desert. We passed through many Arab villages where the people did not look friendly. Several times far out in the desert we drove by a beautiful Roman archway. We arrived for instance quite unprepared beside the ruins of Timgad with not a human being in sight. At last we came to Fez and felt safe again. Even there we seemed to be the only foreigners but we were unmolested. I bought an oil painting of an Arab market by a French artist and had it sent home. Finally we crossed over from Tangier to Gibraltar and spent two weeks in Spain.

153

We had looked forward most eagerly to this part of the journey. We enjoyed the cities and Moorish architecture and the wonderful picture galleries, but we were disappointed to find how little was Spanish. We went to a bullfight in Alicante and were really shocked. The roads everywhere were indescribably bad and we were happy to see France again.

We drove the whole Riviera, then up through Switzerland and Germany to Hamburg from where the girls took a boat to London.

It had been a great adventure and Folke was glad to have me safely home when he heard all about it.

---

[1] Leone does not mention Silvio and Franco, the Sicilian gentlemen with whom the girls apparently spent several days, judging from the several changes in clothing evident in the photos taken with them.

[2] The considerable distances and harsh conditions of this tour implied servicing the LaSalle. David Halton told me that his mother Jean was "handy". He said his father Matthew wouldn't change a light bulb; Jean did all the practical tasks. Leone carried a tool kit; from her WW1 ambulance driver mechanical qualification and her motoring experience she would have been capable of lubricating the chassis, repacking wheel bearings, adjusting brakes and other maintenance that was indicated, or at least recognizing the requirements and insuring that they were executed properly. *Cadillac LaSalle Shop Manual: Adjustments, Repairs and Lubrication; 1928-1929 Cadillac 341A 341B LaSalle 303 328.* Book Number 5032, Service Department, Cadillac Motor Car Company, Detroit, August, 1928.

Chapter 15   1933 – 1934

What Leone Neglected to Mention

Jews Not Wanted Here

The deteriorating situation for her Jewish friends in Germany would have weighed on Leone. Swedish approval of the new Germany would have been contrasted vividly with what Matthew Halton had to say during Leone's visit in December of 1933. In early 1934 Leone spent three months travelling with Matthew's wife Jean, who had earlier, in the fall of 1933, travelled with her husband for two months in Germany while he gathered material for his reports to *The Toronto Star*. Leone knew him well enough to call him "Matt". She was aware of his understanding of Nazism.

Matthew had been in Berlin in March for the *Machtergreifung*, Hitler's seizing of power in the wake of the Reichstag fire that Nazi propagandists blamed on Communist conspirators.[1]   Shortly thereafter Matthew was able to get an extraordinary interview with Hermann Göring:

"I should like to ask you one question about the Jews. In your own interests, is it not a mistake to persecute them?"

Göring snorted. "We know our interest! Our interest is to rid Germany of Jewry. Ask me about it again in ten years from now. But why do you bother? You look like an Aryan!"

I could only blink at this magnificent non sequitur. Göring turned on me suddenly and said slyly:

"I don't know what we should do without the Jews. Hitler hates them. He'll make use of them."

As scapegoats of course. Göring seemed to imply that he himself had no particular hate of the Jews.[2]

After telling Matthew that he expected no difficulties from the Allies with respect to German rearmament in violation of the Treaty of Versailles, Göring went on to give the main reason:

Germany will save Europe and occidental civilization. Germany will stop the rot. Germany will present the 'Untergehen des Abendlands'. Germany will save Europe from Bolshevism.[3]

Matthew was surprised to receive permission to visit Dachau, near Munich, the first of the major concentration camps. In the fall of 1933 it housed 3,000 inmates and 400 guards. The excess of guards was in the service of training staff in the brutality that would be necessary in future concentration camps and progress toward the *Endlösung*, the Final Solution to the Jewish problem.

During his two months of travel with Jean in the fall of 1933, Matthew became convinced of Nazi Germany's intention to realize Hitler's goal - to make Europe an Aryan nation, free from Jews, with himself as its leader. Everywhere Nazi policies furthered this end. Men and boys were being trained in military skills. Women were encouraged to have as many Aryan children as possible. Unmarried mothers were "brides of Hitler". Their Aryan children were needed in the Reich to exceed the numbers of Jews and other degenerates, and to provide enough Germans to organize the rest of the world during the Thousand Year Reich.

On the Lighter Side

Matthew's son David Halton and Leone's daughter Mona gave me many photos of the three month motoring trip taken by Leone, Jean and Kathleen. Among these are several of the girls with two Sicilian gentlemen, Franco and Silvio, taken over several days. In her draft autobiography of January, 1970, Leone gives Sicily less than a paragraph and does not mention Franco or Silvio at all. We shouldn't suspect her of concealing something untoward: she wrote about dancing in the moonlight on the Appian Way with "three handsome young Italians"; there is only one ill-focused photo of the Italians, yet there are several photographs of Franco and Silvio.

Leone's two friends were the Campbell sisters, Jean and Kathleen, from Lacombe, Alberta. Both were graduates of the University of Alberta: Jean in 1929 with a B.A. in Ancient History; Kathleen in 1931 with a B.Sc. which included mostly courses in home economics and classics. [4] Katherine was single and Jean in September, 1932, had married Matthew Halton, her university sweetheart and the London-based correspondent for *The Toronto Star*.

J. W. Bayne   S. T. Bowden   K. M. Burgess   J. M. Cameron   J. J. Campbell

SID. BOWDEN

BORN—Without doubt.
    Educated—Uh! Huh!
Married—No? Never????
Ambition—To keep the fourth floor (St. Stephen's) in order.
Chief pastime—Wine, women, song, and religion.
Chief characteristic—A man of prayerful petition.
Favorite expression—"Please sign here."
General reputation—A good sport, full of enthusiasm and energy.

JEAN J. CAMPBELL

JEAN is, indeed, as the Handbook has it, a super-lative argument in favor of co-education; more than that, she is far, far above the common conception of co-eds in that she disdains the superficiality and the caprice attributed generally to the type. As Secretary of the Wauneita Society last year, and Vice-President of the Senior Class this year, she has justified the confidence placed in her by her fellow-students. And finally, she more than justifies the old aphorism: "The statement that beauty is but skin-deep is but a skin-deep statement." (Ask the Editor of The Gateway!)

JEAN MACMILLAN CAMERON

ADVENTUROUS and independent, Jean sallied forth from Glasgow to Alberta looking for new fields to conquer.
    Regardless of the time spent in teaching Grade VIII with "Excellent" results, she took her full Varsity course in her spare moments—in the usual time.
    Naturally with such a delightful Scotch burr-r-r the ancient alliance between the French and the Scotch was renewed in "first-class" style.
    Though working under difficulties, she is always jolly—bubbling over with mirth, vitality and optimism. Versatile and idealistic, she is a charming companion.
    Her only weakness is that she can't refuse a favor.

KATHLEEN MILLER BURGESS

"VIVID," says Mr. Webster, "means spirited, animated and bright"—the best the poor man could do, not having known Kay. That's where we've got the bulge on him. And vivid is the word, be she dispensing dogs to a starving populace at the Arts Hike, or cutting a dash down the ice in the wake of a winged puck. It's a rare girl who combines the subtle danger of a Mexican vamp with the clear head of a good student and the loyal heart of a real friend.

158

G. V. Gowan   M. H. Halton   D. I. Hamilton   R. B. Harding   T. R. Haythorne

GEORGE VICTOR GOWAN

BEHOLD the "High-minded Man" of Plato's pamphlets! Vic's abilities, which are considerable, often go unnoticed because he makes little effort to display them. Plays golf, tennis and basketball proficiency, and has a musical bump, which he smoothes out on the fiddle and piano—not a virtuoso, but a musical fellow. Has been on the executive of his class, Vice-President of the Literary Association and an active member in Dramatic circles, both as actor and director. His scholastic record is excellent; good grades have been gathered in consistently, and good sense has guided all his conduct. Plans to be a lawyer, and if I ever find myself in the toils of the law, I'll trust my person, and my pocketbook—yea, to the very last scud—to Gowan.

MATTHEW HENRY HALTON

MATT possesses in a generous measure all the attributes common to Pincher Creek citizens. Without enlarging upon the commoness of these attributes a rough idea of their nature can be gathered from the fact that starting as secretary-treasurer of the Freshman Class he successfully handled a succession of important student offices including the editorship of The Gateway and finally capped his industrious career by winning the I.O.D.E. Scholarship. His two weaknesses are both a weakness for beauty. Nuff said!
Good bye, Matt, and good luck in London.

DOROTHY ISABEL HAMILTON

DOT is one of those English sharks
   To whom the Profs give brilliant marks.
Nothing escapes her drag-nets' toils—
With a mind alert for all things new.
She is willing, efficient, friendly, too.
The Shakespeare prize was one of her spoils.
She played her part most expertly.
In making sandwiches and serving tea
"As a matter of fact," "Say, listen," says she,
"For 'n instance," "Make it snappy," that's Dorothy.

TOM R. HAYTHORNE

TOM is a native of Edmonton. His summers have been given to farming, however near the city. Strathcona High School saw him for four years, and then he came to Varsity.
Tom has taken his college education as he would a new and thrilling game. He has played it, not to the exclusion of everything else, but yet with a never-wavering enthusiasm. A ready tongue, a ready smile, and a cheerful disposition have helped to win him many friends. The vocational barometer at present points to Journalism.

Leone, Matthew and Jean were all prominent in student affairs at the University of Alberta. Leone was vice-president of the Students' Union in 1924. Matthew, as editor of the student newspaper, wrote a famous editorial criticizing organized religion which almost resulted in *The Gateway* losing its funding.

In the 1920s W.G. Hardy was classics professor and coach of the University of Alberta hockey team. Energetic and colourful, he inspired many students to take an interest in classics. Jean and Kathleen were prepared by university course work to appreciate their time on the shores of the Mediterranean.

The girls' three-month journey began in the early spring of 1934 - snow is still visible in a photo taken in northern Italy. A LaSalle Cabriolet on European or African roads in 1934 would have caused a sensation. Created by General Motors to be the sporting version of Cadillac, the "The Standard of the World", the size, power and sheer presence of a LaSalle would have made the girls conspicuous wherever they went.[5]

You will meet a tall dark stranger. Well, maybe not that tall, but a nice dresser. With a villa. And well bred horses. In Sicily.

Silvio and Kathleen

Kathleen   Silvio   Franco   Leone   Jean

Roof garden café.

[1] *On March 6, the day of the first framed Nazi election, I was in Berlin again. The windows were hung with swastikas and with the black, red and white colours of Imperial Germany. There was not one flag of the Republic, the republic which few Germans had accepted in their hearts. Fourteen thousand soldiers marched through the Brandenburg Gate and down the Unter den Linden, and over the wailing of the fifes and the rolling of drums there was a thunder of "Sieg Heil" from a hundred thousand throats.* Halton, Matthew, *Ten Years to Alamein*, S.J. Reginald Saunders & Company, Toronto, 1944, p. 22.

[2] ibid, p. 23.

[3] ibid, p. 24.

[4] From course records in the University of Alberta Archives, Edmonton.

[5] In response to a letter from a Vienna friend who had just returned from North Africa, Leone wrote in 1972: *Thanks for the beautiful card from Tunis. We were often frightened on that trip (1934) but we were 3. No other women drove cars in Sicily or North Africa then. We were most afraid of the hoards* (sic) *of Arabs on camels, screeching for money. Weren't the Roman ruins lovely?* Medical Women's International Association Archives, letter to "Dear Girls" (Dr. Martha Kyrle, General Secretary, and Hertha Dax, Secretary), dated June 22/72.

Chapter 16   **1936 - 1945**

In what follows, Leone loses the chronological thread for a while, before addressing the events immediately before and during WW2. I suspect that she would rather not have written about that difficult time at all. The material concerning various friends and learning French, out of order and parenthetical, delays discussion of 1939-1945. When she at length arrives at this period, she skips lightly over it.

On my trip with Kenneth and Carol before my marriage I became interested in the life of Isabella d'Este. Luckily I found in Stockholm two volumes of her letters translated by an Englishwoman, Julia Cartwright. They fascinated me from every point of view, not the least medically. Her dearly loved sister Beatrice died at 21 after the birth of her second baby. Women in those days in Italy died so often in childbirth that Isabella's long life was a miracle. Her knowledge of art, history, music and literature was beyond that of any woman of her time. Ever since I discovered her I have followed in different countries and in different galleries her undertakings and this interest has widened my knowledge of the history of that period. [1]

When I had been in Stockholm about five years, there arrived two Vancouverites, younger than I and very nice. They married Swedes also. Helen's husband, Torsten Frey, is now Professor of Psychiatry and Helen is the best translator of medical papers into English in the country. Catherine's husband, Baron Gustaf Djurklou, is in Public Relations for Shell and Catherine has charge of the Fulbright Fellowships for Northern Europe. We three girls had all kept a picture of Canada where everyone was exactly like our best boy and girl friends there. Marrying Swedes made us very observant of all Swedes. Our husbands were all unusually attractive and clever but naturally they had some typically Swedish characteristics. It has taken us all these many years to realize that we preferred to marry these foreign men just because they were different from our Canadian friends and that we must accept the fact that there are advantages and disadvantages in our

situation. We are all six devoted to one another and our husbands are still fond of Canada. [2]

I have one friend through all these European years that I have had to learn how to get along with. She is an American, Outram Mott, who was studying to be an opera singer in Hamburg long before I got there. I saw her first by accident as she got off a street car and I remember thinking, "That is the most beautiful girl in the world." A week later I met her at a party. She was already engaged to a Swede, Hans Mott, who was Folke's junior in the Swedish-owned iron works outside Hamburg. They married about four months before we did. They came to live in Sweden with their four children shortly after the war broke out. We have at last learned to understand, forgive and appreciate one another, but it took us a long time. It is so unfortunate that it takes so many years of one's life to learn to be tolerant of people who are different but at least as valuable as ourselves. Nowadays [3] I would explain my difficulty of long ago by the fact that Outram is a combination of Mama and Phyllis and I already had difficulties there as a child.

I have ever since high school days been regretting that I did not have an opportunity to learn French thoroughly. At the University of Minnesota I took a six weeks intensive course until my reading ability was quite good. On and off since then I've started taking private lessons. Usually the teachers have been poor pedagogues and that I cannot endure. As a result I can get rooms, food and drink and take care of a car in French but I cannot converse comfortably as I do in German and Swedish. In 1954 and 1955 I decided to remedy the situation and drove down to France with Viveca, an older Swedish friend. We stayed at Reid Hall, which then belonged to the International Women's University Association, and we took lessons at the Alliance Francaise. We met many interesting women in Reid Hall, even some men, and enjoyed our daily lessons. Our French improved somewhat but not enough. In Reid Hall I found, however, two French women who became my friends and who gave me practice in French. The one, Magdy Watteau, was the widow of a descendant of a famous painter. She is very interested in psychoanalysis and this gave us a relatively easy subject for me to practice my French on. She is now married to a retired British Ambassador in Mallorca and Folke and I visited them last Xmas. My other French friend, Claude Estadas de

Ripouilh, was a divorcée, much younger than I, an artist of talent and the head of a school of therapeutic art for children in Toulouse. She has been a devoted friend and has visited us many times in Stockholm, hoping with her energy and gifts to make me fluent in French. [4]

Two summers ago I drove with another friend, Caroline Olin, to Strasbourg to attend the summer session for foreigners in French. We lived in a beautiful new dormitory, had excellent teachers and loved the student life. The lectures on politics, art, history and literature were on the highest level I have ever encountered. We listened to these all day and relaxed for lunch in the garden of the Orangerie and for dinner in the restaurants of the lovely little villages in Alsace. There are almost no tourists because this province has not been fashionable since the turn of the century. As a result the villages are charming, the old restaurants are excellent and French is spoken everywhere. If the arthritis in my hip had not commenced that summer, the two months would have been really ideal. Folke was happy with his golf here in Stockholm and was well taken care of by our angelic little German housekeeper, Fridel, who has been with us for 22 years. Folke has never wanted to take a course in anything since he finished university. All educated Swedes hate schools and courses and can hardly understand anyone who feels otherwise. Folke has always teased me by calling me "the eternal student."

This summer after Folke's death [5] I was lucky to have Claude and Helen Frey to stay with me through July and we all spoke only French so we two Canadians at least made some real improvement in this language.

By the time I passed my licensing exam in Sweden in 1937, I was expecting my first baby. Monica arrived in October and was the joy of our lives. I engaged an excellent young German nurse from the children's hospital in Hamburg and we all had a wonderful year. Monica was healthy and pretty and clever. At that time I was of the opinion that mothers even with good help should stay at home with their children during the early years. Donald arrived two years later and until they were 10 and 12 years old I was only away from them for two trips. When Monica was one year old Folke and I sailed for Buenos Aires and Rio for three months. It was a wonderful experience but I was very lonely for Monica. I remember flying in a small plane between Buenos Aires and Montevideo and thinking, "If anything happens to us,

Monica will be alone in the world." The voyage between Southampton and South America took three weeks and was very gay. There were many famous people on board, I had beautiful clothes and was placed on the Captain's left. I found South America inspiring. There seemed to be such a need for doctors. Everything was developing. The Germans and Swedes out there were very enterprising, successful and more international than in Sweden, or so it seemed to me.

In 1939 when Donald arrived and the war broke out we had just moved into a very large and wonderful flat in the most beautiful location in Stockholm, looking out over the water and lovely parks and yet in the center of the city. I had a cook, a housemaid and a nurse. We had at once to turn our car in to the government as gasoline was rationed and soon food rationing set in. [6]

Donald helps our understanding of their situation: *Just before the war my father understood that it was coming and had ordered from Argentina several huge wooden crates with corned beef, beef essence and coffee beans. They served us well as payment for goods outside the reach of rationing cards or amounts allowed. Once we had coffee beans ground at a department store in Stockholm and were riding back on the street car. Well, freshly ground coffee in about 1945 in Stockholm was about as likely to smell as having a million dollars falling on your head from above. It started with someone beside us sniffing and moaning from pleasure, and then another one, and on, etc. This time only admiring eyes followed our later retreat when leaving the street car.* [7]

167

Donald   Nana   Leone   Monica

We were never at all hungry but the food we could get was very boring. It was difficult to keep a staff of three contented in such a mixed-up world, especially as they were all of different nationalities. The cook was Czech, the housemaid Finnish and the nurse German. The children learned Swedish, English and German at the same time and had a great advantage in this way when they came to school.

I think they also became less nationalistic than children in general. Except for the great general tragedies of the war [8] and the constant fear of invasion, [9] the chief discomfort for me was due to the wood and coal rationing. Folke and the children never seemed to notice the cold but it was never warm enough in the evenings for me so I acquired the habit of doing all my reading and studying in bed after dinner. The children were in bed too, and Folke spent most of his evenings playing the piano. Besides my medical journals and the literature on psychoanalysis, I read all the volumes of Toynbee's "A Study of History" and derived great comfort from them.

During the war summers I was with the children and the nurse in Falkenberg, a small town on the west coast of Sweden in a hotel on the beach. Folke could only join us for a month each summer [10]. The children were very happy there and we all made many friends. The American Consul General Billy Corcoran and his Jamaican English wife were also there every summer. Dulcie now lives as a widow in La Jolla but we will never lose track of each other. We are kindred spirits despite our very different childhoods. Billy was a remarkable man and a comfort to everyone who ever had to do with him. It was he who was able to discover the source of the rockets which were destroying England during the war. [11]

Falkenberg: Donald Leone   Monica   Nana

Falkenberg: Donald Folke Monica   Nana

As I received almost no mail from abroad during the entire war, I never asked to have my mail forwarded from Stockholm to Falkenberg. In this way I did not receive Phyllis's telegram about Charlie's death in 1942 until six weeks after she sent it. There she was a widow at 41 with two children, Marilyn and John, and I could not even write to her. I sent a telegram but was very sad.

In about the fourth year of the war I met at a party a tall, beautiful American girl, Frances Hepp from Denver, Colorado. She was about 10 years younger than I but we were congenial at once. Our children were the same age and our husbands liked each other. She had married in Denver a charming, gifted half-German, half-French man. He had been living in the States for years but had still his German citizenship. When war broke out he had to return to Germany and Frances came with him out of love and loyalty. She lived with his parents in Stuttgart until he was able to get them all to Stockholm. Some years after the war they emigrated to Chile.

Before they left we visited back and forth with our children and were able to make many wonderful trips around Stuttgart which is in such a

historical district. We never tired of Rothenburg, Dinkelsbühl and Tübingen (where Ernst's ancestors were professors) and the Black Forest where we picknicked.

This is, however, somewhat ahead of my story. When the war ended, our cars were still confiscated, our food rationed and our fuel supply very short. It seems impossible to believe now but there I was in a flat with three bathrooms for eight years without any hot water due to fuel rationing and on top of that a constant chill in the flat.

---

[1] Isabella d'Este (1474-1539) inherited sovereignty of Ferrara and 30,000 subjects. Her childhood recalled Leone's: a brilliant, accomplished girl, handsome but not strikingly beautiful like her younger sister. Marriage to Gianfrancesco Gonzaga united the adjoining states of Ferrara and Mantua. While Gianfrancesco traveled on military adventures, Isabella governed. Her husband, who later died of syphilis, had an affair with Lucrezia Borgia, risking the epic, jealous wrath of brother Cesare. Isabella was a passionate collector of art objects and a sponsor of artists. Much of the Gonzaga collections were lost, but surviving are portraits of Isabella, her husband and her children by Leonardo and Titian, and commissions by Mantegna. Items from Isabella's collection are prominently displayed in museums throughout the world. Isabella was vain; she had an enormous collection of expensive clothes and paid much attention to her appearance even into her sixties. *Ercole Fedeli, a famous Jewish goldsmith, took four years to make her a pair of silver bracelets.* Marek, George R., *The Bed and the Throne: the Life of Isabella d'Este*, Harper & Row, New York, 1976, pp. 96-97. Isabella was on good terms with two Popes and was, for her time, remarkably tolerant of Jews.

[2] In the original typescript an "and" after "husbands" has been crossed out (covered with "xxx"). Of course this changes the meaning, but it also makes more sense. Take your pick.

[3] Since my psychoanalysis.

[4] From Donald Hellstedt: "My mother struggled with French, but mostly ended up knowing the grammar by heart, but less being able to use it. This frustrated her quite a lot. Knowing the problem with languages both my parents sent Mona and me abroad most summers to improve our proficiencies."

[5] Of cancer in 1969.

[6] The 1937 Lincoln Zephyr was impounded by the Swedish military but not used. Its 12 cylinder engine used a lot of the gasoline which was precious during WW2. After the war it was returned to the Hellstedt's in perfect condition.

[7] Only the Finns drink more coffee than the Swedes.

[8] Leone here sidesteps discussion of WW2. More than 50 million deaths, including those of six million defenceless Jews, are attributed to WW2. Total fatalities in Sweden amounted to 0.0022 million, most of these from mines laid by Swedes to placate the Germans.

[9] Alternating between the Russians and the Germans, fear of invasion drove Swedish government policy.

[10] Prominent among his responsibilities, Folke was chairman of the board of AB Separator's German daughter company, Bergedorfer Eisenwerk. In this capacity he could be expected to travel regularly to Germany. Leone's daughter Mona told me that her father was away much of the time on business during WW2. Leone's son Donald mentioned his father's dangerous wartime flights to Germany.

[11] Neutral countries, especially Sweden and Portugal, were hotbeds of intelligence during WW2. Knowledge of activities around the Baltic Sea, like the rocket research base at Peenemünde, its advanced technology and personnel (e.g. Wernher von Braun), could be gathered from Stockholm. At Strandvägan 53 Leone lived in the Stockholm embassy neighbourhood. Both the Allies and the Germans placed spies in their legations. Donald Hellstedt told me that Allied diplomatic personnel were often guests of Leone and Folke during the war. For a well-written insight, see Denham, Henry, *Inside the Nazi Ring: A Naval Attaché in Sweden 1940-1945*, Holmes & Meier, New York, 1984.

Chapter 17   1934-1945

It is safe to say that Leone changed her mind about Nazi Germany. When
we don't know. That is, she expressed admiration for the "new Germany" in
her December, 1933 interview with Matthew Halton. Like most Swedes,
she must have been favourably impressed by the economic miracle
occurring in Germany.[1] The Swedish economy was at a very low ebb, the
level of unemployment unprecedented.[2] But Germany had long been
Sweden's biggest trading partner; Sweden's economy was improving in step
with Germany's. Sweden's industrial leaders and hereditary upper class
favoured the new Germany. Since Leone was now a member of the
Swedish elite, her views could be expected to be similar. But as the Hitler
regime developed, and its inhumanity worsened and became more evident,
even Sweden turned against Germany.

Although I have been unable to find much explicit evidence of Leone's
Weltanschauung, her autobiographies and especially the letters written to her
friends in Vienna reveal, little by little, her attitudes toward religion,
overpopulation, work ethics, feminism and other social issues. Many of
these small revelations accord with ideas expressed by Carl Jung; and
because Leone took lectures from Jung in Zürich 1934-1935, and because
she became a psychoanalyst (as was Jung), it occurred to me that an
interpretation of Leone's behaviour, under the provisional assumption that
her views accorded with Jung's, might be useful. That is, it could tie
together the bits of Leone lore into a plausible picture, if not entirely
consistent, at least more easily understood. However, her training analyst
during her 1934-1935 stay in Zürich was Gustav Bally, who was considered
to be after WW2 among, "A few analysts, who generally remained true to
Freud ...." (Kaspar Weber, enotes p. 2). Freud and Jung had split in 1913.
Jung's followers in Switzerland had divided into further schools of
psychoanalytic thought by the time Leone was in training analysis. If
Bally's loyalty to Freud was the same in 1934 as it was post-WW2, then
Leone would have been subject to classical Freudian influences. The
training analysis which led to her qualification in the Swedish association
was with the academic Tore Ekman, who returned to Sweden in 1943 from
his teaching positions in Leipzig and Berlin. My impression from reading
Freud, Jung, Ekman and Leone is that her view of psychoanalysis was more
along Freudian lines - with emphasis on biological origins for psychic

phenomena and practical medicine instead of Jungian symbolism. Leone also shared Freud's conservatism and high regard for accomplishment.[3] She, like Freud, was a bit of a snob; both preferred being with and being seen with successful people.

On her three month motoring tour with Jean and Kathleen, which Leone had taken in part to "...see Sweden in perspective....", Leone reflected:

It was a wonderful journey, and when I got home, I told Folke that I would have to change my speciality. He was willing to help me in every possible way. I had decided that I would train to be a psychoanalyst, and as this was not possible in Sweden -- there was not even a professor of psychology in the country -- I arranged to work at the Neurology Clinic in Zürich, to start my training analysis with Professor Gustav Bally, to observe at Burghölzli, to take part in child psychiatric seminars at the university, and to take Carl Jung's and Pulver's lecture courses.

These were fascinating months. I was in the medical field I would have chosen from the beginning. The analysis fascinated me. I decided while there to submit once again to a licensing examination, and on my return to Sweden, I applied to the authorities for permission to qualify. After due consideration I was granted a Swedish matriculation in exchange for my Ph.D. and could thus enter the medical school. In exchange for my M.D. I was allowed a Swedish candidate examination, which credited me with the equivalent of the two years of basic sciences in Canada. I was also permitted to repeat the two last years of medicine. This was the first and last injustice I suffered in my entire medical life. I did not want to leave my husband, but there seemed no other way out. I got my license in 1937. Only two foreign physicians before me had ever applied for legitimation in Sweden.[4]

While setting up a household in Stockholm in 1932, doing laboratory work with carcinogens in late 1933,[5] planning the trip and traveling with Jean and Kathleen in 1933-1934, and beginning psychoanalytic training in Zurich in 1934, Leone was not earning money. For someone who had practically paid her own way since the age of 14, and who expressed disdain for dependent women, [6] this must have been uncomfortable. Folke was supportive and certainly able to maintain a wife; [7] but Leone wasn't being much of a wife either, living in Zürich while her husband lived in Stockholm.

The overall outcome was that Leone dropped her psychoanalytic training and returned to Stockholm. In 1934 - 1935 she translated two substantial medical books from Swedish into English.[8]

Best Before 1935

Einstein, at age 36, had produced one of history's most imaginative and dramatic revisions of our concepts about the universe. The general theory of relativity was not merely the interpretation of some experimental data or the discovery of a more accurate set of laws. It was a whole new way of regarding reality.[9]

From 1935 - 1937 Leone was occupied with the last two years of medical school at the Karolinska Institut in Stockholm. She received a license to practise medicine in Sweden in 1937. However, she earned no income in the next few years. Her daughter, Monica, was born in October, 1937. Leone was apparently occupied with taking care of her child and her husband in 1937 - 1938. In 1939 she accompanied Folke on a business trip to South America. Monica was not with them. Ship manifests indicate that they were on board ship from Buenos Aires to Southampton *nine months* before Donald McGregor was born October 31, 1939. On the manifest under "Occupation", Leone was listed as "Housewife" and Folke as "Industry".

One of the wonders of Swedish socialism is the publicity of everyone's taxable income. The following, taken from Swedish government records, indicates that Folke had a very good income from 1935 - 1955, in the top 1% of Swedish wage and salary earners; and that Leone earned nearly nothing during this period.

The Swedish crown was worth about twenty cents Canadian or American throughout this period, and around fifteen cents today.

Ernst Folke Hellstedt
SEK Swedish Kronor

INIT. DATE 17 4 12

Year	Rent	Income from employment	Income from capital	Income from real estate	Income from other	Net income	adjusted for price level 2011 SEK
1935	4200	54350	660			55010	1614818
36	6500	53290	2240			55530	
37	6500	55080	4480			59560	
38	6500	60620	4350			64970	
39	6500	89460	5950			95410	
40	8500	79360	4700			84060	1981714
41	8500	72260	8640			80980	
42	8500	65170	10570			75740	
43	8500	65390	8000			73390	
44	8500	67133	5908	8492		81523	
45	8500	64959	5864	12775		83598	1632501
46	missing	missing		missing			
47	8500	79641	6997	24072		110710	①
48		165365	10545	15354		191264	
49	8500	98897	11648	25726		136271	
50	8500	109225	11566	24387		145178	2540615
51	8500	109005	13360		26546	148911	②
52	8500	128979	14327	18704		162010	
53	8500	138588	14165	12161		164914	
54	8500	133826	13686	22780		170292	
55	8500	138526	13997	33772		186295	2500451
56	8500	149022	17522	25782		192326	
57	8500	95209	17932	23068		136209	
58		46579	22062	21247		84888	
59		44600	18090	18076		80766	
60						37950	424243 ③
61						33215	
62						52608	

① 5.8% inflation in 1948
② 16.9% inflation in 1951
③ change in register entries

All entries in SEK. Between 1930 and 1950 the price level in Sweden doubled. By the 1960s it had increased by about 360%.

Leone McGregor Hellstedt
SEK Swedish kronor
income

Year	Rent	Income from employment	Income from capital	Income from real estate	Income from other	Net income	Adjusted for price level 2011 SEK
1935		3790				3790	
36		10390	70			10460	
37		1810	170			1980	
38							
39							
40							
41							
42							
43							
44		3200				3200	
45							
46							
47							
48							
49							
50							
51							
52							
53							
54							
55					1021	1021	
56		680			21911	22591	
57		580			41652	42232	
58		647			46644	47291	
59		657			53995	54646	
60		655			55397	56052	
61		660			66847	67507	
62		62913				62913	

177

While conducting research for this book, I had occasion to discuss Leone and her career with friends - to them it must have seemed my *only* topic of conversation for nearly two years. Some asked, "Why would you write about her ... what did she accomplish?"   And indeed, Leone left nearly nothing for us in the psychoanalytic literature; her activity in medical research apparently ended in 1935, at age 35. Only after Folke, nine years her senior, retired, did she become active in the Medical Women's International Association and begin urging women doctors to write their autobiographies as part of her crusade to enlist gifted girls into the medical profession.

Thirty-five is a pivotal age. From *The Book of Common Prayer*, Christians learn that it is downhill from 35 to the end: *The days of our years are threescore years and ten.* Matthew Halton was privileged to get an interview with Carl Jung in London, October 4, 1935.[10]   Leone knew Jung; she had taken lectures from him in Zürich; perhaps she helped Halton get this interview.   Jung agreed to only a few minutes, but Halton was able to charm the world famous psychoanalyst, who lit a cigar and talked for two hours. During the interview Halton described one of his dreams. Jung's interpretation involved telling Halton that he had started dying. "When life is half over everybody starts dying. Death begins at 35."   Although Halton was not yet 35, his life was in fact more than half over: he died at age 52.

Freud, like Jung and Leone ,[11] expressed nostalgia for the vigorous, expanding intellect of his youth:

When I was a schoolboy it was quite natural for me to be able to repeat from memory the page of a book which I had read; and shortly before I entered the University I could write down practically verbatim the popular lectures on scientific subjects directly after hearing them. In the tension before the final medical examination I must have made use of the remnant of this ability, for in certain subjects I gave the examiners apparently automatic answers, which proved to be exact reproductions of the text-book, which I had skimmed through but once and then in greatest haste.
Since those days I have steadily lost control of my memory;.... [12]

Today's pop psychology contains alarms like, "After age 35 our brains lose 100,000 cells per day". Biological correlates have been found for senility and dementia; medical science is making steady progress in identifying causes and producing cures for mental diseases associated with ageing.

Intelligence declines with age, but normally not precipitously until one is near death.

Among Freud's speculations for which, despite his having repeatedly identified them as speculations, he is criticized for having presented as science, is the idea of death instincts. He recognized a related strain in Schopenhauer's philosophy, that death is the result of life and in that sense the purpose of life.[13] Freud thought that the processes of ageing unto death would, one day, be understood in biological science:

The deficiencies in our description would probably vanish if we were already in a position to replace the psychological terms by physiological or chemical ones. ....

Biology is truly a land of unlimited possibilities. We may expect it to give us the most surprising information and we cannot guess what answers it will return in a few dozen years to the questions we have put to it. They may be of a kind which will blow away the whole of our artificial structure of hypotheses.[14]

Can the effects of ageing account for Leone's abrupt change from a driven, productive research scientist and doctor to a ... *hausfru?* Probably not. But she might have recognized that her "best before date" as a scientist had passed. The idea that a scientist's vigour is dissipated by mid-life was underlined in 1937 by the publication of Eve Curie's biography of her mother, Madame Curie. Leone was aware of the career of Marja Slowdowska, born in Warsaw in 1867, the first woman to win a Nobel prize and the first person to share in two Nobel prizes. Like Leone, Marie Curie was the daughter of well educated parents, was reading at age four, was first in her classes in school, knew several languages, was gifted in mathematics and drawing, was irreligious, was a schoolmarm at age 17 to earn money for advanced education; and in her twenties devoted herself to scientific research, resulting in significant accomplishments - a doctorate from the Sorbonne and important scientific discoveries, including radium for which she and her husband Pierre would be honoured by the scientific establishments of London and Stockholm in 1903, when Marie was 36 years old. In later life Madame Curie gave up active science in favour of helping girls to realize careers in science.[15]

What is society's interest (she asks in one of her reports)? Should it not favor the development of scientific vocations? Is it, then, rich enough to sacrifice those which are offered? I believe, rather, that the collection of aptitudes required for a genuine scientific vocation is an infinitely precious and delicate thing, a rare treasure which it is criminal and absurd to lose, and over which we must watch with solicitude, so as to give it every chance of fruition.[16]

Having said that we must not allow the talented girl's gifts to wither, Madame Curie did not recommend the same level of devotion to the laboratory as she herself had maintained. Her daughter wrote about their conversations later in her life:

Mme Curie avoided even that element of vanity that might most easily have been forgiven her: to let herself be cited as an example to other women. "It isn't necessary to lead such an antinatural existence as mine," she sometimes said to calm her overmilitant admirers. "I have given a great deal of time to science because I wanted to, because I loved research ... What I want for women and young girls is a simple family life and some work that will interest them."[17]

In Leone's Medical Women's International Association correspondence of her later years, she recommended this biography of Madame Curie.

The Teskey Women

Leone reported her Teskey genes:

My father's paternal grandparents, born in Ireland of Scottish parents, also settled in Ontario. A son Thomas married Sara Ann Teskey, of Huguenot descent, and in 1889 they moved from Ontario to Carnduff in the Northwest Territories. Their fourth son Matthew, who became my father....[18]

In September of 2011 I enjoyed a series of telephone calls and meetings with Calgary people who knew Leone's only sibling, Phyllis, and who had met Leone: Rod McDaniel, Bill Selby and Marmie Hess.

Rod McDaniel married Phyllis's daughter Marilyn. At the time of our interview in the congenial confines of the Calgary Country Club, where Rod and Bill Selby were long-time members, Marilyn and her mother had been long deceased.

Rod met Leone just once that he could recall. After their conversation he realized that she had learned a great deal about him and he had learned nearly nothing about her - which he attributed to her skill as a psychoanalyst.

From Rod I first learned that Leone pronounced her name *Lee own'*, not *Lee own' uh* (as it would be pronounced in Swedish or German). When I visited Leone's daughter Mona in Stockholm, she confirmed Rod's two-syllable version.

From Phyllis Rod learned that Leone did not get on well with her children. In her typescript autobiography of January, 1970, Leone mentions that neither she nor Folke were prepared for the unruly behaviour of their children when they reached puberty. Leone also said that Phyllis believed a mother should be occupied in the care of her children (unlike Leone, who paid a nurse and had a career) and that Phyllis had a different understanding of their mother. Leone said her mother was demanding and mentions instances when her mother was overly strict; and she observed that Phyllis was able to charm her mother into letting her get away with much less disciplined behaviour. Daughter Mona told me that she felt unequal to the very high aspirations that Leone had for her: for example, when Mona was an M.D., Leone talked about a marvellous young woman, her patient, who was becoming a *dozent*, a professor of medicine at the Karolinska Institut - which Mona perceived as invidious comparison. The repetition of a mother-daughter pattern seems evident here (Leone's mother was also overly demanding). However, I feel unqualified to speculate on the subtleties of mother-daughter relationships.[19] The more general question of the upper class practice of children being raised largely by servants (e.g. Mona and Donald did not eat dinner with their parents until the age of 12) is another which I am unqualified to discuss.[20] Neither Mona nor Donald ever addressed their parents by the familiar "du" in Swedish.

Rod remembered Phyllis very well, of course, and he placed her in the category of "Teskey Women", about whom he had an interesting theory: they married prominent men; not just successful, but conspicuously successful men, even unto the rich and famous. Rod gave as examples the wife of the current prime minister of Canada and the wife of Ron Southern, a prominent Calgarian and one of Canada's wealthiest men.

Rod believed in blood lines. He had bred horses, and his father was Dorsey P. McDaniel, a cattle and horse breeder and a legendary figure in southern Alberta ranching lore.[21] One might think Rod's theory fanciful, but I can't help considering that the considerable business which Rod built in Calgary was centrally concerned with exploding fanciful theories. McDaniel Consulting was (and is still, although Rod is retired) relied upon by banks and investors to independently evaluate the assessments of oil and gas companies regarding their assets.[22]

Whether the Teskey female talent was for supporting their men or just for picking winners, Rod said he didn't know. In Phyllis McGregor's case, however, it was clear that she had married an already successful man: Dr. Charles Bouck was established as a highly respected surgeon at the time of their marriage. The Boucks lived in a large house in Calgary's posh Mount Royal district.

Rod told me that Phyllis was a strikingly beautiful woman and a gracious hostess. Bill and Marmie agreed. She was not accomplished in her own right, however, Marmie pointed out. Rod thought that Phyllis was a nurse, but the library of the Alberta Nurses' Association was unable to find the academic record of a Phyllis McGregor at either of the nursing schools of the time, Calgary General or Holy Cross. Many years ago a fire destroyed some of these records. However, page one of the *Red Deer News* of May 17, 1922 reported:

Miss Phyllis McGregor and Miss Nettie George have been accepted as nurses in training by the Calgary General Hospital, and will take up their duties about the first of June.

Leone's daughter Monica (Mona) was told by her mother that Phyllis was the gold medalist in her class of nurses at Calgary General, and that she graduated in the same year as Leone, 1925. In her draft autobiography of January, 1970, Leone regretted that none of her family could afford to attend the Calgary General Hospital nurses' graduation ceremony in 1925, the disappointment all the greater because Phyllis was the gold medalist. High school class standings, published by the Red Deer News, indicated that Phyllis was a top-quartile student, but not in the top five or ten of her class. She was, however, notably successful in extracurricular activities: team and individual sports, piano, choral singing, drama, president of CGIT and Methodist Church groups.

Phyllis taught school at Fabyan, near Wainwright, the year before she entered nurses' training. It is practically certain that she became a nurse and that is how she met her husband, Dr. Charles Bouck.

Leone also married a highly successful man, more support for Rod's theory. In her correspondence Leone mentions from time to time that someone "married well" - this enterprise seemed part of the Teskey family culture.

Dr. Charles Bouck died in 1944, a well known and much loved figure in the Calgary medical scene. His surgical skill and generous nature were attested to in eulogies from many patients and colleagues. Phyllis remained in the big house, where she was visited by Leone on several occasions following the war.

Genius on Hold

About five months after I got my Swedish medical license in 1937, my planned little daughter Monica was born, followed two years later by my son Donald. I had a cook, a housekeeper and an excellent registered German children's nurse; I was actually living in luxury.[23]

Leone's situation in 1938 did not lend itself to the independent pursuit of fame and fortune. She had a new baby, Monica. She had a husband, senior executive of a multinational corporation. They lived in a lavish apartment in the best district of Stockholm, where Folke had numerous friends, relatives and business associates. Leone's social obligations were many.

But she also had excellent domestic help. She and Folke were planning an extended voyage to South America, where Alfa Laval had affiliated companies for which Folke was responsible. She had time to read. Among the books which were then hot topics among psychoanalysts was the Otto Rank heresy, *Art and Artist: Creative Urge and Personality Development* (1932). Rank disputed Freud's attribution of artistic creativity to the sublimation of libidinal energy, instead proposing a will to immortality as the artist's motivation. They agreed, however, on the nature of genius:

exceptional natural endowment and access to the unconscious, expressed not in neurosis but in productivity.

In Chapter One I called Leone a genius. With what justification? Einstein was a genius. Mozart was a genius. Leonardo da Vinci was a genius. Andy Warhol? Hmm. Your member of parliament? Doubtful. In the early days of intelligence testing some psychologists used labels to denote IQ levels. For example, for the Stanford Binet test, a score of below 70 = "moron", 100 = "normal", more than 140 = "genius". These labels of convenience have largely disappeared from our currently inoffensive world.

While high intelligence is a property of genius, most of us understand that it must be coupled with rare innovation or accomplishment, something of lasting importance. Otto Rank described the common understanding of "genius" in terms of its etymology: *...the idea contains, as well as the notion of begetting, that of the descent also and indeed that of the continuity of all life .... the Roman idea of Genius contains from the beginning, in addition to the individual urge to reproduction, a collective element which points beyond the individual ....*[24]

Leone was highly intelligent. Of that there is no doubt. She was also a leader - the first MD from the University of Alberta, the first woman and the first gold medalist. By 1935 she had made some lasting contributions: her doctoral thesis of 1929 was cited in medical textbooks into the 1970s;[25] she published other contributions to pathology and sought a mechanism involved in the aetiology of cancer; she translated two substantial medical books from Swedish into English. Late in life she would lead the Medical Women's International Association and further several important causes.

Rank said that the genius uses his exceptional talent to create works which come from and contribute to the unconscious of his collective. These works are immortal; and they make him immortal, realizing for him his ambition, which is the unspoken ambition of us all - immortality. Those who make no lasting contribution to art/literature/science/civilization/posterity (i.e. nearly everybody) seek immortality through the most ordinary of means - by having children. That is what Leone did. In 1938 her genius was on hold.

Ernst Folke Hellstedt: Husband, Father, Breadwinner

At a party in the home of the Canadian Trade Commissioner I met the man whom I married eight months later. Folke Hellstedt was an economist and the director of the Bergedörfer (sic) Eisenwerk, a large Swedish factory located outside Hamburg. He was a Swede, nine years older than I, and he had lived all over the world as an industrial expert. He was a very broad-minded man who understood my ambitions and wanted me to have a professional life. We married at the end of my fellowship year, and I moved into his beautiful, large flat. Four months later he was made vice-president of Alfa Laval, and we moved to Stockholm, where his head office was. This was 1932.[26]

Ernst Folke Hellstedt was born in Eskilstuna Parish, County of Södermanland, State of Uppsala, Sweden on February 11, 1891. At the age of 15 he moved with his mother and siblings to Stockholm. There they resided at various addresses: his mother Margareta Albertina Selma Emilia, maiden name Berglund, born 1852; sister Dolly Margareta, born 1886; brother Ernst Gustaf Åke, born 1887; brother Ernst Svante, born 1892; sister Emmy Maria, born 1894; and brother Ernst Olof, born 1898.

While a 17- year- old student, Ernst Folke represented Sweden in the high jump at the London Summer Olympic Games of 1908; his best of 1.67 metres was good for 17th place in the final standings. In 1912 he held the title, "Reserv löjtnant (reserve lieutenant) in the Swedish navy.

The Swedish *Vem är Vem,* (Who's Who) said this about Hellstedt, E. Folke:
   Director, MBA, Stockholm, born in Eskilstuna 11/2/91 by merchant Ernst Hellstedt and Emelie Berglund;
   Diploma from the Stockholm School of Economics, 1912; employed Separatorkoncernen Sweden and overseas, 1919-1922 and 1925-1931; chief executive officer Separator Stockholm 1932-1956;
   Memberships - chairman Swedish Economic Association 1937-1940;
   Distinctions - Royal Vasa Order

In a letter to her Viennese friends, Leone said that Folke spent 1917-1918 in Omsk, Russia. This was the time and place of the last stand against the

Bolsheviks. When Kolchak's tsarist regime fell, the world's largest country entered a chaotic period of communism.[27] Folke and Leone's children, Mona and Donald, told me that Folke was visiting his brother, an architect who was building in St. Petersburg at the critical time for the tsar's family. When St. Petersburg fell to the Bolsheviks, Folke moved to Moscow, which in turn became dangerous for foreigners. He carried on to Omsk, still in the hands of the Kolchak regime, then across on the Trans-Siberian Railway to Vladivostok and on to New Zealand. Later photographs depicting Folke beside a large centrifugal separator in the Opotiki (North Island of N.Z.) Dairy suggest that in 1918 he was already working for AB Separator in a sales capacity. There are a surprisingly large number of photos of New Zealand in Leone's albums; Donald said that his father considered becoming a sheep farmer in New Zealand.

From a good family, intelligent, educated at top Swedish schools, fluent in several languages, Ernst Folke rose steadily within one of Sweden's most successful companies, AB Separatorconcern (or ABS, since 1963 called Alfa-Laval). On September 26, 1925, he moved to Germany, to manage the Separator daughter company, Bergedorfer Eisenwerk.

In 1859 Bergedorfer Eisenwerk began manufacturing farm machinery in the town of Bergedorf, near Hamburg. AB Separator was founded in Stockholm in 1883 to exploit the patent of Swedish engineer Gustaf de Laval through manufacture of a milk separator. In the first decade exports accounted for more than 80% of sales. Purchase of a superior technology in the form of the Alfa patent, from a German in 1889, allowed continued success in competition with a growing number of milk separator manufacturers in Europe and America. In 1904 the German agent, Bergedorfer Eisenwerk , became a competitor. ABS's response was to buy controlling interest in 1907 when Eisenwerk was converted to a public limited liability company, and continue to buy shares until 1914 when Eisenwerk effectively became a daughter of ABS.

When Folke joined Bergedorfer Eisenwerk in 1925, the company had long since (in 1901) abandoned manufacture of farm machinery. Several products were made for the milk industry: separators of course, margarine and butter forming machines, heating and cooling apparatus. A division for industrial applications of separators and other apparatus had been founded in 1920. A new installation for the manufacture of separators for the purification of lubricating and heating oil on board ships started in 1925.

During Folke's management tenure Eisenwerk made improvements to old products and created new ones. New markets included smaller operations wanting heaters and coolers, chemical and pharmaceutical industries (conical homogenizers), textile manufacture (weaving machines) and plate type heaters for pasteurizing and condensing milk. Technologies developed during this period allowed Eisenwerk to exploit lucrative monopoly opportunities in the 1930s, e.g. oil separation and freezing equipment for processing on whaling mother ships.[28]

From Eisenwerk's beginnings the company had the difficult problem of pouring intricate and precise castings. Their success was a matter of great pride to the company. This special expertise attracted clients with special casting requirements, and thus the opportunity to charge more. *Aus der Not eine Tugend machen.* ("From a necessity make a virtue", an Austrian - German specialty).

Folke Hellstedt's management role in the parent company, as nearly as I could determine, was what we would label, "Vice-president, Marketing" or "VP International Operations". He travelled the world, studying the feasibility of subsidiaries or joint ventures, establishing operations abroad, negotiating and selling. His facility with languages was a great asset in this enterprise. When Rod McDaniel met Folke in Maracaibo ca. 1954, when Leone wanted a report regarding Rod's suitability as a husband for her sister Phyllis's daughter Marilyn, Rod said that during the course of their dinner Folke spoke fluent English to him and fluent Spanish to others. And Folke had come from Brazil, where he spent a year before the war, presumably speaking Portugese. Folke spoke German in Bergedorf and at home[29]. In 1917-1918 he spent considerable time in Russia. He knew the language. Donald Hellstedt told me his father was fond of Russian literature.

Opotiki is on the North Island of New Zealand

Folke with New Zealand clients and their separator 1924

Bergedorfer Eisenwerk's 100th anniversary publication notes the development of new stainless steel and aluminum products in 1937. Significant among these was, *Grosslieferung von 400 Schlammseparatoren für Deutsche Hydrierwerke* (large delivery of 400 mud separators for German hydrogenation works). In 1937 Hitler was pressing IG Farben to demonstrate large scale production of gasoline from coal. The process used by IG Farben, which featured hydrogenation, was licensed from Standard Oil of the United States. Political difficulties were thus added to the technical problems. Because Hitler believed that Germany must be self-sufficient in fuel for the tanks and aircraft needed in the military operations he planned (Germany had no oil fields), the German government was prepared to support IG Farben - with money and by ignoring the legal niceties involved in exploiting American technology. The success of ersatz fuel production was a precondition for the series of invasions: Austria, Czechoslovakia and Poland.[30]

Ernst Folke Hellstedt was the chief executive of Bergedorfer Eisenwerk in 1930-1931, and remained on the board of directors until at least 1946.[31]

The history of Bergedorf Eisenwerk, 1859-1959, commissioned by the company, contains nearly nothing about its activities immediately prior to and during World War Two.[32]

Sweden and Germany Before World War Two

Although a qualified physician, Leone apparently did not work during the period 1937 - 1943, only a bit in 1944, then not again until 1955. She was dependent on Folke's (substantial) income.

Leone's daughter Mona told me that it was difficult for a physician to get a job in Sweden during this time. My guess is that Leone was busy with raising children and the social obligations attending Folke's business and his many relatives and friends in Sweden. Mona said, however, that Folke travelled most of the time, leaving Leone in Stockholm, and that the servants took care of the children.

In the summers prior to the war, Leone and Folke took motoring holidays in Europe. Following are pages from their photo albums.

Circa 1935

The following photos are from June-July, 1938

From Leone's photo albums: a poster showing Jews as degenerates

Leone   Berchtesgaden and Obersalzberg

Hitler's Home
Obersalzberg

Garmisch Partenkirchen

Leone and Folke visited friends in Hamburg on their return to Stockholm.
The Lincoln is a 1937 Zephyr model.

Psychoanalysis At Last

The war broke out, and as a result, Swedish training analysts returned to Sweden, the Swedish Psychoanalytical Association was founded, and I was able to continue my education in this field. I gradually became an analyst and was admitted to membership in the International Association of Psychoanalysts. I soon had a full-time practice. I became vice-president of the Swedish Psychoanalytical Association, and during this period the international congress was held in Stockholm.[33]

The European war began September 2, 1939 and Leone did not qualify in the Swedish Psychoanalytical Association until 1951. Thus she said nothing in her published autobiography about the biggest event in the lives of her generation, WW2. In the 77-page typescript January 1970 autobiography Leone wrote about the practical problems of lack of fuel for hot water and heating, boring food, inability to travel abroad and having to do without their Lincoln Zephyr. Another hardship, Mona told me, was the absence of her father much of the time during the war, while he travelled on business.[34] Folke told Donald that his flights to Germany and back were dangerous.

From the beginning of my research I was keen to learn the identity of Leone's training analyst. Neither the Swedish Psychoanalytical Association in Stockholm nor the International Psychoanalytical Association in London could/would tell me. For more than a year it was a mystery. Was it the notorious Alfhild Tamm, homosexual and masturbation advocate? Was it the Jewish socialist Stefi Pedersen? Was it the Hungarian Jew Szekely who wrote in several languages of his interest in creativity? Finally, Leone's daughter Mona told me it was Tore Ekman, a lektor in Berlin and Leipzig who returned to Sweden in 1943. Ekman was not a Jew, of course - he could not have been a professor or even survived in Germany in 1943 had he been Jewish. When he returned to Sweden he was criticized by colleagues, many of whom were Jewish, for staying in Germany as long as he did.

The biggest failure in my study of Leone lore was an inability to penetrate the WW2 taboo. Nowhere does Leone write about her thoughts or feelings about the war. She was, after all, from Alberta (outstanding in its loyalty to the British Empire) and she was studying to become a psychoanalyst (at that time, not so long after Freud, psychoanalysis was considered almost a

Jewish profession); at the same time her Swedish neighbours were pandering to the Nazis and her husband was a director of a company fully committed to Nazi ideology and the German war effort; if Folke did pass information to the Allies about his observations in Hamburg and Bergedorf, he could not admit it to anyone. [35] In her hundreds of letters and her typescript autobiography, the closest Leone came to these topics was to mention, "...the general tragedies of the war and the fear of invasion....", [36] and "...a different national background made problems in our marriage. Communication is easier between people of the same country and between those who have gone to school in the same epoch. It takes great devotion and loyalty to overcome such difficulties." [37]

There are four dramatic stories in Leone's life, each worthy of its own movie:

(1) her struggle through poverty and the ancient prejudice against women in medicine to achieve success in a medical career; [38]

(2) the domestic drama of servants raising children in the absence of parents absorbed in their important roles in the adult world ; [39]

(3) her crusade to bring equality to women in medicine, especially the recruitment of gifted girls into M.D. programs; [40]

(4) and the conflict inherent in her status during WW2 - a Canadian with Jewish friends and colleagues in a country favouring Germany, dependent on a husband whose income was derived in part from supplying the German war effort.

Leone told about the first three of these dramas in her autobiographies and correspondence. Because she said nothing about her life during WW2 apart from the loss of their Lincoln Zephyr, the shortage of fuel and the boring food, we are forced to speculate about the fourth drama. Moreover, the issues in this drama are highly charged ethically and emotionally. Accordingly I decided it best to leave its discussion to an appendix, where its provisional, speculative nature will be clear.

[1] For example, close to home, Leone would have learned from her husband, still on the board of Bergedorfer Eisenwerk, the company in Germany that he managed from 1925-1932, that it was about to report its first annual profit in several years.

[2] *In the fall of 1931, Sweden left the gold standard without being able to break the generally declining economic trend, and at the end of the year approximately a quarter of the union workers were unemployed.* Söderpalm, Sven Anders, in *Sweden's Development From Poverty to Affluence, 1750-1970,* edited by Steven Koblik, translated by Joanne Johnson, University of Minnesota Press, 1975, p. 267.

[3] Roazen, Paul, *How Freud Worked: First-Hand Accounts of Patients,* Jason Aronson Inc., Northvale, New Jersey, 1995, p. 87.

[4] Hellstedt, Leone McGregor, editor, *Women Physicians of the World,* Hemisphere Publishing Corporation, Washington & London, 1978, p. 203.

[5] McGregor, Leone, MD, PhD, Pathology Dept., Radiumhemmet, Stockholm, *Reactions to Radiation in Lymph Nodes Containing Carcinoma Metastases of the Squamous Cell Type,* Acta Radiologica, January, 1934.

[6] letters to MWIA Secretary and Recording Secretary (who were colleagues and friends) in Vienna.

[7] tax return records.

[8] Ahlbom, Hugo E., *Mucous- and Salivary-Gland Tumours: A clinical study with special reference to radio-therapy, based on 254 cases treated at Radiumhemmet, Stockholm,* Kungl. Boktryckeriet, P.A. Norstedt & Söner, 1935, 452 pages of text, 46 pages of plates. Although Leone translated this entire book, she is not mentioned on the cover or on the title page. Only in the last paragraph of the Preface is any mention made of her: *Finally I wish to extend my thanks to Dr. Leone McGregor-Hellstedt who has spared herself no trouble in the difficult task of translating the Swedish text into good English .... p. 11 .* The other book translated by Leone was: Knutson, Folke, translated by Fru Leone McGregor Hellstedt, *Urethrography: Röntgen examination of the male urethra and prostate after injection of contrast material into the urethra. Experience from 154 patients in Maria Hospital, Stockholm. Vol. 28 of Acta Radiologica: Supplementum.* Kungl. boktryckeriet, P.A. Norstedt & Söner, 1935, 150 pages.

[9] Isaacson, Walter, "Einstein: His Life and Universe", Simon and Schuster, New York, 2007, p. 223

[10] Toronto Star, October 18, 1935.

[11] correspondence with secretaries in Vienna re forgetting and lack of mental energy.

[12] Freud, Sigmund, translation by A.A. Brill, *Psychopathology of Everyday Life,* Wilder Publications, 2010, Blacksburg, VA, p. 62.

[13] Freud, Sigmund, translated and edited by James Strachey, *Beyond the Pleasure Principle,* W.W. Norton & Company, New York, 1961, p. 59.

[14] ibid, p. 72-73.

[15] Curie, Eve, *Madame Curie, a biography by Eve Curie, translated by Vincent Sheean,* Doubleday 1937, second edition, Da Capo Press, 2001.

[16] ibid, p. 340.

[17] ibid, p. 357.

[18] op cit Hellstedt, p. 199.

[19] Dramatic presentations of the daughter's view of a mother with a career can be frightening: *Autumn Sonata*, the film directed by Ingmar Bergman, with Ingrid Bergman as the mother and Liv Ullmann as the daughter; *Mommie Dearest*, the biography of movie actress Joan Crawford written by her daughter.

[20] Even to those of us who claim no expertise, some parenting practices seem ill-advised: *When my children were young, I would never let them leave the dinner table until they had finished their martinis.* Levant, Oscar, *The Memoirs of an Amnesiac,* G.P. Putnam's Sons, New York, Third Impression, 1965, p. 13.

[21] Bush, Wendy Marie, *Dorsey,* Friesens, Altona, Manitoba, 2006.

[22] Donald Hellstedt recalls: *I have wonderful memories of Calgary from the time in 1965, when I stayed with my Aunt Phyllis Bouck and was allowed to do some office work at McDaniel Consultants, which belonged to Rod McDaniel who was married with Marilyn, Phyllis's daughter . ... That was where I learned office discipline and work principles, which I later on applied to my own company. Phyllis was very different from my mother. A lot of fun and very easy going. She had been married to a successful surgeon Dr. Charles Bouck, who unfortunately passed away quite young in the 1940s. Marilyn's brother,*

John C. Bouck, a lawyer, moved early to Vancouver where he in due course became a member of the BC Supreme Court. He moved to Vancouver as he had some difficulties, when starting out in Calgary, with constantly being reminded that he was "the son of Dr. Bouck."

[23] Ibid, Hellstedt, Leone McGregor, p. 204.

[24] Rank, Otto, *Art and Artist: Creative Urge and Personality Development,* Alfred A. Knopf, Inc. 1932, first paperback edition W.W. Norton & Company, 1989, p.20.

[25] C. Kaplan, B. Pasternack, H. Shah and G. Gallo, *Age-related incidence of sclerotic glomeruli in human kidneys.* Am J Pathol 1975 August: 80 (2) ; 227-234.

[26] op cit Hellstedt p. 203.

[27] Manchester, William, *William Spencer Churchill, The Last Lion, Visions of Glory, 1874-1932,* Dell Publishing, New York, 1983, pp. 673-695.

[28] *Alfa Laval Astra, 100 Jahre Bergedorfer Eisenwerk : 1859 -1959* (company publication of 55 pages). The chronology in first few pages notes that in 1936, *Deutschlands grösste Walfang-mutterschiffe "Unitas" und "Walter Rau" werden mit DeLaval-Separatorenanlagen für Walöl ausgerüst.*

[29] Mona Theorell told me that when she was growing up the family most often spoke German at home. Speculating on the reasons for this, several occurred to me: Mona's beloved nurse until she was 10 years old was German; Leone could read German well and had developed some proficiency in speaking during her time in Hamburg, and according to Mona she spoke Swedish with a brutal accent; born in 1937 she would have passed through her facile language learning phase (age 3-7) during the time when Germany was favoured by Swedes to win the war, and the German language was popular in Sweden.

[30] On March 12, 1938 Hitler despatched troops across the Austrian border and the next day declared *Anschluss*, the reunion of Austria and Germany. In October of 1938 German troops occupied the Sudetenland, the part of Czechoslovak bordering Germany and Austria, containing three million people, most of whom spoke German, and sophisticated industries (including arms manufacture). The invasion of Poland in September, 1939 precipitated WW2.

[31] The Bergedorf Museum archives provided me with minutes of Bergedorfer Eisenwerk management meetings, newspaper articles regarding Eisenwerk and local histories which contained references to Eisenwerk.

[32] op cit, *Alfa Laval Astra, 100 Jahre Bergedorfer Eisenwerk: 1859-1959,* Bergedorfer Eisenwerk Aktiengesellschaft, Astra-Werke, Hamburg-Bergedorf, 1959.

[33] op cit Hellstedt p. 204.

[34] As one of the three directors of Bergedorfer Eisenwerk, Folke would be expected to travel regularly to Bergedorf, a suburb of Hamburg. AB Separator had subsidiaries, joint ventures and substantial clients all over the world. Its German, American and British affiliates were all important suppliers to those countries' war efforts.

[35] Donald Hellstedt told me that during the war diplomats affiliated with Allied countries were frequent guests in their apartment. His father's reticence regarding the war was rarely breached. Leone mentions their friendship during the war with the Corcoran family, in Sweden for the American diplomatic mission.

[36] From Leone's typescript draft autobiography dated January 1970, p. 64.

[37] ibid p. 76.

[38] The Horatio Alger stories, dozens of Hollywood dramatizations of rags to riches, ugly duckling stories.

[39] e.g. Ingmar Bergman's *Autumn Sonata* and *Mommie Dearest.*

[40] e.g. Jackie Robinson leads negroes into major league baseball - *The Jackie Robinson Story.* Shirley Muldowney leads women into top level drag racing - *Heart Like a Wheel.*

Chapter 18   1946 - 1960

Gradually letters began to come from Mama and Phyllis and my American friends and in 1947 (sic)[1] I left on a freighter for Canada. It was a stormy voyage through the mine fields around Denmark but we finally arrived in Boston, the same day that a large boat had crashed up on shore and stopped all the city traffic. However, Carol met me and had a wonderful party that night with all our old friends including the Arthur Hertigs and the Tracy Mallorys. The food was divine after our war rations. I took the train to Toronto the next evening. Roland Michener was to meet me and I was to spend the day with Norah and him but we had a minor train wreck and I only got to Toronto in time for dinner with them. Norah was getting her Ph.D. in philosophy and both she and Roland were quite shocked to hear that I was interested in psychoanalysis. That evening I took the train for Calgary. All airplanes were still reserved for returned soldiers. I awoke in the morning to the crunch of dry snow on the station platform in Winnipeg. It was a sound from my childhood and I felt right at home. We arrived in Calgary on a long train such as one never sees in Europe and with a whistle which I love. Phyllis and her beautiful 16 year old daughter Marilyn were at the train. Mama and Papa were living by this time in Phyllis' house. I wondered how I had ever come to leave them all. It was so heavenly to be with them again. I threw my arms around Mama and said, "Mama, how could I?", meaning how could I settle down so far from home. Phyllis' home was very luxurious and comfortable, the atmosphere was relaxed and I was overjoyed to be under the same roof as my parents. Mama was still handsome and very wise, well read and interested in everything. Papa was taking medicine for Parkinson's Disease but was able to get around quite well and to read a great deal. He was his usual optimistic, gentle self and this comforted me. I was very surprised that all my old friends remembered and gave parties for me. I had expected that everyone would have forgotten me. It was 22 years since I had been in Calgary or Edmonton.

Phyllis' two children were clever and handsome. Marilyn was just in puberty and a bit difficult. It was my first encounter with youth in this state. Puberty had not yet arrived in Europe. I could not imagine my well behaved little cherubs Donald and Monica being in a state of revolt but I saw that I should be prepared. However, I could not get Folke to even consider such a problem. He could not conceive of such a situation. He had obeyed his parents and our children would obey us.

Phyllis and I drove up to Edmonton and stayed at the Macdonald. My childhood friend Mary Simons McDonald and Mrs. Ower and many others had wonderful receptions for me. I could hardly believe it was all true. Pembina Hall was just the same as when I lived there, although I was told that the girls could now smoke. It was thrilling to meet my youthful idol Dr. Pope who had just retired and who also had a party for me.

When I left Calgary by train after two months I travelled via Minneapolis to see Dr. Bell again. Unfortunately the whole day we had planned was lost, for the train was hours late. Nevertheless he was there and we walked up and down the station platform for the two hours allowed us. He was just as inspiring and amazing as ever and I wondered how I had ever left him. I flew from Chicago to New York where I stayed with Wilda Blow, now Mrs. Bernard, in her apartment on Fifth Avenue. We had not met for 17 years but we were still friends. The problem of getting an exit permit and a boat passage on the same day was almost insurmountable and took me three weeks. I finally got home to Sweden on a freighter and was so happy to see Folke at the dock in Gothenburg with our nice new car back again in our possession after eight years. The children were wonderful and glad to have me back and there was now no war.

That summer I was able to get permission from the Allied authorities to drive with Monica and Donald down to the Millstätter See in Austria for the summer. The condition was that I did not eat any German food or buy any gasoline in Germany. So we had food and big dunks (?) in our Lincoln Zephyr. The children were now 11 and nine. They found Hamburg and Austria beautiful. I bought them American maple walnut ice cream and Wolfgang treated them to German Kirschentorte with whipped cream, so they were thrilled. We had to get to Kassel that night. This was quite a drive as all bridges were provisional and there were troops on every road. We slept on straw-filled gunny sacks in the basement of what was left of a hotel which was now occupied by the Allies. The whole center of that once beautiful city was only rubble and it was a horrible sight. American soldiers and German girls danced all night long in the room beside our cubby holes. There was a puncture in one tire in the morning but we finally got on our way and crossed the border into Austria that day. The saddest sight of all had been Würzburg where I could not even find my way in the rubble. That night we reached the nice hotel at the Millstätter See. Donald hopped out from our balcony window into the garden in his enthusiasm and broke his tibia, so he had to wear a cast all summer. However, the people and the little town were lovely. The trees in the hotel garden were loaded with fruit and nuts. We took short car trips in Austria and one long trip to Venice [2]where we stayed at the Danieli on the Grand Canal. Monica sent Folke a postcard saying that Venice was more wonderful than Maria Montez in "The Queen of the Sudan" which was her favourite film. On the way home we picknicked in the gardens under the grapevines in Northern Italy. Finally we started home but this time without hotel reservations in Germany. The military people allowed us to sleep in a hotel in Ulm and we reached the Danish border the next day, thanks to a nice American soldier who gave me his gasoline tickets. It was heavenly to get away from occupation troops and to be in security in Denmark.

Donald Hellstedt recalled this trip:

Compared to Mona, I believe, that I in general remember more from our childhood and our parents. At least that is what she often contends.

It struck me that I never quite understood why we travelled to Millstatt in Kärnten in Austria on the tour with mother and us two in the Lincoln. Of course, it was a beautiful place on the lake and far away from the consequences of the war. Millstatt was in the British sector, but they were not as visible as in Germany. Most everyone wore Lederhosen and all the women gorgeous Dirndl. Mona met a boy, Christopher, with whom she corresponded many years afterwards. He told my mother that Mona looked like a fairy princess.

In the context of Millstatt I now begin to believe that it was a trip "à la recherché des temps perdus" for my mother, searching for reminiscences from easier times and in particular the encounter with King Alfonso in Millstatt, the latter at least partially or perhaps not.[3]

On this occasion we also drove the Lincoln down to Venice and over the Grossglockner pass, but I believe it was only my mother and I with possibly another guest.

Driving in Italy at that time was a drama. We had to lock the doors and roll up the windows, because the roads were full of unsettled people walking in both directions, with huge bundles and pulling small carriages, impeding the traffic, which besides these human masses consisted of bicycles, military trucks and very few cars. When we had to stop, now and then, because of the congestion, we were immediately surrounded by people trying to open the doors of the car and get a free ride, sometimes quite aggressively and insisting that it was their right.

In Venice I was treated with my mother's "culture transfer drill". It consisted of lively compact lectures on most everything of interest in Venice. I still remember parts of those talks. As compensation she bought me a small toy cap gun, which I found in a showcase shop window. Before we left Millstatt for the excursion I had managed to splinter a bone in my leg and I wore a plaster around my leg under the knee.

My mother was always extremely well read about sights and important historic and cultural features and was able to place them in context. She could beat the Baedecker or at least keep up with it. Once she lectured me somewhere in Germany about a cathedral, of which there remained, in front of us, only a sorry heap of bricks. However, it re-appeared in her description in my fantasy. Walking through a museum with her was a delight. She had a way of stopping in front of certain selected items and hammer in their importance – for life. She was an expert on the Roland saga and we always stopped to look when a village or city displayed statues of him, which hundreds in Germany do.

Leone   Mona   1948   Donald

That fall, once again with Folke's blessings, I was able to recommence my own training analysis and to take the necessary courses. My analyst was Swedish but he had done his training in Berlin.[4] We found it most profitable to let me talk English and he talked Swedish. I was really fascinated by psychiatry and analysis and for five years was fully occupied for most of the day. I could do a lot of the reading at home and thus be near the children. My best Swedish friend with whom I had taken my licensing exam had returned to Sweden with her Dutch husband. Both of them were analysts and one of her oldest friends here had become a child psychiatrist so we all had much in common. During these years, Folke had great responsibilities in his work and had to travel to many countries. The children were abroad each summer for three months in either England, France, Germany or Spain to perfect their knowledge of languages. Two summers we took a house for the four of us in Sitges in Spain, at that time a charming small village with a good golf course which was fine for Folke. The other summers Folke and I motored around Europe looking at historic sights and staying in quaint country inns. Several times my oldest friends from the U.S. and Canada came over and travelled with us.

Donald in Venice, 1949

Above: pointer & Folke;
Below: Leone & Outram (?)

Gradually Donald entered a Swedish boarding school about 60 miles north of Stockholm and Monica was ready for gymnasium (High School). Donald thrived in Sigtuna where both the house mother and father were very musical, which made him feel at home with them.

Folke was also very musical so we have always had all classical records and the children were very accustomed to hear good music.[5] When Donald was only five he used to insist that we play Tchaikovsky while he went to sleep. Monica gradually became an expert with her bedside radio and spent half each night listening to music from all over Europe.

In 1951 I had a short holiday in Canada to see Mama and Papa, for the last time, as it turned out. Mama was still in good health and a joy to behold and to talk to. Papa was already in a nursing home and as cheerful as ever, but it broke my heart to see him so helpless. Except for the change in Papa, it seemed to me both times I was home in Calgary that nothing and no one had changed since I left in 1921. This time Phyllis had sent me an air ticket as a present and it was a wonderful feeling to fly over Canada. I had already flown a great deal in Europe, but it was not the same. Phyllis and I drove down to California and visited my friends Dulcie and Billy in La Jolla. The drive down and back was very beautiful. Then my old friend Bill Genereux came up from Saskatoon to see me and everyone I had ever known had parties for me.

When I returned to Stockholm I was ready to start my psychoanalytic practice. I was lucky to have such a large home as there were and still are no available offices for rent on account of the housing shortage. I was able to use one of my living rooms for the couch and consultation work and my large hall as a waiting room, without causing any inconvenience to the family. My practice grew very quickly and I soon had far too much to do. I enjoyed the work immensely. My practice gradually came to consist of young university students with contact difficulties or examination phobias. After writing a paper on one of my cases, I became a full member of the Swedish Psychoanalytic Association. I attended my first congress in this field in Geneva and was amazed to discover how many of those famous people were noticeably inhibited and anxious. It was thrilling, however, to see and hear and meet Ernest Jones, Heinz Hartmann, Anna Freud, Marie Bonaparte and Jeanne Lampl de Groot.

Gradually I became Vice President of the Swedish Association and had a good deal to do with getting lecturers from abroad and entertaining them while here. Our most famous visitor during this period was Jeanne Lampl de Groot who stayed in my home and whom I am lucky to count as a real friend.

While I was Vice President we had the International Congress here in Stockholm and I entertained the Central Executive and our senior members at a dinner for 40 persons in my home. It was very exciting to meet such a number of famous analysts privately. I placed them at four large round tables. The tablecloths were of pink linen. One table was set with Chinese porcelain from 1700 which Folke had inherited. Another was set with my antique Japanese porcelain from 1780-1800. The other two tables were set with my powder blue flower-embossed Spode and my Eden Spode. The large rose linen serviettes were folded high like boats in the Swedish custom. The flat silver was my Danish Jensen, King's Pattern. There were cards in the hall for the gentlemen to tell them whom they should take in to dinner. The ex-Europeans living in America enjoyed the temporary return to European customs. I sat between Heinz Hartmann and Maxwell Gitels and felt very honoured and happy. Folke had Anna Freud on his right. He made a nice speech of welcome in the Swedish fashion and everything seemed to go off very well.

[1] Articles in issues of the Calgary Herald during January 1946 (not 1947) refer to the current visit of Dr. Leone McGregor Hellstedt to her sister Phyllis in Calgary.

[2] About 250 km.

[3] According to Leone's January 1970 autobiography the three weeks of daily golf games with King Alfonso were at a golf hotel on the Wörther See, about 60 km from Millstatt am See.

[4] Tore Ekman.

[5] Donald Hellstedt loves Mahler's music, as did his mother. Mahler interested psychoanalysts. He lived in Vienna and consulted Freud, who noted Mahler's fixation on his mother. Mahler denied this, despite such evidence as asking his wife Alma to change her name to Marie, his mother's name. Donald remembers,
…his wife Alma Mahler published her book "Mein Leben". My mother, always on the forefront together with emancipated women, was impressed by the book. I was quite skeptical and referred to her as a "groupie" dedicated to collecting geniuses and less interested in them as such. This developed into a principle ongoing discussion between my mother and me on emancipation and the available options for gifted women of Alma Mahler's generation. I contended that someone who manages to marry Gustav Mahler, Walter Gropius and Franz Werfel as well as entertaining numerous additional relations with other famous artists, such as Oskar Kokoschka et al cannot be taken really seriously. We usually ended the friendly disputes with listening to a "long playing records" recording of "Das Lied von der Erde" with Bruno Walter conducting. Of course Alma Mahler was an extraordinary woman and my mother of course saw her as a leading light with her unorthodox ways and life style. Perhaps she even envied her in some ways. I also believe that she discussed Alma Mahler during her encounters with Anna Freud and other psychoanalysts – I guess she was a "case".

Chapter 19   1946 - 1960   Out of Confinement in Sweden

The end of the war did not see the end of hardship for Leone. Shortages of goods persisted. Folke's income, while still high by Swedish standards, had stagnated during the war. The family's Lincoln Zephyr was returned, however, and the beloved motoring trips were again possible.[1]

In January, 1946, Leone was able to get a freighter to Canada (returning troops filled the ocean liners). She spent two months with Phyllis in Calgary and enjoyed visiting her friends in the relative material splendour of Canada and the United States. She ate well and bathed in nostalgia.

For Mona 1947 was not a good year. Nanna (Käthe Greve), her nurse since infancy, moved back to Germany. Another German girl, Fridel Lehmann, came to work in the Hellstedt household, where she remained for 30 years.

In the autumn of 1947 Leone returned to training analysis: typically "on the couch" for one hour per day, four or five days per week; plus study of theory and case histories. Her analyst was Tore Ekman.

Donald sent me impressions of his mother, formed critically in 1948:

She loved the Lincoln Zephyr 1939 (sic-1937), *pitch black, grey seating, a huge space in the back, and with a straight* (sic-V) *12 cylinder engine. In 1948, with special permission by the occupying allies, we received permission to drive through Germany to Austria on vacation. I believe that most people in Stockholm thought she was a bit mad – driving through occupied Germany with two rather small children to, of all places, Austria.*

It was quite an experience with all the border controls, rationing cards and military convoys, bombed out cities as also with most bridges out. My mother drove all the way with Mona and myself in the car. I wore the popular "Monty Costume", a khaki type of uniform from the North African campaign, with breast pockets. In those pockets I kept our cash in dollars. No border or military person would question a small boy's pocket content – it was not allowed and a bit risky if found out.

My mother counted on her nationality, if questioned, and I remember that she was anxious to reach the American sector as fast as possible. The

English were quite imperial in their sector it seemed. We were instructed to only speak English in the presence of allied military.[2]

Here is an anecdote from that trip. We were supposed to stay overnight in a hotel in Kassel. We arrived in the dark and received direction from an English officer. After driving for some 20 minutes in the pitch dark with me as the card reader (nine years old) we couldn't find the hotel and most buildings round us were flattened. So, we took directions in the opposite direction. Same thing. Finally a military patrol in a jeep drove ahead of us to the hotel, headed by a British Captain. We looked at it and it had only the remaining first floor left, with the entrance leading down the cellar stairs. Once inside it was full of military personnel, who had put out their cigarettes on the floors and counter, for several years. I remember staring at this overall material and human made destruction. After we were assigned our room it turned out to have stacked beds with straw filled mattresses and straw filled cushions.

My mother wanted to see all her old friends who had survived the war and longed to get out of the seclusion of Sweden since 1939. It was a profound experience for me and it formed my opinion on not only Germany, Europe and war, but on human relations in general. I remember listening to all the conversations she had, understanding some. One was with Wolfgang Rittmeister, whose brother was executed by the German regime as a resistance agent. Wolfgang had wished to marry my mother and he was like a second father to me for the days we spent with him and his wife in Hamburg on that trip. Many more encounters followed through Germany. Everyone was so excited to see my mother again and treated us so well. A totally new world appeared to me and it probably influenced me to move to Berlin in 1986, where I lived for some 20 years, before moving to Luzern.

Millstatt, Austria, 1949: above, Mona & Donald; below Leone & Folke

1950: Mona and Donald visited by Nanna (a.k.a. Nana, Käthe Greve), out of the service uniform she always wore before she left in 1947 to take care of an infant in Sweden. She married and eventually settled in the U.SA.

Leone managed a short visit to Calgary in 1951. She saw her parents for the last time then. Her father died in 1951. Her mother's obituary in the Calgary Herald in 1953 listed her address as 1014 Prospect Ave.; apparently Mama had been living with Phyllis.

Leone said that she began her psychoanalytic practice in 1951, that it grew rapidly, and that she presented the case history which qualified her for full membership in the Swedish Psychoanalytical Association in 1953.[3] Government records show no net income for this period; in fact, insignificant income from employment until 1956. I don't know how to account for this discrepancy. My best guess is that the expenses of her training in psychoanalysis were deductible and could be carried forward according to Swedish tax law: thus she could earn fees from her psychoanalytic practice and deduct expenses of prior years to arrive at zero net income.

Donald, Mona and friends, 1951

Schloss Elmau   Xmas Holidays
January 1953

Mona   1953

In 1957 Leone applied for resignation from the Church of Sweden, to which all Swedes automatically belonged.

A heavy case load and activity in the Swedish Psychoanalytic Association characterized the late 1950s. Leone was Vice - President when the International Congress of Psychoanalysts was held in Stockholm.

A significant event during this period was attendance at the biannual Congress of the Medical Women's International Association in Baden Baden in 1958. There Leone began her activities in aid of women doctors which was to become her "hobby" and then almost fully occupy her during the last decade of her life.

The Medical Women's International Association (MWIA) was founded in 1919 following a meeting of women doctors in New York. Leone dedicated "Women Physicians of the World" to the twelve founders of the MWIA:

Esther Pohl Lovejoy	United States
Alma Sundquist	Sweden
Clelia Lollini	Italy
Tomo Inouye	Japan
Yvonne Pouzin	France
Martha Welpton	United States
Grace Ritchie	England
Christine Munch	Norway
Regina Stang	Norway
L. Thuillier-Landry	France
Maria Feyler	Switzerland
Radmila Lazarevitch	Serbia

Esther Pohl Lovejoy was the first president of the MWIA. In Leone's time International Congresses were held in a different country every two years; today the International Congresses are at three year intervals. National Associations and Geographical Regions typically meet more often. Members are those who belong to National Associations (NAs) of female MDs. From countries which have no NA, individuals can join, providing they have MD qualification in their country's medical association.

Leone's immersion in MWIA affairs brought her into contact with ordinary women doctors from around the world whose work was difficult, exhausting and even dangerous. While interning at the University of Alberta Hospital in 1925 she told herself and others that she preferred academic medicine and research to treating patients. Accordingly she made a career far away from the sort of practice described by Dr. Mary Percy in letters from the Notikewin district of Alberta in 1930.

I'm up to my eyes in work. I've been up three nights running, and done 78 miles on horseback in the last 48 hours too! Wednesday I was out all day, got home at 12:30 a.m. very cold - it was freezing hard - to find a man waiting to take me to a case 20 miles away; so I had to repack my bag, snatch a biscuit or two, and start off again; they'd had to send for me to go on a saddle horse, as the trail was impassable to anything else - miles of it under water, and a couple of creeks to swim! When we were two miles from our destination a man met us and told us they wanted us in a hurry, so I did the last two miles of a 45-mile day at a dead gallop. Found the woman pulseless, cold and clammy, so it was a very good job we hurried. Stayed there till 6 p.m. (from 4 a.m.) and got in at 10 p.m., looked to the horse, made supper and went to bed. At 1 a.m. a man's voice outside my window - Could I go and see his wife? - he thought she had appendicitis - and the trail to his house was only fit for a horse. So I dressed, packed my bag, and off again. Sure enough, she was starting an appendix. I was arranging to take her down to Peace River to hospital, when another man arrived. Could I come at once to his wife? He had had to follow me over to this case, taking an extra hour, so we hurried on. Back home to fetch my bags, and then a 9-mile hurry up there. And here I've been all day, and look like being here most of the night!   letter to her parents in England, April 11, 1930 [4]

The rush continues. I've had 1 1/2 nights in bed in the last 8 days, and have done 180 miles on horseback in the time, and also 100 miles down here with an acute appendix. I'm just off to the hospital to give the anaesthetic and then am off back to the Battle.[5] We've had another heavy snowstorm, so we had to bring the appendix case out with a sleigh pulled by a caterpillar tractor!! It was the only way. I kept her nearly unconscious with morphia, but, oh boy you don't know how trying the rat-a-tat-tat of a caterpillar is till you've done 70 miles behind one.   letter to her parents, April 16, 1930 [6]

In the 1960s and 1970s Leone would work tirelessly and effectively to improve the lot of women in medicine throughout the world, but she did it her way - mingling with people at the highest levels of society while she stayed in five star hotels.

Leone   Folke

[1] Leone loved driving and was a car fancier. Her 1937 Lincoln Zephyr was followed in 1951 by a series of Volkswagen beetles. On September 3, 1967, Sweden changed from driving on the left side of the road to driving on the right side like Norway, Denmark and Europe. The change was not popular with Swedes, but the government did it anyway (reminiscent of the change of Austria and Czechoslovakia to the right side of the road after German occupation). Most vehicles in Sweden in 1963 were already left hand drive. In the 1970s Leone wanted a red Ford Mustang, Mona told me. Alas, she never got one. Mona also told me that Leone was an aggressive driver and in her seventies was involved in minor accidents.

Donald recalled: *During the war the Lincoln had been compounded, but not used by the Swedish military, so we received it back in 1945 and kept it for some years. My father had GM stock, so he decided for a Chevrolet, probably about 1952, quite a distinguished car in Stockholm at that time. Later on he got fed up with it and we bought two VW beetles, which were used for many trips abroad, in tandem. I think he lost interest in the image of a car and my mother too. Separator (today AlfaLaval) had a Volvo 1946 or -47, which picked up my father each morning and back in the evening. I used to stand at the window after breakfast and call out when it arrived: "Johnson är där!" (Johnson has arrived!). Johson was the driver.*

[2] Mona and Donald had been raised speaking German first. Their nurse, Nana, was German.

[3] Typescript autobiography dated January, 1970, p. 69.

[4] Cited in Jamieson, Heber C., *Early Medicine in Alberta,* University of Alberta, 1947, p. 139.

[5] Locals in the Manning - Hawk Hills area call the tributaries of the Notikewin River the First Battle, Second Battle and Third Battle (River).

[6] Cited in Jamieson, op cit, p. 140.

Chapter 20   1960-1970

On my arrival in Sweden (in 1932) I was at once taken as a guest to the Women's Medical Club, but was not asked to be a member as I did not have a Swedish M.D. After I took their licensing examination in 1937 I was admitted to this group of rather eccentric, elderly pioneer women. Like most educated people of their generation in Sweden, they were very stiff and reserved so the meetings seemed to me boring. I paid my fees but never attended. Suddenly one day in 1960 I decided to give them one more try. At this meeting, Märta Holmström, now one of my best friends, and at that time one of the seven International Vice-Presidents of MWIA, made a report on the coming Congress in Manila in 1962. She was so natural and charming in every way that I decided on the spot to attend the Congress in the Philippines. The trip turned out to be one of the most enriching experiences of my life. The Philippine women doctors were amazing in every way. They all seemed to have large families, good jobs, beautiful homes, and they even were often on the boards of large business enterprises. An entire university in Manila is staffed by women. There were 7000 girls studying medicine at the different medical schools. The Congress was perfectly organized and was held in a wonderfully beautiful new building. The opening ceremony with all those Asian women, beautiful by nature and still more lovely in their native costumes, touched me to tears. I had not known that we white women were so much less attractive in every way. The entertainment was magnificent. This was the first international medical congress in Asia and it was the pride of the Philippines to do it well. It was here that I became friends with our Canadian Vice-President, Henrietta Banting. After the congress I took the tour over Japan, Hong Kong, Bangkok, India and home.

Japan was cold but the country and the historic sites were for me overwhelming. The Japanese women doctors of my age could not speak English but they were charming and made us feel very welcome. I bought something I had been looking for for 30 years, namely antique Japanese porcelain. These I found at Yamanaka's in Kyoto. Folke had often been in the Orient, and we belonged to the Japanese-Swedish Society here. One of his oldest friends who had lived in Japan had once served us a dinner on Japanese antique china and I fell in love with it. I was able to get groups of six dishes for three courses for 24 people, so now my children can each inherit enough for 12 persons.

We were also gloriously entertained in Bangkok. The premier and his wife gave a garden party with supper at small tables outdoors. The cooks made the dishes to be served over open coals before our eyes. Thailand girl dancers in beautiful costumes did the entertaining. I was asked to thank the hostess over the microphone. Then the cabinet ministers thanked me with the words, "May Buddha bless you." The temples, the boat market and the silk weaving were all fascinating. I gave a television interview. The women doctors there seemed to have a very good position. One evening we visited Dr. Pereira's hospital and home, with her some 80 adopted illegitimate babies, the children of unmarried university students. She cares for them and educates them at her own expense. The mothers may readopt them at any time.

I came home from Asia with quite a different picture of the world. Europe and America seemed so small and Asia so large. Folke and I had much to talk about. The physical beauty of most of the Asian peoples had been a surprise to me as well as the existence of Japanese and Philippine medical schools entirely staffed by women doctors. I felt as if I had many more sisters in the world than I had ever dreamed of.

Monica had first done two years in the school of political economy of the university before she decided to enter medicine. In medical school she met Klas Theorell, the eldest son of Hugo and Margit Theorell. Hugo is a Nobel Prize winner in Biochemistry and all his three sons are doctors. Klas and Monica still had a year until graduation but they were lucky enough to get the flat of his parents and they decided to marry. The wedding was in the Anglican Church near us with the service in Swedish. As is the custom here, the wedding was at five p.m. and followed by a formal dinner for 100 in the festival flat of the Wennergren Center. I felt as I imagine most mothers do on this occasion, sad to lose my little daughter and deeply desirous that she should be happy.

MONICA AND KLAS THEORELL 1962

Two years later we attended the International congress for Medical Women in Oslo and Monica, looking very lovely, read the report from Sweden.

In 1964 Folke and I had one of our best trips together. He had never really understood my longing to see Egypt but to please me he arranged for a three weeks stay over the Xmas holidays. He came home just as entranced as I. He could not bring himself to drive or walk through the villages but he was fascinated by the old Egyptian temples, pyramids and tombs. We met on the airplane a charming Finnish couple, Vera and Kay, who took me to all the places of present day Egypt which Folke refused to visit. Vera has an antique shop in Helsingfors and Kay is a shipper. Their son is studying medicine in Heidelberg. Their interests are wide and international. Aside from the beauty of the old city ruins up the Nile, I think I was most impressed by the paintings on the walls of the tombs. The colours were as fresh as if they were painted yesterday. All human occupations were depicted but I never saw one showing any form of human cruelty.

Two years later Märta Holmström and I attended the congress of the MWIA in Rochester, New York. There was a heat wave and an air strike, so after several days in the country home of my Chautauqua friend Mary Chorn Hazard (outside Pittsburgh) I had to take three buses to get to Rochester. Somehow or other I developed an acute appendix that day and had to be operated on that night. Märta and Lorna Lloyd-Green, incoming president of MWIA, diagnosed my condition and got me to a surgeon and a hospital.

Everything went well and I was allowed to get up and give my paper two days later, as long as I promised to sleep two nights more in the hospital. When Märta and I flew home, we landed in Scotland and I'll never forget the lovely cool, refreshing air after the heat wave in the States. My nice colleague, Beth Baxendine, kept me as a guest in her home a few days and then Märta and I returned to Sweden.

Soon after this Donald married Tuula Juramo, a Swedish-Finnish girl, the daughter of a naval officer and an artistic mother. I could not have found a better or more beautiful daughter-in-law in the whole world. Folke and I loved her immediately. She and Donald are both engaged in different parts of the tourist and congress administration business and seem to us to be a very happy couple with so many interests in common.

DONALD AND TUULA 1967

Monica and Klas now have three children: Andreas, Leone and Mona, who are a joy to us all. Monica is resident physician in the Seraphimer University Hospital and will be finished with her specialty training as an internist within a year. She and Klas have a lovely modern country home close to that of his parents out in the archipelago, to which they retire weekends.

In June, 1968, Märta and I took part in the Vienna Congress of MWIA. The weather was perfect, the city and the state entertained us 900 women doctors royally and I was chosen as president-elect. This means that I will be installed as president on the last day of the congress in Melbourne in 1970 and I will preside in Paris in 1972. I was proposed by Canada and Sweden, and am very happy to have this opportunity and recognition in my old age. Our week in Vienna was particularly enjoyable because all officials are especially well-placed at the entertainments. Märta and I saw the opera, the Riding School and all the other wonderful sights from the very best seats.

LEONE McGREGOR HELLSTEDT   STOCKHOLM 1968

These almost two years since have been unbelievably sad because Folke developed a sigmoid cancer and despite three operations gradually died in hospital on June 13, 1969. We had spent Xmas in Mallorca with Märta and her daughter, hoping that he had recovered. He had played golf as usual in October and November. He died as he lived, with great dignity and holding my hand. To lose one's life companion after 38 years of marriage is an experience that no one can be really prepared for. However, as most women are destined to become widows, one must and one can learn a new way of life and how to be a useful person even if you are alone. In this great emergency in my life, I have been amazed to find how my men and women friends, from my youth and from later years as well, have done their very best to comfort me. I will never be able to repay them. My gratitude is boundless.

I still have my psychoanalytic practice which I will now gradually reduce so that I only receive patients in the mornings. For the last 10 years I have begun at 7:15 and have continued until 4:00 p.m. This is now too much and I will need more time for the MWIA, at least until after the Congress in 1972 when I will be presiding.

Thoughts in 1970 about those closest to me

Mama belonged to those women who all their lives are attractive to men. Her father's devotion to her plus her stunning apparition must have given her from early life an inner security which almost nothing could disturb. She was very dark, tall and slim, with a beautiful figure and thick blue-black hair. Her hair was naturally curly until she caught typhoid fever at 16. When it came out again it was thick but straight and very long.

She did not marry until she was 26 but this was not from lack of suitors. Even after her marriage, all interesting men were fascinated by her. As life was in the small towns in those days, the educated people met often, no matter what their economic situations were. My parents' friends were always the judge, the doctor, the lawyer, the clergyman and the teachers. Mama was an excellent cook, although she loathed housework, and she was always glad to have guests. I do not remember any woman of our acquaintance who received so much attention from other men. My father adored her all his life. She had a keen intellect, was exceedingly well read and could discuss almost any subject. In addition, everyone told her or longed to tell her all their troubles for she was utterly reliable. Her many women friends from her youth and adult life were all devoted to her. She was my mother and I could not have had any other.

As I look back on my father, I think of him as a warm-hearted optimist who loved his wife and daughters dearly. He had an unusual gift for expressing himself orally or in writing. He could make a speech on any current subject with very little preparation. He could compose a poem on the spur of the moment. He was totally unworldly and apparently unable to settle down anywhere for good. Like Mama, he belonged to those people whom everyone wants to confide in. He liked people and was always helping someone, no matter how complicated his own life situation was. Except for economic reasons I couldn't have wished for a better father.

My sister Phyllis, like my parents, has been with me in my heart all these years, no matter how far away I have been. She married young and we have been separated for the greater part of our lives. Now when we meet we are amazed to discover how many ideas we have in common. Her picture of our mother is entirely different from mine, but we have identical memories of our father. Phyllis believes that women should stay at home and take care of their children. I am not at all sure about this and in fact suspect that mothers are often not good for their children. However, on the whole, we are very much in agreement. She and Mama have been the ideal from which I have selected my wonderful collection of women friends. I wish Phyllis and I could have lived nearer each other so that we could have shared more of our life experiences. She has repeatedly come to me when I have needed her and for this generosity I am most grateful.

Monica and Donald have been my treasures. They were planned and wanted and loved. They have turned out to be enormously active, independent creatures and I do not think they will realize until they are as old as I am now, how their father and I wanted them, watched over them and tried to be good to them. We were often unwise due to how little we knew about the bringing up of children. We were almost completely unprepared for how early they desired complete independence. We can only wish them all success with their own children and forgiveness for the faults in their parents.

When it comes to my men and women friends, I do not know how I could have lived this life without them. I have been terribly fortunate that they are so numerous and that they have remained so faithful. When I listen to my young patients, I think how simple life was in my day and how lucky I was in my boy friends and later in my men friends. And all the way along, my girl and women friends have provided me with the proof of the wisdom of Mama's principles.

I was lucky to marry a man like Folke who considered me an equal and who from the beginning of our acquaintance always understood my desire to practise my profession in some way as well as to have a home and children. I did not have to talk him into these ideas. His father before him had the same outlook and was equally concerned that his daughters as well as his sons should have professions. Folke's success in his own career made it possible for me to live these 38 years in a country and in circumstances where I always had plenty of good help so that I seldom needed to do anything in my home except organize it. From the beginning of our marriage he placed the money at my disposal for the household and for me personally directly in my bank account. His position was luckily such that we never once needed to have dinners for business reasons. Our guests have only been our friends. He was nine years older than I and this plus a different national background made problems in our marriage. Communication is easier between people of the same country and between those who have gone to school in the same epoch. It takes great devotion and loyalty to overcome such difficulties. I am more than grateful for the 38 years we have spent together.

Thoughts in 1970 on women in medicine

As to women in medicine, it has always been clear to me and still is that women are at least as suitable as men in this profession. This will not be obvious to the general public until girls on an average become as well educated as boys on an average. As long as girls do not choose a profession for life, they will be regarded, and justly, with suspicion. The great problem of how to get their children cared for must be solvable. Perhaps enough mothers will be willing to take special training in the care of children in order to stay at home and work part time in kindergartens. Perhaps compulsory community service for all girls, as there is compulsory military service for boys, will stimulate many girls to get further education in professions for the care of children. It is already quite obvious in Sweden that men cannot earn enough money to support a wife and children in the way they want to live. This means that the wife must earn her living and also be able to contribute to the cost of the household. As soon as girls are taught from early life that this is their responsibility, they will more and more choose the professions which really interest them, rather than a job to keep them busy until they marry.

At any rate I am convinced that we still need national women's medical associations until girls are allowed to study medicine everywhere and to receive the same pay for the same work. We need the International Association (MWIA) to encourage women in countries where they are not yet treated as equals in the medical profession. In the meantime our International association provides us with stimulating and interesting contacts all over the world. When equality has been reached, our association will probably be superfluous and we can be quite content in the fold of the medical organizations for both men and women.

Chapter 21   1961 - 1977

Just Between Us Girls - Tales from the Vienna Woods

No collection of facts is ever complete, because the Universe is without bounds. And no synthesis or interpretation is ever final, because there are always fresh facts to be found after the first collection has been provisionally arranged.   Arnold Toynbee in *A Study of History* [1]

The alternation between eating and digestion, between gathering facts and interpreting them, what scientists call experiment and theory respectively, Toynbee said, is the nature of scholarship and of history itself. This chapter continues the emphasis on facts that I have intended throughout - leaving most of their interpretation to the reader. Because individuals are complicated and have unconscious motives, psychological facts are revealed only little by little through what they do and say; therefore collecting enough for a "psycho-analysis" and a "provisional synthesis" is a long, arduous process. This chapter deals with my selection of a sample of about five per cent of the Vienna Medical Women's International Association set of Leone's correspondence. It is still a lot to digest at one sitting; a recitation of facts can be tedious. More than one meal might be made of this chapter, depending on the reader's appetite for Leone lore.

From 1967 until her death in 1977, Leone was very active in the Medical Women's International Association (MWIA). The office of the MWIA was then in Vienna. Leone became best of friends with the Executive Secretary, Dr. Martha Kyrle, and the Secretary employed by the MWIA, Hertha Dax. Leone traveled to Vienna every few months, Martha and Hertha visited Leone in Stockholm and "the girls" took advantage of MWIA congresses to spend time together.

Fortunately many of Leone's letters to and from Vienna are in the MWIA archives, now in the Drexel University Library in Pennsylvania. I was able to take copies of these and get permission for their use in this book.

In those days before electronic mail, inexpensive long distance phone service and photocopying, people wrote letters and relied on postal services. Leone disliked ball point pens. She wrote on personalized blue stationery with a pencil or fountain pen in the same handwriting style that was taught to me in Alberta schools (50 years later). The happy result? I can read every word.

Some of the Vienna correspondence is personal and some of her letters to Martha and Hertha are marked "Confidential", "Not for archives" or even "Burn after reading" in Leone's handwriting. As one would suspect, these are quite revealing. Fortunately, in Vienna, the home of Freud, they were filed for future reference.

The reader of this book will not have the luxury, as I did, of reading all the MWIA correspondence several times. I have 548 letters to and from Leone in my files, some as long as 14 pages. To convey their significance in a summary fashion, this chapter is organized along topical lines. That is, a topic that was treated by Leone in several, perhaps many letters, will be identified and Leone's thoughts about it summarized. Reference will be made to particular letters in which the thought occurs, according to the dating system which Leone usually used: month/day/year. Leone and the Viennese girls normally dated their correspondence; all the letters which were not dated I was able to place unequivocally through analysis of context.

Some pages are included in their entirety, in Leone's handwriting. These help convey a fuller sense of her personality, especially her good taste, generosity and love of life.

When I qualified for my M.D. in Canada in 1925, I did not know that the Canadian Medical Women's Association had just been founded the year before. There were at that time only about 280 medical women in Canada. In 1934, when the Medical Women's International Association (MWIA) met in congress in Stockholm, I attended and joined but did not interest myself in the local organization. However, in 1958 I drove with a friend to the MWIA congress in Baden Baden, which I enjoyed so much that I decided to attend the next meeting in Manila in 1962. That congress was a revelation for me. It was the first international medical congress of any sort in Asia. I can never forget seeing the women of all nations standing in their costumes before their flags and listening to their national anthems. The organization that the Philippine women had carried out under Fe del Mundo will never be surpassed. Esther Pohl Lovejoy, the founder of the MWIA in 1919 was present. We were invited to private homes. Everything was perfect. We had toured Thailand before the congress, and we traveled in Japan and India afterward. We were welcomed everywhere by our medical sisters.

Since the Manila congress my hobby has been the MWIA. It was therefore very gratifying for me to become president-elect in Vienna in 1968 and president in Melbourne in 1970. I served in this capacity until 1972.[2]

MWIA Correspondence	Significant events
1965-67 - 7 letters	
1968 - 20 letters	vice-president and president-elect, MWIA
1969 - 31 "	husband Folke dies after a short bout with cancer
1970 - 64 "	as president Leone is responsible for the Paris conference
1971 - 131 "	difficulties with French colleagues preparing conference
1972 - 141 "	Paris conference in September, Leone presiding
1973 - 63 "	on good terms with successor Alma Morani
1974 - 47 "	gathering autobiographies, advising executive
1975 - 44 "	editing autobiographies, promoting MWIA

For Love of Folke

At a party in the home of the Canadian trade commissioner I met the man whom I married eight months later. Folke Hellstedt was an economist and the director of the Bergendörfer (sic) Eisenwerk, a large Swedish factory located outside Hamburg. He was a Swede, nine years older than I, and he had lived all over the world as an industrial expert. He was a very broad-minded man who understood my ambitions and wanted me to have a professional life. We married at the end of my fellowship year, and I moved into his beautiful, large flat. Four months later he was made vice-president of Alfa Laval, and we moved to Stockholm, where his head office was. This was 1932.[3]

After a three month motoring trip through Europe and North Africa with her Alberta girl friends in 1934, Leone ... *told Folke that I would have to change my specialty. He was willing to help me in every possible way. I had decided that I would train to be a psychoanalyst, and as this was not possible in Sweden - there was not even a professor of psychology in the country - I arranged to work at the Neurology Clinic in Zürich, to start my training analysis with Dr. Gustav Bally ... and to take Carl Jung's and Pulver's lecture courses.*[4]

Some guy loitering at the entrance to

Strändvagan 53, August 2012

Both Leone and Folke traveled a great deal during the 1930s, sometimes apart and sometimes, most happily, together. They had two children, Monica born in 1937 and Donald McGregor born in 1939. When Donald was born they moved (with three live-in servants) [5] into a luxurious apartment, the fourth floor of Strandvägan 53, overlooking a canal in Stockholm. This was their home for the rest of their lives.

In 1969 my husband died of cancer, and two months later I was operated on for a hip arthrosis. Two more operations completely cured the arthrosis, but nothing can replace a life companion, especially one who was in complete sympathy with all my medical interests and aspirations, as well as with all matters pertaining to the further development of women in general.[6]

Leone believed that loving a man was part of being a real woman. She mentioned this in connection with the lack of trust of women displayed by a particularly difficult MWIA colleague. Such paranoia is in some women an abnormality associated with an inability to love a man or a child, Leone said.[7]

Ernst Folke Hellstedt came from a large, upper class family. At the age of 17 he represented Sweden in the high jump event at the 1908 Olympic Games in London. In 1907 he also trained on the sailing ship *Saga*. Among the other cadets aboard *Saga* on that training voyage was young Jacob Wallenberg of the famous Swedish banking family.[8]

Folke graduated from the Stockholm School of Economics in 1912.

In 1917-1919 Folke was in St. Petersburg, then Moscow, then Omsk at the time of the Kolchak White regime, then across Siberia to Vladivostok and onward to New Zealand.

It is likely that by 1919 he had joined Separator AB. His aptitude for languages served him well in overseas assignments. He rose quickly in the organization. In 1925 he was transferred to the daughter company Bergedorfer Eisenwerk near Hamburg. There he was a manager, probably vice-president for finance. On October 11, 1930, the senior manager P. Wenck died; and Folke became managing director on the three-member board, his colleagues Ludwig Voges and Hans Ohle.

Folke's older brother, an architect, during the tsarist era "built a city in Russia", according to Leone .[9] Svante, Folke's younger brother, was head of immigration in the Swedish foreign office during the difficult time immediately before and during WW2.[10]

Donald Hellstedt provided some memories:
   My father first became a navy cadet, thereafter he enrolled with the Svea Livgarde, the first of the two Life Guards, the other one being Göta Livgarde (where I did my military service in 1961). To be accepted at that time, one was required to have recommendations from the parish priest and from some additional persons of standing. He stayed on to become a lieutenant in the reserve. Thereafter he attended the new business school in Stockholm, Handelshögskolan, and graduated as the first or second class. [11]

When my father graduated he apparently was interviewed for a possible position with another company. When asked what his education was he answered that he had just graduated from Handelshögskolan in Stockholm with the title "Civilekonom". The person asked: "Don't you have a real education?" "Well," my father said, "I am a Svea Livgarde Reserve Lieutenant." Everyone in the room lit up and became really interested in him.

1913-1925 is not quite clear to me either. As I see it my father was an extremely discreet person, Mona would say secretive, my mother would say strong and silent. He never bragged or told stories about his career or encounters, except in a few cases. He admired his older brother Lennart, who was in construction and also active in St. Petersburg. That is where I believe he went in 1917 and was caught up in the revolution in 1918, which forced him to "back out" eastwards to Vladivostok from Moscau and then on to Australia and New Zealand. I believe he was looking for opportunities and even considered sheep farming. This is a bit blurred I am afraid. One thing, however, is clear. He always had a certain purpose in mind and was no romantic wanderer.

Leone and Folke married in September, 1931. Folke was promoted to head office and returned to Stockholm in January, 1932.[12] He remained vice-chairman of the Bergedorfer Eisenwerk board at least until 1946. I was not able to find minutes of board meetings from the Bergedorf Museum archives, although I laboured through hundreds of pages of minutes of management meetings, notices and contemporary newspaper articles. Hellstedt is listed as one of the three directors of the company from 1946-1960, but is not mentioned after 1960.

In 1937-1940 Folke was chairman of the Swedish economic association.

Folke lived in Rio de Janeiro for a year, 1938-1939.[13] His daughter, Dr. Mona Theorell (whom Leone called "Monica") told me that Leone joined him for part of this time:

Mamma was in South America for 3 months. I think I was already then cared for by "Nanna", the German nurse whom I loved and was very close to until she left us (and I kind of died) maybe 10-11 years later. My parents' first flat in Stockholm was on Valhallavägen, then they moved to Villagatan 10 - I don't know the year - where I was born, and that was the flat where Donald years later, to everybody's surprise, discovered that it had already been inhabited by our parents (when some pieces of wood were torn from

232

the kitchen wall during Donald's restoration works, it was written "Hellstedt" on their back). My parents moved to Strandvägan 53, a bigger flat, when Donald was born in 1939, and there were besides Nanna, Ester our marvelous cook, and a housemaid, all living-in.[14]

Early in 1939 Folke and Leone returned from Rio de Janeiro together. [15]

From 1935 to 1955, Leone earned practically no income. Folke, as befit a senior executive of a multi-national company, was very well paid. Unfortunately the grotesquely high Swedish income tax rates took most of every Swede's salary, and 80% or more of the top earners'. Until Folke retired circa 1962, he would have given the vast majority of his life's earnings to the Swedish government.

In 1968, the year Leone was elected vice-president of the Medical Women's International Association, Folke was stricken with cancer. On July 3 Leone wrote that she made an urgent return from London because her husband was not well. In her letter of November 3 to the girls in Vienna, Leone said, *My husband seems really well now and plays golf daily - so I am relieved.*

Leone and Folke shared a fondness for golf and for music. Donald tells us:
   My father was a Wagnerian and he had lived through the period when many considered both him and his music immoral. He joked about it and often played parts of his music on the grand piano at home. He also played some Tjajkovski. It is correct that he played less in later days. His golf companion (every morning in retirement) *was a retired management board director of a large construction company, perhaps SIAB. His last name was Sjögren, but I don't remember his first one. I think they became informal you only after several years. My father often took part in matches and won quite a few handicap* (Folke's handicap varied from 12-17) *based ones. I believe they played two-balls most of the time.*

During the time Leone was president-elect, she was unable to perform some duties and attend some meetings:

233

Thursday June 12/69

Dear Martha,

I am very sorry to have to tell you that my husband is dying in hospital of the toxemia from his cancer. He has suddenly become much worse and I'm sure you will understand that I cannot leave him.

I have just cancelled my air tickets and I have sent a telegram to the Bristol Hotel.

I had hoped to learn a lot from how you & Loina conduct the executive meeting, but this was not to be.

Would it perhaps be possible for you to come to Stockholm (at my expense of course) and stay with me a few days a little later on (say in September which is a beautiful month here) and you could perhaps go through with me the major points which will come up next week? I would appreciate this very much.

My best wishes to all in the executive.

Yours sincerely
Leone

234

FOLKE HELLSTEDT   HAMBURG 1931

  Many of Leone's letters contained memories of Folke occasioned by people
and places which reminded her of him. Telling the Vienna girls about a five
day trip to Zürich to consult a surgeon regarding a problem with her artificial
hip: *While in his waiting room in came Folke's first girlfriend (now 81 &*
Baroness av Uglas) - he had operated on her in Sept & she walked like a
girl of 15! [16]

And in response to a post card: *Thanks so much for the pretty card from Trogir. I loved Jugoslavia almost 40 years ago. We motored all over (4 of us - Folke and me - & an American couple - old friends of mine). The roads were terrible & the hotels awful - but it was wonderful anyway.*[17]

Disagreements between Leone and Folke, at least as revealed in her letters, were few. In early 1972 Leone and the Vienna girls were thinking of candidates for MWIA honours. Leone wrote to the girls about fellow Swede Andrea Svedberg:

Märta H. has the idea that Andrea has been a V.P. I have no idea about it. But she had an amazing career - married to a Nobel Prize winner - & later to a Cabinet Minister. Salon Communist, but always denied it. Beautiful. Close friend of Alva and Gunnar Myrdal. Oberärztin for Internal Med. Laboratories. Lenin Prize. After that Folke would not let me have her in the house. (I had met her at Harvard in 1928). In any case she has always worked for women in medicine in Sweden & was for years the local president. In view of all this we must know if she was once an MWIA V.P. She & Alma Sundström organized the 1934 Congress here (when I translated!). In 1929 I was working in a hosp. in Hamburg on a research fellowship from USA & Andrea invited me to come up to Stockholm & talk to the women's medical association here & to stay with her (I did not know Folke then), which I did.[18]

Folke was very much opposed to Communists. He would have been influenced by his time in Omsk, 1918-1919, during the last throes of the White Kolchak regime opposing the Bolsheviks.[19]

Socialism as practised in Sweden, however, seemed all right with Folke. Eighteen months after his death Leone was forced to reduce the size of the apartment they had lived in since 1939, and wrote to the girls:

Until now I could easily have had you both staying in my flat. From next week on I'll have only 1 guest room. Would love to have either of you. I decided in Dec - under pressure from the new house owner to let him have 2 rooms and bath, etc (separate entrance from the elevator hall). All socialists are furious at elderly widows in big flats. They write scandalous articles in the papers & quote our incomes etc. So this seemed to me the wisest action. My children were very upset & opposed but I think Folke would have approved. I still have 7 large rooms.[20]

Leone thanked Folke for much of her success as a person, for her ability to lead a richer life than she could have imagined before meeting him. His generosity [21] and grace, coupled with his social standing, defined *noblesse oblige*. In a letter to Alma Morani, the American who succeeded Leone as president of the MWIA, Leone addressed the suitability of Dr. A. Reza Arasteh, a psychoanalyst, to conduct a study for the MWIA:

First of all, Arasteh - I have now read 3 other books by him. He is undoubtedly a superior person. I think it is an advantage that he is a foreigner who has had to adapt himself to a new world and has thereby enriched his mind and capacity - Just as I think your Italian origin enriches your personality & creativeness - Just as I think my transposition to Europe at 29 & all the efforts I had to make to survive as a person (despite money & a completely understanding husband of high social and intellectual position) has given me a wider view of humanity & in particular of women's matters.[22]

Family Planning

In her autobiography and in her correspondence with the Vienna girls, Leone stated that she was a planned child and that her sister Phyllis was not. The value of orderliness was a theme frequently addressed by Leone. Planning her own children was important, as was the earlier choice of an altogether genetically superior mate in Folke.

She recognized the global environmental tragedy attending overpopulation. In 1971 many English newspapers carried the message, "two children are enough", and the American MWIA proposed that maternity leave benefits be confined to a maximum of two children. Leone approved of these initiatives[23] and sympathised with the African physicians hampered by the tribal mentality of self-aggrandizing government leaders who said that, "...it is the duty of every woman to have as many children as possible." [24] This policy was reminiscent of Nazi Germany's "Brides of Hitler" program: unmarried women were encouraged to have children by Aryan fathers in order to provide the additional Germans who would be required to lead and control the Thousand Year Reich.

In the matter of what the MWIA could do, Leone agreed with her successor as president of the MWIA, Alma Morani, and said that "family planning should be on every program" of MWIA meetings[25]. Leone was enthusiastic about MWIA cooperation with UNICEF in promoting family planning via women physicians. [26]

Invited to give a speech in Finland in 1971, Leone talked about pre-marital eugenic consultations. [27]

Among the important influences on Leone's intellectual development were advocates of rigorous birth control. Dr. Edgerton Pope, her favourite professor at the University of Alberta, was a founding member of the four-person Alberta Sexual Sterilization Committee and served on it for many years. A similar government organization operated in Sweden until 1985; the Alberta Sexual Sterilization Act was repealed in 1972.

According to Alix Strachey, who was analyzed by Freud and then became a member of the British Psychoanalytic Society, Freud said, "... the greatest benefactor to mankind would be someone who invented a sure and cheap contraception." [28] Certainly Freud did not neglect the power of the sexual instinct and narcissism, nor did he praise the ability of mankind's collectives to control these forces in the service of rationality and civility. [29]

Monica and Donald

About five months after I got my Swedish medical license in 1937, my planned little daughter Monica was born, followed two years later by my son Donald. I had a cook, a housekeeper and an excellent registered German children's nurse; I was actually living in luxury. The war broke out, and as a result, Swedish training analysts returned to Sweden, the Swedish Psychoanalytical Association was founded, and I was able to continue my education in this field.[30]

Monica was born in October, 1937, five months after Leone completed her work at the Karolinska Institut to qualify for a Swedish medical licence. Donald was born in October, 1939, nine months after the voyage of Leone and Folke from Rio de Janeiro to Southampton. In 1937 Leone hired a German nurse to help her with Mona. "Nanna" stayed until 1947.

Monica and Donald are mentioned frequently, with affection and respect, in the MWIA correspondence. For example:

6/14/70 *Sort of expect to drive off (to Vienna) on Sat July 4.*

I hope to have Mona - MD pediatrician, 34, mother of 3 (3,2,1) - with me as well as Tuula, my daughter-in-law (Finnish). Mona is with her children and maid in the country now. If none of them (the children) get sick etc - all should work out. Tuula has not yet gotten permission to have her holidays just now. They are lovely girls & I like so much to have them along.

6/20/70 - Leone looks forward to driving to Vienna with Monica;

9/15/70 - Monica working in town and living in the country while carpenters modernize her kitchen;

10/19/70 - *Monica's kitchen is in order so she & Klas & the children are in their own flat.*

Donald just phoned that he has been chosen for all of Scandinavia to represent Congress Administrators in Amsterdam this week - & everything seems to be looking up.

4/6/71 - *Have a nice woman friend here for Easter. She is a psychoan. from Paris. Monica and family in the country. Donald & Tuula divorcing. There is no peace in this life!*

5/3/71 - *If any nice young girl you happen to know about would like to come for 1 yr to Sweden & take care of Monica's children (3)- get her name for me. They speak German (the babes!). The girl would have her own flat about 3 blocks away from Monica's. She can learn Swedish "free" in the evenings at the courses for foreigners.*

6/2/71 - Donald is clever and Monica is fluent in Spanish.

Doktor Leone McGregor Hellstedt
Strandvägen 53
115 23 Stockholm

June 2/71

Dear Hertha & Martha,

Have just come home from lunch in our nicest restaurant – where I intend to take you two! Also have solved the guest-room situation – Donald told me how to do it – So if you two can bear to share my guest room – a little crowded with 2 beds – but a whole bathroom plus a separate toilet or wash place for yourselves – then I can have you both next Sept – when we relax after Paris. Paul will have to do without you both for at least 10 days here – or more if you like. (Provided of course that the Parisians don't murder me) –

Now down to earth. As I mentioned Monica has as a guest at her clinic

Dr Hilda Raizman
V. Liniers 1336
Capital Federa
Argentina

Put this name somewhere – so that Alma can use it later. (or you graduated)

She is about 35 – pretty – charming & clever – a pediatrician. Monica is fluent in Spanish so the head of the U. Clinic handed this girl over to her – She is definitely something to count on for the future for MWIA

240

9/12/71   Monica is bringing over the three little ones today.

9/18/71   Leone relays advice from Donald regarding congress fees - authoritative, because Donald is in the business of organizing large meetings.

11/19/71   *Just hope I can get together with "my" young people who are always so busy. Monica is on TV (one whole day with a doctor in the children's clinic) & she has a new German maid. Donald is newly engaged to another lovely girl. Everything is rushing so fast.*

12/6/71   (on page 14!) *Donald is engaged - & she is lovely. Lunch at the co-parents yesterday. Monica is also delighted. Hoping for the best.*

1/9/72   *Have saved up all my Xmas cards in a bundle for my little granddaughters to look at in 10 years or so. Fashions change & old cards are curiosities & interesting.*

Monica leaves on Tues. with her colleague for Ceylon. She is already wishing she hadn't decided to do it. She just can't leave the children. Hope it will turn out well.

20/1/72   *Monica had "worked-in" 6 weeks holidays at the U. Hosp -. & the children are too young to travel - & she loves to swim - & Ceylon is cheap - so that is why she went off, rather unwillingly because she thinks she should never leave those children. However, Klas has had a letter & she loves Ceylon. So I am very pleased for her.*

Had my new daughter-in-law-to-be Elisabet last night with all the others. She is so beautiful - & altogether a darling.

2/28/72   *Monica announced last night that she is coming to Paris. I had not asked her or even mentioned it - so I was very pleased. Where will we put her?*

3/29/72   Leone wrote the girls that the husband of one of her closest friends died of intestinal cancer, that she does not normally go to funerals, but she had no choice in this case.

Then the next day was Donald's wedding - which was charming. Both 32 - & looked as if they knew what they were doing. They are in Tobago for 10 days. She is a lovely girl.

Monica dragged me downtown to see the clothes she thought of buying - & I said no to everything - so now she is quite calm. She is going to a special 7 day course on "neonatal diseases" in Denmark in 2 weeks.

5/7/72   *...Monica rang from the country to tell me that she had read in the paper (she reads the liberal paper) that a Ceylonese exhibition of wall hangings was to open at 1 today.* Leone's political sentiments were to the right of Monica's, more Albertan than Swedish.

5/10/72   As president of the MWIA, Leone was concerned with the organization's finances, especially the cost of "her" international congress in Paris in September, 1972 and her wish to avoid a deficit. Much of her correspondence with the girls in Vienna dealt with questions of who should pay for what, and the usual policies of international organizations in these matters. Her son Donald was a professional congress organizer; she offered his services to the secretariat in Vienna. *My darling son is just home from USA & rang me. So I asked him some questions. He would be delighted to hear from either one of you & will answer of course at once. Just write, "Dear Donald, Strandvägan 7C, Stockholm Convention Bureau."*

5/26/72 letter from Hertha Dax in Vienna to Leone. *I was delighted to make your Donald's acquaintance, he is very good looking and very much like you - actually a baby edition of our President. He looks very young, very efficient and very intelligent. I shall "return" him next week when Martha has met him too.*

5/27/72 *Donald's Elisabet is expecting a baby. They rang last night to tell me & I am delighted. Don't know when but they are very happy.*

5/29/72 *Tomorrow my two little girls will be 3 & 4 & will get their Austrian dirndls & Andreas his hosenträger.*

1/5/73 *Stephanie arrived Jan 3 - & is the picture of Monica at her age. Everything normal. Monica & Donald stayed with her all through the delivery. "Their" abdominal & other muscles were all worn out from sympathetic contractions. I visited them yesterday & took Stephanie a little turmaline heart framed in gold & a gold chain.*

1/22/73 *Monica is in Bangkok & Donald in the Argentine (10 congress organizers in the world are the guests of the Gov. there).*

Stephanie is a dream.

6/4/73 letter of Dr. Martha Kyrle of Vienna to Leone, about her experiences at a conference in Göteborg: *Donald's presentation was by far the best and you can be proud of your son. He is absolutely charming and certainly most efficient. I hope that he and Elizabeth will have more Stefanies in the future.*

4/10/73 *On Thurs, Fri & Sat Donald & Eliz are guests of honour at the opening of the big Congress Center in Hamburg in the Park "Planten und Blumen". Friedel & I will have Stephanie.*

4/16/73 *In the meantime Stephanie will be christened, something drastic in our family!*

5/3/74 *Can you imagine. Donald & Elisabet & Stephanie are moving in 2 weeks into the flat Folke & I lived in 1932-33. It's a dream of a flat - well planned - 7 rooms, 2 baths & a hall toilet. They are repainting it & redoing the whole kitchen - so they will be broke - but I hope they will always be able to afford to live there.   Donald sold his flat & they now rent. I am crazy about Stephanie.*

   8/3/74   All grandchildren flourishing. Children good friends with me for the time being.

   4/21/75   Leone was chided regularly by the Vienna girls for her lack of interest in religion. Donald was not religious, either, according to Leone. Nevertheless the grandchildren were baptized.

   Catherine Emilie (sp. corrected) is now available for heaven. And Andreas has now added Donald to his names.

   9/27/75   I think I must have told you that Monica has bought an enormous sail boat & has lost her mind about sailing. No inheritance from her mother. Donald's two are so beautiful that I fear they will be ugly when they grow up!

   Friedel feels as if she were a member of MWIA - she enjoys all of you so much.   Affectionately, Leone (her usual ending salutation)

   12/10/75   Was at a gorgeous party 2 nights ago. The Theorells gave it for their Nobel Prize special friends. 90 of us at the top of the Wenner-Gren Center (23rd floor). All small tables. I had Prof Cori zu Tisel. He is so charming - Recited Rilke for me all through the dinner. Linus Pauling opposite me. Very amusing. His wife made the last speech for Women's Year. She told of Baroness ? who was Nobel's friend for 40 years - & who wrote "Waffen Nieder". Szent Györgyi is 90 & was there with his 4th wife - very pretty & only 26. Monica & I talked to her after the dinner. He had told everyone that they had been married only 10 days. She told me that she paints but hasn't much time to do that just now as she has a small baby! Several wives are high power researchers as well as their husbands. I wore my muu muu & it was much admired. Hope Martha is making a success with hers.

   12/28/75   We were at Donald's for Xmas Eve - & he and his family were here for Xmas.

Friends

As her voluminous correspondence suggests, Leone valued her friends. The feeling was mutual, as far as I could determine.[31] In Stockholm she had visitors whom she had known for fifty years or more. Her luxurious apartment was often the Stockholm base for a few days, sometimes a week or more, for a friend or two from abroad. And she assiduously sought new friends, by making acquaintances at meetings, dinners and parties, then inviting those she liked to join her at meals or to stay at her flat when they visited Stockholm.

Here we are concerned with correspondence from the last decade of Leone's life, 1967-1977; accordingly most of the allusions to friends concern those prominent in Leone's life at that time; and not, for example, the Campbell girls with whom she toured Europe and North Africa in 1934. Another theme in Leone's circle was professional affiliation: nearly all her friends were medical doctors, psychoanalysts and academics; neighbours and people from Folke's business associations apparently did not interest Leone. She rarely mentioned Bergedorfer Eisenwerk, and when she did she misspelled it - a Freudian slip or a ploy to suggest how little she knew of this company's activities? (Folke's role in Bergedorfer Eisenwerk and its role in the German war effort are discussed in the next chapter).

When Leone became vice-president of the Medical Women's International Association in 1968 she began extensive correspondence with Dr. Martha Kyrle and Hertha Dax in the MWIA office, Vienna. Leone became fond of "the girls" and of Vienna. They returned her affection and throughout her presidency, 1970-1972, her considerable activity in support of Alma Morani, president 1972-1974, and the enterprise of gathering autobiographies which Leone led until her death in 1977, Leone and the girls supported one another in MWIA activities and exchanged candid views in their correspondence. Leone's observations regarding her friends were frequent.

June 20/70

Dear Hertha.
Your voice on the telephone
is exactly like that of a daughter of
a friend of mine in Hamburg! It will
be so nice to meet you & Martha again
Enclosed Cherrel's latest
symphony. Mona & I leave here Sat. a.m.
June 27. That night in Copenhagen -
June 28 Hamburg Hotel Vierjahreszeiten
" 29 Rothenburg
an der Tauber " Eisenhut
" 30 Arrive in Vienna late
in the afternoon.
Could you & Martha eat
with us somewhere? I can
understand if Martha perhaps has
social engagements with her
husband - but it would be nice to
have you both - We like
restaurants with "atmosphere" —
See you soon.
Affectionately
Leone

7.20.70   *The dinners in your homes were charming & I enjoyed every
minute of being with you both - you enrich my life and I am grateful.*

7/10/70   *Wed. 15th I fly to Paris to motor for 2 weeks with a friend. ...Petitmaire* (fellow MWIA officer) ... *arrives here Aug 2 for a few days to stay with me.*

9/5/70   *Martha (Märta Holmström) is still at the West Coast in a small village with a friend and I miss her very much.*

Am still hoping fate will allow you to come to Paris with Hertha & me - but if you cannot - then I must have Hertha.

10/19/70   In a letter to Hertha Dax, written after a busy day in which Leone went to the dentist, the physiotherapist, saw seven patients for 45 minutes each and ran a lot of errands: *My dear, you were an angel & such a loyal help in Paris in every way & I thank you from the bottom of my heart. I think you realize how much I mean this - & that you are welcome at any time in my home.*

I've written Simone, Marguerite, Chevrel, my psychoan. friend Margaret Williams & Alma - so now I can think of you. I hope you could have some nice days with Simone. She is a darling.

3/6/71   *Am dying to have you girls here.*

4/3/71   *My American woman psychoanalyst friend from Paris - Margaret Williams has just arrived for 10 days.*

Not for <u>archives</u>

May 18/71

Dear Marte and Hertha,

Read Das Konzert on
the aeroplane & enjoyed it so much –
Have worked 2 days
& have the patients under control, I hope –
Have written the
million letters you "two tyrants" drive me to,
& I do hope they are well done –
The Pres & Sec & Treas
of Internat Akademikers Assoc are away for
3 weeks so I can't get the % which is sent
abroad.
I have such lovely
memories of these days in Vienna – You two
are absolute darlings – & I've enjoyed
it all so much. Thank you for
everything & most of all for yourselves as
human beings. You enrich my life.
Imke whom I love is just
entranced with my print. If it is possible to
find 2 different (one like mine & one other in
the same size) Kokoschas – please reserve them
& write me – I'll send you the money at once –
Monica & Klas are off at a

8/3/71   *To amuse you: There was a man from Malta (born on Malta) at the Congress in Leicester without his wife and 4 children. Orthopedist & Pres. of the Maltese Med. Assoc. Handsome, charming - about 56 - perfect for Hertha - if his wife was to disappear. If I were 56 I'd compete! Am afraid he's happily married. Still it was an idea! Also - did you have any notion that the Maltese Med School & Hospital is the oldest in the Br Emp & probably in Europe. Founded of course by the Knights Templar - I think in eleven hundred.*

10/3/71   Leone called "The Tale of Genji" a "gold mine for psychoanalysts" and recommended it to her friends.

Am so glad you are also reading Genji. It is fascinating how he fell in love with all those <u>related</u> women. How Murasaki ever wrote all that in such a pure and simple form is beyond me. Life seemed to be composed of flowers, poems, clothes and perfumes, and now and then a pregnancy. Also very much discussion of beauty of appearance. Did you notice that if a woman died in childbirth - they killed the baby? That they could all play on a zithern? When I have finished the two volumes, I am going to reread them.

1/20/72   In her 70s Leone gave parties on her birthdays. This letter to the girls was headed:

72 years old!

Thank you so much for your pretty and warm-hearted telegram. I had 28 friends & I think we all looked very elegant (considering!) & I feel very happy today. It's fun to be a child for one evening.

Still Jan 20/72   *Excuse the incoherence in this letter - but it's the day after the night before.*

3/6/72   Letter from Martha to Leone: *Many kind regards and alles liebe, also from Hertha.*

5/7/72   *Just received a note from Zürich which says I am to be operated upon in Klinik Hirslanden Nov 2. Just one joy after another, I'd say.*

Your letter of April 20 also here. Hope your arm is better. Burns are horrible, even when small.

Also a long letter from Rosa Lee. Do not file this letter! Alma has a beautiful home. Mrs Johnson who lives with her is an artist and <u>very</u> rich. Wonderful pictures etc. Alma is 3rd generation of well known sculptors. Perhaps it is Mrs Johnson who might pay for the PR for MWIA.

5/24/72   *Just home from a reception (lots of champagne) & a morning disputation of a PhD thesis by a friend - an Art Historian. She was with me in Australia (Caroline Olin - from the south of USA).*

5/30/72   Hertha was planning a vacation in North Africa. Leone wrote to Martha: *Tunisia was wonderful in 1933 when I & 2 Canadian girls drove everywhere in an elegant Cabriolet - Arabs on camels after us. Saw the first homo or perhaps transsexual in my life in a night club at some oasis. "He" on the stage dancing. Nowadays it will be different - but always interesting. Fascinating Roman ruins, etc. Nice for Hertha.*

With the same letter Leone enclosed a newspaper photo taken from her flat: Leone's friend Margaret Mead in the foreground, behind her an open window through which the building where the environmental congress was being held is visible. Mead was attending the congress.

6/22/72   *All back at work I'm sure. Thanks for the lovely card from Tunis. We were often frightened on that trip (1934) but we were 3. No other women drove cars in Sicily or North Africa then. We were most afraid of the hoards (sic) of Arabs on camels screaming for money. Weren't the Roman ruins lovely?*

I have my Pres Report to the Exec all ready except whatever I have to say about what we decide in Edinburgh. It is quite long & I won't read it. The Pres Speech or Report to MWIA will be very short and I'll do it today.

Alma is right on my tail (quite justifiably I think) to get the Assessment Committee named. Either Dr Mermod or Dr Methwen should be chairman. They can then report to Alma at the last Exec - on the grass roots opinion. Alma wants to continue this in Rio. It is the only way we'll ever find out what the ordinary members think.

The better I get to know Alma, the surer I am you two will be saying daily next year, "How did we ever put up with Leone?" My only excuse is - Leone did her best. Alma will be dealing with the kindest, most polite people in the world. Unfortunately they are very inefficient. I was in Brazil once, 1938, with Folke for 3 months. I am ashamed to say it, but I haven't the slightest desire to see the country ever again.

9/29/72   *My oldest (also 72) friend & her husband are here this week - staying at the Hotel Diplomat - & mostly eating with me. We have been friends for 50 years & it's wonderful to have them. Both are brilliant.*

Thanks once again for your letter. Your stay was for me a joy.

                    Affectionately, Leone

10/25/72   *Had to dress up and go to a big (36) women's dinner last night. I have one Jewish woman friend - she is also a widow now - & it was she who gave this dinner. Sat beside the wife of the Israeli Ambassador who is very nice. Then talked a good deal with Gertrude Philipson (Berlin Jewess now married here). She is apparently fully occupied with these "save the children" programs, etc. & had just spent last weekend with Dorothy &*

Eric Warburg in Hamburg - & my friends there. You girls went to school with Dorothy's sister, I think.

11/20/72 After hip surgery in Zürich, Leone flew home and wrote this letter to the girls while in bed, after doing her physiotherapy exercises. It ended: *Am thinking of you both so often & send my love.*

12/4/72 Leone expended a lot of her time and money recruiting foreign doctors into the Medical Women's International Association. She was particularly frustrated in this enterprise by the barriers erected by Communist countries: the refusal of China to allow doctors to join if the MWIA had members from Taiwan, and vice versa; and the reluctance of Soviet bloc governments to allow their doctors to go abroad to MWIA meetings - because of the risk of them defecting. In this letter Leone suggested some strategies for gaining Russian members, told the Vienna girls about some hours spent entertaining delightful Russian doctors at her flat and contrasted the warm and fun-loving Russians with her fellow Swedes.

Apparently "mutual trust" is one of the themes in women's education in the schools in Russia. This is sadly missing in the western world.

The Swedish Women's Med assoc had their annual luncheon last Sun. A bunch of deadly bores - with a couple of envious monstrosities. Be glad you did not have to meet them. The contrast to these Russian women is almost incredible.

12/23/72 In this letter to the girls Leone talks about her friend Jeanne Lampl - de Groot, an M.D. and psychoanalyst trained by Freud in Vienna.[32]

Dec 23/1972

Dear Girls,
    Just a little note to tell you that I am now
on my second reading of Maria Theresa + enjoying it
still more. Isn't it simply heavenly that we were not
alive then? It's complicated enough now. One of the
most interesting sections is about that Hollander van
Swieten who founded the medical school in Vienna.
        A propos that, a letter from Holland tells me
that their regional congress this next spring on
"too much medicine" for patients - will include a
lecture by Jeanne Lampl- de Groot - MD+
analyst - 76 - I think at least as clever as Anna
Freud. They are great friends - Jeanne had her
analysis in Vienna (I presume by Freud but
am not sure) Then she married Lampl - an MD
analyst+ Jew - much older - They lived in Berlin
until the political situation made them move to
Holland. Jeanne is not Jewish - she is a wonderful
woman - she was driving their car about seven
years ago - + they had an accident. He was killed
+ she was in hosp a whole year. The subject of
excessive medicinering is of course purely
psychological, as my two little pupils in Vienna
will realize! - so Jeanne's lecture will be
fascinating - when she lectured up here to the
analysts, she stayed with me - + we are very good
friends.
        Am having dinner guests these days +,

2/12/73   The hip will be " replaced" on Feb 19 Monday if all goes well until then. I'll be 3 weeks in hospital & can then come home and get a physiotherapist to exercise me. <u>Do not</u> spend any money on flowers, telegrams, etc. Instead write me <u>one</u> little letter a week and I'll be very pleased.

Am invited to 4 dinners this week. I'll have to starve all my 3 weeks in hosp to make up for it.

Am writing this as usual in bed. It's 3:30 PM. It's snowing for the first time this winter - & I'm having a "man" to dinner. My nice brother-in-law!

3/12/73   It was wonderful to get 2 letters from you today. I felt really loved again!

4/16/73   Am still a wreck - but continue with physiotherapy, etc. The surgeon and others who should know say I am doing fine. Hope I can go to Holland May 31. Would much prefer Oberammergau with you & Alma.

8/14/73   Leone had strong opinions and shared them candidly with her friends. In this letter to Hertha Dax, secretary of MWIA, Leone assures Hertha that a series of errors and omissions which damaged the MWIA were attributable to Dr. X, not Hertha: *X is of course (I hope) not a crook - but she has holes in her brain. For goodness sake, Hertha, don't be sentimental about her & feel sorry for her. All she has needed to do since last Sept. is to <u>resign.</u> She is just plain stupid.*

10/17/73   *Alma and my oldest friend in the world Mary Hazard were both made Distinguished Daughters of Pennsylvania last Tuesday. They had never seen each other before.*

12/9/73   Alma Morani, a plastic surgeon in Philadelphia,[33] succeeded Leone as president of the MWIA. She was more successful than Leone in raising funds for the MWIA, although Leone had tried hard - even giving generously of her own money in an effort to lead others. Scandinavia and Europe were much less affluent than the USA in the 1960s and 1970s. Morani's situation in the cradle of North American women's medicine, Philadelphia - her many contacts there - helped the MWIA.

In Alma's case, it is <u>her friends</u> who are donating the money. No usual MWIA president could do this. The U.S. is still rich and she has many admirers - & she deserves them.

2/12/74   I had Märta here to dinner two nights ago. She had rung and asked to come. She looked absolutely well - not any outward sign of illness. All "values" are normal except hemoglobin which is only 50%. I don't dare mention the Hon Treasuryship until she has had her holiday in the Bahamas & has come home. I suspect that when she was so close to death, she suddenly thought it would be better (if she survived) to devote her time to her 2 still very unsettled children Ann & Jan. Actually she is not a help to them at all - & it would be better for all concerned if she had something else to do. Ann is now engaged to an Englishman & expects to marry in Oct or Nov but we have all been through 4 engagements (to weak counts & barons) with her - so we are keeping cool. I think it was very wise & nice of you to write to Märta as you did. Another such letter in April or May would be a good idea & might do the trick. She needs to feel "wanted".

4/9/74 I am going to make a speech in Toronto at the mixed banquet Can Med Assoc and Fed of Canad Med Women. Am visiting old friends in Boston first for a week - then a week in Toronto during which a cousin (woman MD) will drive me to various places where my mother grew up & studied. Mama was born in 1972 (sic) *& went to Toronto U. in 1990* (sic).

Margaret Meagher has invited me to visit her in Halifax where she will be retired this month but as yet I am not planning on it.

After Toronto I think I'll join my best USA friend & husband in Pittsburgh for a few days & then fly home.

1/7/75 Have no special reason to write this letter except to forward Alma's request & also to say that I miss my little Austrian girls!

4/14/75 Anyway we two voteless can live at the Bristol .... Could you please reserve me a single room & bath there? I'd be alone at the Continental & that is no fun.

Now 86 histories in progress.

Margaret Meagher will be staying with me for 3 days from the 24th. Then she moves to other friends.

Am going to Igls & then for a week with Susanne Ohman Schwarzenbach in Zürich. Märta H intended to accompany me but as usual changed her mind.

6/17/75 .... Spicy tidbits for my girl friends - who think presidential & ex-presidential & pre-presidential letters should be truly business-like!

Vienna

Initially Leone had occasion to visit Vienna because she was an officer of the MWIA and the secretariat was then in Vienna. But then acquaintance with the Honorary Secretary, Dr. Martha Kyrle, and the employed secretary Hertha Dax, led to friendship. "The girls" visited Leone in Stockholm, they got together at meetings of the MWIA, and Leone visited them in Vienna.

Leone's fondness for Vienna was a product of several factors. In Vienna was #19 Berggasse, the home of Sigmund Freud and the birthplace of Leone's profession, psychoanalysis. Leone loved Vienna's music. That is hardly a distinction, who in the world doesn't? But she also evidenced a fondness for the distinctive graphic art produced in the Vienna of 1900-1910: Klimt [34], Schiele and especially Kokoschka. Many paintings of Kokoschka are understood to be illustrated dreams, more like nightmares perhaps - they appeal to psychoanalysts. Indeed, Kokoschka was influenced by Freud [35]; as were other members of the radical intellectual and artistic community in Vienna of this time which was to have a cultural influence out of all proportion to its size. Gustav Klimt's painting, "Adele Bloch-Bauer I", sold for US$140 million at auction in Los Angeles in 2006.

Leone stayed in several Vienna hotels and their perceived merits yield insights into her personality. She liked the old and the grand as long as it was well-maintained and not outrageously expensive. When she was in any city as a member of a group, she preferred to stay in the same hotel as her colleagues, and thus lowered her standards in order to stay in a hotel which they could afford.

7/6/70   *I am so glad you put me in the Sacher. I got fonder and fonder of it.* (following a week in Vienna for MWIA meetings)

7/10/70   Martha and Hertha wrote to Leone: *It was wonderful to have you here with us and we are happy to hear that you have safely returned to Stockholm.*

We are glad to realize that you are slowly approaching the level of Austrian snobism by liking the Sacher. It is a must to adore it!

9/1/70   From Martha: *I have just telephoned to the Sacher and they promised me a room for you from October 11-14 - so far they have not heard from you directly. October seems to be a difficult month and at the moment the hotel could not confirm a private bathroom, however, I am sure that this can be settled. I shall also keep an eye on the Opera programme, in case you would like to go there either Monday or Tuesday.*

1/23/71   *Thank you so much for the Sacher Torte. Several of us are enjoying it morsel by morsel!*

5/18/71   *I have such lovely memories of these days in Vienna.*

If it is possible to find 2 different (one like mine & one other in the same size) Kokoschkas - please reserve them and write me.

6/20/71   From the girls: *With regard to your hotel reservation, please don't be upset if we tell you that we have not been able to get either the Imperial or any of its equals so far. We shall do what we can and you may* *be sure that you will have decent accommodation when the time comes. Lorna asked for the Bristol, naturally, we could not get it and by mere chance got her a room at the Regina. We won't put <u>you</u> in the Regina! There is a good chance that we shall get you into the Intercontinental which is not what you prefer, we know, but it is at least clean and well run and quite near from the Office - perhaps a little bit further than the Ambassador was (we could not get this either).*

1/20/72   One thing I must mention - when I'll tell you my address on a trip, or the hour of my arrival in Wien ... I do not expect to be met - but I must admit it's a lovely feeling to see you both there in Wien.

5/29/72   Tomorrow my two little girls will be 3 & 4 & will get their Austrian dirndls & Andreas his Hosenträger.

7/20/73   I plan to arrive in Vienna on Monday 14th. Would like to stay at Intercontinental if you can arrange it. Imagine Märta H will come with me. She is in Nassau and returns today.

Sunday A.M. In bed.
7⁰⁰ a.m.
March 23/73

Dear girls!

Am a bit "the day after" - Have been to two very
swank formal dinners there last 2 days -

My histories are now 82. About 10 have already come
in. Fascinating - several move one to tears - They will be
invaluable in the history of women. Hope I can keep my
wits about me until I get them all in, arranged, & the
questionaires I'll soon send out returned. I wrote Dr Hitzenberger
as you suggested.

As to hotels in Sept - where do Alma Lorna+Bno & Helga intend to
stay? I'd rather be where they are - I think the Regina is awful -
Am quite content at Intercontinental but its no fun to be there
alone. I think Lorna prefers the Bristol + I'm glad to be there
too - or else at the Royal as you suggest - although I
don't know it. The Sacher + the Regina are so depressing -
& shabby. According to my calendar Sept 2 is a Tuesday
(not Wed as you write) - Didn't know Marta+I were
coming by train but its alright with me! Will look into
this matter as soon as I can - I can act immediately -
but Marta is out on her "colony" (Schreber Garten) -

Charming informal letter from Mrs Sipilä - She is
completely behind the Project - May perhaps go to the General
Meeting here on the 7th -

Affectionately
Leone

```
Dr. Leone Hellstedt
Strandvägen 53
STOCKHOLM
          Schweden


                           Vienna, April 17, 1975

        Dear Leone,

        Many thanks for your letter of April 14 (took 3 days!).

        I shall book the Bristol for you but please let me
        have the exact dates of your arrival and departure
        as soon as possible. Many thanks.

        Martha is in Switzerland with Paul for a short holiday
        and returning on Sunday. She is intending to go to
        Igls and if she goes by car I may come with her.

        Are you coming through Vienna or flying directly to
        Munich. We should very much like to know if you will
        be touching Vienna at all either before or after Igls,
        if so, we want to see you here. (Thinking of you in
        Vienna, our theatre outing always comes to my mind
        when her Royal Highness in white silk and white mink
        swept through the foyer while the ordinary folk receded
        with awe struck expression on their faces to let you
        pass - and little me in your wake as the chosen Lady-
        in-Waiting. I shall never forget how proud I was of
        my royal mistress. Nor shall I forget our visit to
        the jeweller in the Avenue de l'Opéra (or was it ?)
        in Paris. Don't think that I do not remember the
        remarkable dinner luncheon given in your honour in Paris chez
        Madame Déjérine-Sorrel and her pleasant family and
        the sweet Madame Chevrel in black gloves holding the
        menu. We did have fun, did not we ?

        Thanks for your suggestions for the agenda of the
        Executive Meeting, we shall consider them. Your report
        will be one item anyway.

        How are the young Hellstedt girls ? And how is Monica
        and family ? I should love to have a good chat with
        you.  All the best to you and kindest regards,

                                   yours
```

Alberta and Canada

Before and during WW2 travel from Sweden was impossible for Leone.
With the war over and her children in school, however, Leone made several
trips to Canada: to see her sister Phyllis, to speak to medical women's

257

organizations and to visit friends. Her correspondence with the girls often indicates loyalty to Canada. Her Alberta roots are perhaps suggested by occasional outbursts against the French, although the proximate cause of most of these is the careless and arrogant behaviour of those responsible for the organization of the MWIA's international congress in Paris during Leone's presidency.

11/3/68 *It is really far too much to expect any of you to write my French letters, but is most generous of you to make such a suggestion. If I get into difficulties (or before I do) I shall turn to you & I thank heaven that you will be at my side to whisper in my ear in Paris!*

In the meantime I know that both Dr Henry and Prof. Chevrel read English perfectly. Therefore I have proposed to them that I type my letters in English & that they answer in French. This saves so much time and each of us is sure of what she has said. I have read so much French medical & non-medical literature in my life that there is no reading problem. If I must, I can of course write a French letter that anyone can understand - but it's far from perfect. I very much envy you Viennese who have had better school training in languages than we in Canada long, long ago.

8/31/70 From Leone's farm background: *No one was prepared to consider the matter as it had not been announced ahead of time - & as all large audiences are like "cows" & get frightened at anything new - they voted "no".*

Alberta vernacular surfaced occasionally in Leone's letters to the girls: 8/13/71 *shotgun marriage;* 10/26/71 *to tell you the gospel truth;* 2/16/72 *reminds me of mama, "Have you a clean hankie?"*

1/23/71 *I had 30 women friends to a gala dinner - had the Can. Ambassador as guest of honour.*

6/29/71 *This is Dominion Day, the national Canadian Holiday - so Margaret Meagher is forced to receive. Her home is very lovely - a big residence on the waterfront on an island which forms a suburb of Stockholm. Have to go.*

11/29/71 *Tomorrow Margaret Meagher comes to dinner. I want to hear what she thinks about the Chinese (MDs I mean). I do not see how we can continue to have on our official paper "China" for Formosa. What do you think? Can you imagine, Dr Hammerling Nova Scotia now Pres. in Canada has been Margaret's personal doctor for years? Recently when she was home in N.S. Dr. Hammerling asked her if she knew me.*

2/14/72 *I asked Marie Storrie to look up anything she could about Dr Leacock & Dr Windsor who practiced in Calgary when I was 10 years old. They were beauties & terribly popular. Dr. W. married Rosamond*

Leacock's brother later. Stephen Leacock was Prof in Math at McGill & the best writer in Canada at that period. Marie says Rosamond is dead & no one knows who Dr Windsor was! The whole matter interests me - especially as I remember hearing it said that the most prominent men in town (150,000 at that time) were all deserting their men doctors for these 2 women. That in 1910.

6/13/72 Have been at a few Environment meetings. At this stage it is all political. Am good friends with Mrs Strong plus the wives of the men of Environment for Canada & his vice-. Have had them all here.[36]

12/27/72 This statement should be in the hands of the president & of the secretary of the local congress organizing committee. It should also be included in planning a congress. Of course no rule would work with the French. As to the 7 years war - we in Canada - even the English speaking - have always sympathized with Quebec & Montcalm which at that period of our history seem to be romantic. No more, no more!

1/22/73 The party went off well. Margaret Meagher was here & 2 Russians & my usual 30 friends.

11/1/73 Also I do hope Buerk instead of Marie Storrie is elected. Both are Canadians. Buerk is so much more travelled & representative & has so much experience.

11/13/73 My sister in Canada is quite ill ....sister phoned, can't go to Rio.
15/1/74 Sister Phyllis in Canada is still quite ill.

12/9/73 I have been asked to make the speech at the banquet in Toronto when the Can. Med. Women have their 50th anniversary in June. The mixed congress is also there & they say a lot of men will be present.

1/21/74 Your 27th & other letter just arrived a few minutes before Helga departed today. Thank you for the birthday wishes. I had 23 persons including Kaisa & Helga & I think it went off very well. Anyway I enjoyed it very much myself. Helga says she is coming to my 75th! Had a telegram from Margaret Meagher - now teaching in Dalhousie U. in Canada for one year. Also sweet letters from two of my beaux from the days of my youth.

11/18/74 I asked Enid McLeod (Nova Scotia Can) - Prof in Physiology - very competent - to get me a list of superior Can women MDs who could afford to be Vice Ps. or Com Members. She sent me 8 - all willing to come to Vienna etc & to pay their own way. I know them all & they are tops. So any time you need them I have their addresses.

3/8/75 Received the enclosed from Alma & found it very interesting. Only 68 women MDs in Canada in 1934. I had no idea. I graduated in 1925. Norway 66. You probably have the same paper in your archives.

4/14/75   Margaret Meagher will be staying with me for 3 days from the 24th.

6/17/75   A letter here tells me that the Can Fed of Women MDs meets in Calgary next week & wants me as a guest. Am very surprised - & pleased.

8/3/75   Must now write 18 thank you letters for parties in Calgary.

8/8/75   Helga apologizes to Leone regarding some errors in the use of Leone's name in publications and writes: *Don't forget that I did remember to include McGregor - I had remembered that you had asked for it some years ago and I definitely wanted to please you. This trespass will not repeat itself either, I promise.*

Sweden

Leone found the women of the Swedish MWIA National Association to be overly reserved and boring. Her daughter Mona told me that Swedish women thought Leone rather brash. The result was that Leone, although a member long before WW2, was not active in the Swedish Association for the first 30 years of her acquaintance with it. When she began to help the Swedish NA, it was for the benefit of the MWIA administrative office in Vienna.

7/7/67   Leone provided Dr. Martha Kyrle, Honorary Secretary in Vienna the best list available, incomplete, of the names and addresses of women MDs in Sweden.

1968.   At the XIth Congress of MWIA in Vienna, Leone was elected Vice-President. She began an exchange of correspondence with Martha Kyrle and the employed secretary, Hertha Dax, with updated and expanded information regarding women doctors in Sweden.

23/1/71   Regarding the contemporary issue of women MDs wanting to do their specialty training part time - to accommodate family obligations - and the Austrian medical association's policy of a full time requirement, Leone wrote: *Now about part time work and training. I agree with the Austrian women M.D.s. However, I've had to change my mind while living here in this rapidly changing society. There still exist some maids in Austria & some grandmothers, aunts, etc., I imagine. Here there are none. I tell you truly I do not know a single person who has a maid - except myself. The tops of the gov. have no maids. And we do not have as yet not 1/10 enough child day-care centers. If we do not get half time jobs & specialty training for women (& men also of course), no woman will be able to continue to work - or to specialize or still worse to get back after 5 or 10 years. You must remember that almost all Swedish women are working. Therefore there is no help in the homes.*

6/29/71   Friedel will take three weeks of holiday in July.

7/13/71   On the topic of soliciting donations to MWIA: *I think the donations in wills should be stressed on every occasion. It hurts no one while she lives & the death duties will take it anyway when she dies.*

12/6/71   Women of the NA in India had asked to be members of the MWIA without paying MWIA dues, and to have the MWIA pay for their trips to Paris: *Bhatia's letter is <u>really cheeky.</u> <u>... As</u> to not being able to pay fees abroad, or travel abroad, aren't all people in the world at some time or other in such unfavourable situations? I remember during World War II, I was expelled from the Amer. Assoc. of Path.'s - which is terribly difficult to get <u>into</u> - because I could not send money from Sweden.*

1/10/72   *Am busying myself with my birthday dinner party on Wed. - 30 guests, all women. Gratifyingly enough, several husbands have asked their wives to ask if they also are invited! Soon there won't be any husbands left to invite.*

8/19/72   *In a country like Sweden (which is going to the dogs) the whole idea is to wipe out any suggestion of sex in regard to a degree or a piece of research. ... If you happen to see a new book, borrow or steal it: "The New Totalitarians" by an Englishman ... I think his name is Huntingdon.*[37] *He has lived here for about 12 years.*   Leone regretted the movement toward extinction of individuality and personal responsibility in Sweden, but she recognized its proud past.

11/27/72   *Am glad Herta that you can enjoy Swedish history. Despite great poverty, poor soil, no roads and enormous distances, the Swedes have done a good deal that they can be proud of.*

1/22/73   *Now about Alma's *[38]* money raising ideas. She says she does not accept the fact that Helga & I cannot raise funds for MWIA in Sweden & Germany. It is impossible for her to understand our financial problems. Americans always translate directly as in a bank. For instance, 1000 Sw. Crowns = $200. They forget that we have to work as long & as hard for 1000 crowns as she does for $1000. I gave MWIA 5000 Crowns and that is for me in working hours, etc. $5000 - but for Americans it's only $1000. No one else in Sweden but Märta and me would do this.*

7/20/73   I plan to arrive in Vienna on Friday 14th. Would like to stay at Intercontinental if you can arrange it. Imagine Märta H will come with me. She is in Nassau & returns today. She will not stay more than for Ono's Finance Com - as she wants to be here to help kill the socialist gov - & then listen to their groans on TV that Sunday. I'll vote ahead. Am equally desirous of Palme's fall.[39]

1/15/74   We do not need to have an Eng. brochure translated in Sweden. Everyone reads English. We have not distributed it. No one wants it.

2/12//74   Concerning the upcoming conference in Rio de Janeiro: *Am not at all surprised re no mail from Rio. As I told you, Folke lived there for a year & later I visited Brazil with him. They are charming, kind people - but terribly inefficient. Nevertheless the congress will probably go off rather well as Stolz is of German descent. I do not think we should vote for Congress venues in countries which have not yet a good organizing capacity. It is not fair to the country nor to the Executive.*

12/4/74   *Am very busy - as the Med Profession is being totally socialized for Jan. 1- we are not yet sure what will be dictated to us.*

We had a meeting of the Swedish women MDs last week at "Riksstämme" - all MDs. About 40. Many will I think come to Scotland - & even to Tokyo if prices do not gallop too high.

1/11/75   *The new law for MDs started Jan 1. We are now slaves of the state - with thousands of formular to fill out - daily & monthly. Apparently any nation can be completely brain washed.*

3/8/75 *I must tell you that little Catherine Hellstedt is also going to be christened - so you will realize that civilization is advancing in Sweden!*

3/12/75   From Martha and Hertha: *Dear Leone, both Hertha and I are extremely glad to know that civilization is gradually coming to Sweden due to Catherine Hellstedt's excellent example which, we hope, will be followed by other Hellstedt's to come! If this goes on, one day Swedes will be Christians ....*

On the French

As president of the MWIA, Leone was to preside over the International Congress to be held in Paris ca. September 1, 1972. According to MWIA practice, the host country National Association was supposed to be responsible for most of the organization of the International Congress and for its financial success. Ignorance or abdication of these responsibilities, coupled with the unanticipated death of the individual in the French NA most involved in organizing the Paris congress, plus the fiscal irresponsibility of her replacement, frustrated Leone and the girls in the Vienna office. Alarmed, at one point Leone accepted the British NA's offer to replace Paris. This news caused the French to mend their ways and Leone's International Congress, somewhat late, was held in Paris.

4/9/70 *What I need to be told in Vienna is <u>what the French must do</u> & <u>what they must pay for</u> according to our rules. I'm not by nature "statute-minded" but shall do my best.*

5/13/70 *No answer from the French. I wrote very politely and carefully - to C..., P... & one more. Perhaps they have done nothing about the Congress & are embarrassed to say so. I have never met any one of them so I don't think it can be a hate on me "in person". Maybe it's because I'm not French! Anyway, if they don't answer I think it is <u>too early</u> for me to go down there.*

5/29/70 *Here are the answers from C... and S.... The latter sounds nice! Have decided not to go to Paris before Oct. .... I'll write them that I'm not coming just now.*

11/2/70 *A note from C... of Oct 26 arrived today to say the Congress must be Sept 3-7. Does she mean 3 & 7 inclusive? Such a nuisance for you who have sent out all the letters. <u>Bad</u> organization in France. Perhaps we must wait to notify all countries of the change in date. Otherwise they will think both <u>I</u> and <u>C...</u> are lunatics. What do you think? Or is it better to correct the date at once? Sorry you aren't here to talk it all over. They, "the French", need nurses to take care of them.*

1/4/71 *Have you seen recent "Elle" numbers? French women are apparently determined to bring about some changes. I'll enclose for you to look over, these -- please return them. .... Hertha and I already told C... in Paris that $500 was the usual contribution - but I suppose she wanted to see it in writing.*

1/23/71 *I agree that it would be excellent if a French woman would report on the status of women in France. .... No answer from anyone on projects. An American would be best as chairman. They & the Germans are the best politicians. .... I think Ono is the most suitable for 1976 Pres. - even if Japan could not organize a Congress - as she says due to the high cost of living. Otherwise an American. Don't imagine I am American crazy. I'm not at all. I do think, however, that the countries which show such great activity can possibly get more things going in MWIA. It won't be possible to*

263

have an American so soon after Alma. I don't know of a suitable German. The French are impossible. I don't know of a suitable English woman.

5/3/71   Must make my speech in French in Milan. Horrors! J... insists.

6/1/71   Also H... requests that we nominate a French woman for Pres.-Elect in 1972. They are incredible.

8/3/71   I am still so boiling mad - that I don't dare write to L.... Am trying to figure out the most insidious way to put her in her place. Wouldn't it be not to say or write a word to her until Vienna?

.... Then when a venue has been accepted by MWIA, the same paper must be sent again. I suspect it will be difficult to get H... to conform - but of course nothing like the French.

.... Apropos the French. We (Folke & I) sold our brand new flat in Cannes about 2 months before he died. We had 2 garages in the house, so one was still unsold. I forgot all about it. Then suddenly the owner Mme. B... - charming, effective business woman wrote me that she had just sold the garage for 10,000 Francs & she would put them in my bank account in Cannes. I wrote to the bank & asked them to move the 10,000 to Paris. They wrote and said my account was empty. I wrote Mme B.... She phoned her bank in Paris & now after 2 years they write that "by error" they forgot to put the money at my disposal. This is not Mme. B...'s fault - she is correct & honest. But imagine that! the biggest bank in France - to hell with the French!

9/16/71   I think L...'s difficulty is that the pharmaceutical firms in France (who she said did not give a hoot about foreign members) will not support her for some reason and that frightens her economically. I find it very hard to believe that the travel or congress bureau will not give her $10 per person (as she has already promised them $60 per person & they were content)...

.... Otherwise I do not trust L... not to call off the Congress <u>at any time</u> - for instance if the Franc falls or rises. The English would <u>never</u> do such a thing.

9/24/71   Still no letter from you re L...'s sweet epistle. K... and M... have written me copies of their answers - (with private additions about what they think of L...). A note came today from R... (also private) in which she says she will compose herself & write a serious letter on the subject. She calls L...'s letter "superbly insulting". Otherwise I know nothing. Haven't opened my mouth to anyone (not even M...). It's a good thing I'm so used to psychiatric patients.

10/4/71   I quite understand that you as a <u>permanent </u>official find it <u>more unpleasant</u> to have a squabble with the French than I do. After all, I am more or less out of their clutches next Sept. and I don't care any more *whether they leave MWIA. They have <u>never</u> been an asset to us. During over 10 years now, I've been hearing how C... drove the Exec. crazy. Now L... tries.*

Stockholm
Oct 22 1971

Dear Dr L[redacted]   Referring to my letter of
October 7, 1971, I wish to point out that, to date,
no reply has reached me.
                    In my letter, I tried
to explain to you the point of view of the International
Executive in regard to the XIII Congress and to
convey to you the necessity of your following our
unanimous decisions. The absence of a reply
from you, or any other form of communication
with me as President of MWIA has forced me
to take action.
                    After consultations with
the entire Executive of MWIA, it has today been
decided to cancel the Vienna 1968 decision
to hold the XIII Congress in Paris
                    The XIII Congress will be
held in London.
                    In order to save the authors
of the scientific papers from the trouble of
supplying copies of their contributions, we
would appreciate the immediate transference
of these scientific papers to the Vienna
Secretariat.
                    Yours sincerely
                    Leone Hillelett

10/26/71   *Alma & all of them think we should change to London - so do not believe I have acted on my own initiative. L... will of course now do something terrible. I don't know what & even _my_ stable tummy is on the alert.*

10/26/71   Second letter of this date.   *The French have _not_ 500 members. They pay to MWIA for 500 members in order to have so & so many council votes. This is a fact. .... Alma & R... & all find that we are better without them. None of the nice French women doctors will join the Assoc. (French) as it is. They detest the group there. I imagine another group would ask to affiliate if these hop off.*

11/15/71   Martha Kyrle sent Leone a long letter containing the agenda for the Paris Congress and congratulations on her handling of the French crisis. The British NA had offered to hold the Congress in London, but were then graciously assisting its organization for Paris.

1/17/72   *Still not a word from Paris from L... or L.... I answered M...'s letter & also wrote to Hotel Pont Royal to reserve my room, as she asked. (Suspicious creatures, these French. One would think they might trust _each other_.)*

2/10/72   *I don't think we can do anything about forcing the French to get out a final program. L... is a liar and a thief - no matter how much M... thinks I should not indulge in personal opinions. We have no weapon left to force L... to do anything. We must in no case give her our MWIA $500 until she has paid us. .... Have no idea what the conference is. She does not communicate with me. .... Dear Hertha - I sent you the _original_ letter where she promised to consult us about everything? May I not have it back?*

4/2/72   *Am not sure what she means with administrative & technical chairmen. I know of course what the words mean - but she is so tricky.*

4/7/72 Leone quotes from a letter received from L....

"Je suis heureuse de pouvoir assurer votre passage avion Stockholm - Paris aller et Retour, à l'occasion du XIII e Congrès de l'Usioc. Int F. M.

Veuillez me dire quel jour vous désirez quitter Stockholm pour l'établissement du billet que je vous enverrai à l'addresse que vous voudrez bien m'indiquer.

Croyez Madame la Présidente à mes sentiments dévoués."

The signature is 4 cm 2 mm high.

I cannot possibly accept this ticket - for several reasons -

She has refused to pay the hotel in Paris for you 3. She knows from the rules of Planning a Congress that she should pay for at least 2 of you -

She is trying to escape paying for the rooms tape recorder etc for our Exec. Meeting

She still thinks she is putting on a French congress.

Now she tries to bribe me -

5/10/72 *As to L..., I hate to think of what this congress is going to cost MWIA. We cannot do anything about publicity - because we cannot afford to get mixed up in French costs. So forget it. We'll be lucky if we get out of Paris with our clothes on.*

5/28/72   Leone's son Donald was in the business of organizing large scale meetings. Leone told him about the arrangements in Paris and learned: *Apparently the French are No. 1 and the Danes No. 2 in skinning congressists.*

7/6/72   *I have now written, first a friendly letter to R... asking for her co-op. to get the French to report to you & to me; secondly, the two enclosed letters - I do not believe these letters should be more friendly - but if you two find them too hard I could tone them down a little. I am so mad at them it shows in my handwriting. Hope you send them off before those two depart on their holidays. That will be their next excuse.*

12/27/72   Leone is reviewing with the girls MWIA policy regarding publication of Congress reports: *This statement should be in the hands of the president & of the secretary of the local congress organizing committee. It should also be included in planning a congress. Of course no rule would work with the French. As to the 7 years' war - we in Canada - even the English-speaking - have always sympathized with Quebec & Montcalm which at that period of our history seem to be romantic. No more no more!*

3/12/73   The French asked the new president, Alma Morani, if the MWIA would cover the Paris Congress deficit (for which the French NA should properly be responsible). Leone tactfully refrained from telling her more volatile colleagues.

11/18/74   *Dear Martha, ...   If you think I'm still too hard on the French, maybe you can modify a few words in my report.   Affectionately, Leone.*

On Psychoanalysis

7/29/69   Leone writes Herta that she will give two or three weeks advance notice before her next visit to Vienna: *I have the kind of practice where my patients must be warned some time ahead - as there are always several with severe anxiety & it is impossible for them to turn to anyone else because we have such a shortage of psychiatrists. It is not that I think I am indispensable!*

5/24/70   *When do you girls have your holidays? I don't practice in June or July.*

11/2/70   *One of my cleverest patients - whom I got at 18 - was just made Dozent at the Med School. So I listened to her Dozent lecture & felt proud. Her mother suicided a year ago.* [40]

12/5/70   The girls were taking suggestions from NAs regarding future Congress research and discussion topics. Recalling Jung, Leone wrote, *Note the German suggestion, "Aggressivität in der Welt."*

14/12/70   In this letter and earlier in her letter of October 19, 1970, Leone mentions that her schedule consists of seven patients, 45 minutes each.

1/23/71   *I got the information on Aggression in order to be prepared for the Exec Meeting in Sept. Did I mention that the Mitscherlichs are doing a big paper on Aggression for Vienna in July?*

4/3/71   *My American woman psychoanalyst friend from Paris, Margaret Williams, has just arrived for 10 days.*

5/17/71   *Have written to my ex-patient Belgian Dr. Hermine Vogels-Cauter, Antwerp, to ask her if she knows of anyone who would be interested in forming a group there.*

5/18/71   Leone asks the girls to find her two more Kokoschka prints.

5/31/71   Leone is discussing the merits of various possible speakers for an upcoming MWIA conference: *Then Anna Freud occurred to me. Her work (child psychoanalysis and research on children's behaviour) is the basis of all child psychiatry in the world at the moment. She will be in Vienna at the end of July for the Internat. Psychoan. Congress which is to celebrate since her father was born. She is not an MD, but I see the statutes say, "Any woman."*

9/23/71   *In between all these matters I read with fascination "The Tale of Genji." It's a gold mine for a psychoanalyst. Am so amused to think of little Martha reading it at 13 years of age."*

12/7/71   *Your Xmas card is beautiful. I always put them on the mantel - and the patients can regard them from a distance.*

12/14/71   On the topic of who should be eligible for honorary membership in the MWIA: *Anna Freud is such an example. She is really remarkable, but not an MD & not particularly interested in women in med. (I know her moderately well).* Later they became friends; Anna Freud stayed with Leone in Stockholm.

22/6/73   *Except for 3 potential suicides, all hanging on each word I utter, I am feeling much better ....*

For the Medical Women's International Association

Several letters indicate that Leone made a practice of entertaining women from the MWIA who were visiting Stockholm. Some, like her psychoanalyst friends, stayed with her at Strandvägan 53.

11/3/68 I may be mistaken but I find it very hard to believe that any woman doctor would come from the other continents just to listen to a discussion of this subject (toxoplasmosis). *Is it not really so that they come out of sisterly loyalty to other women doctors in the world, hoping that these meetings and this organization will be a moral support for all girls everywhere who wish to study medicine? In addition to that I think they hope to hear one or more outstanding speakers on women's problems in general, preferably from a para-medical specialist. To be really truthful myself, I must admit that my <u>worthwhile</u> memories of 5 congresses are the remarkable women I have by pure chance gotten acquainted with and the speeches by people more or less outside medicine. For instance, I consider your "Presidentin" who spoke the first day - I believe she is social minister - was absolutely inspiring. A man who spoke in Manila - I think he was Minister of Public Health - was on the same level.*

I know that according to the statutes we are supposed to have scientific medical papers, but I think we should face reality and accept the fact that women doing <u>top</u> scientific work in medicine usually have not the time or energy to present their work to our organization. They <u>have to</u> (naturally) present it to the ordinary medical societies for men and women and that is enough work. On the other hand women in other professions who are doing top scientific work would be pleased to present to us parts which would interest us. We have the highest standing in the hierarchy of professional women and therefore they would feel honoured and we would get something really new to think about.

10/29/69 Dear Leone,   Thank you very much for your letter of October 22, 1969. I had no idea that you had been ill until two days before your letter arrived when Dr. Lloyd-Green mentioned that you were again learning to walk after your operation (hip replacement in Zürich) *but she gave no further details. I am terribly sorry to hear of your operation and its painful consequences. That you had to go through this just now when you had no time to recover the slightest bit from the dreadful loss you suffered in June, is really too much for one person. What an awful year you have had.*

I think it is very plucky of you to still consider an excursion to Vienna in December when you will have to face the grand voyage to Australia in February.

4/9/70   *The travel expenses of the Hon. Sec. <u>have always been paid</u> by MWIA and it must be. What is wrong with our organization is that we do not <u>as yet</u> know how to get all women MDs to donate that miserable little 25 crowns per year to MWIA whether or not they have time or the desire to attend local meetings or our big Congresses.*

5/24/70   *I am very <u>opposed</u> to MWIA being used as a labour agency. It is too much trouble. No one has the time. If women want to study or work in foreign countries they should use the combined men's and women's medical associations. These have all the information, secretaries, etc.*

Just as I am opposed to MWIA <u>selling</u> anything. (Again regarding suggested sale of brochures and Leone's letter of April 26, 1970) - *I detest sales of anything. It should be beneath our dignity as educated women.* Recall that Leone sold Chautauqua to skeptical customers in order to pay for medical school.

7/10/70   Concerning Congress head table recognition of outgoing executives: *I agree with Alma. No one should work for 4 years & spend so much money without some form of polite thanks.*

9/27/70   On choosing the best Congress toxoplasmosis panel regardless of sex: *Like Marguerite she thinks we only make ourselves ridiculous if we do not include the recognized specialists, all of whom seem to be men.*

10/27/70   *I quite agree with Alma that the Exec. should be younger....*

3/10/71   *Dear Leone,   The list of our Presidents will support your argument that Japan with its large membership is well due for presidency:*

1.	*Esther Pohl Lovejoy*	*(1919-1924)*	*USA*
2.	*Lady Florence Barret*	*(1924-1929)*	*England*
3.	*Louise Thullier-Landry*	*(1929-1934)*	*France*
4.	*Alma Sundquist*	*(1934-1937)*	*Sweden*
5.	*Louise Martindale*	*(1937-1947)*	*England*
6.	*Charlotte Ruys*	*(1947-1950)*	*Netherlands*
7.	*Ada Chree-Reid*	*(1950-1954)*	*USA*
8.	*Jolanda Tosoni-Dalai*	*(1954-1958)*	*Italy*
9.	*Janet K. Aitken*	*(1958-1962)*	*England*
10.	*Fe del Mundo*	*(1962-1966)*	*Philippines*
11.	*Lore Antoine*	*(1966-1968)*	*Austria*
12.	*Lorna Lloyd-Green*	*(1968-1970)*	*Australia*
13.	*Leone Hellstedt*	*(1970-1972)*	*Sweden*
14.	*Alma Dea Morani*	*(1972-1974)*	*USA*

7/2/71   Leone thought it important that mainland China should belong to MWIA. The obstacle was Formosa, which then called itself China, and the diplomatic intricacies attendant.

Doktor Leone Mc Gregor Hellstedt
Strandvägen 53
115 25 Stockholm

July 2/71

Dear Martha and Hertha,

I met the Chinese Ambassador and took him out on a terrace where I talked to him for about 15 min (with a very handsome interpreter!) - Also talked to his wife, the Consul and his wife etc. I do not know whether it will have any effect but he asked me to send him a brochure etc. which I am doing today. Shall send the golden book and that ugly one-page account of our Assoc. This is the moment when we should have a more elegant and more interesting one or two-page propaganda brochure!

I also asked him for the name of the Min of Public Health & when I get that I'll write to him. It's a start.

Monica has had an Argentine young woman pediatrician at her clinic for 2 days. She says she is very attractive - She did not know that there was a Women's Med Assoc. in the Argentine! Am going to try to invite her to lunch today.

Please send me a new copy of the statutes or the page "Med W.I. Ass" - for myself

Affectionately
Leone

272

12/3/71   On her successor as president of MWIA: *Alma has a mass of ideas, almost all of which are excellent.*

Leone's management style is revealed in the matter of what do about getting the enormous numbers of women doctors in China to join MWIA: *The next "hot" question seems to me to be Formosa. We simply cannot continue to list them as China. Isn't it so that there are 200,000 Chinese on Formosa and 750 million in China? I think we must at least change our writing paper after Paris; or do you think we should wait until they are swallowed?*

I have thought (shall not act until all the Exec have been consulted) that I could perhaps write the Pres on (re) *Formosa & ask her if she has any suggestions as to how to solve this problem. If they were really alert, they should themselves resign; but we cannot possibly ask them to do this - until the mainland Chinese offer to join us. Am interested to hear what you think. Apparently MWA is also struggling with the problem.*

1/13/72   *Without idealistic volunteers, no MWIA ....*

1/18/72   *She* (Alma) *agrees with me that we must strive hardest to acquire international status, which we now have in name only. We can only get this by getting by hook or by crook - China & Russia in with us.*

2/28/72   *... Zontas in Europe pay $6 a year to their international and MWIA members $1. It's a scandal.*

5/10/72   *Wrote you an answer to yours of May 5 this a.m. Saw my patients. Paid my bills. Phoned the family. And now at 2 p.m. lying on top of my bed and thinking over your letter still more. ... My leg drives me crazy too - so both of you must remember ... no matter what difficulties we have ... you both still have 4 legs that function!*

5/28/72   *This matter works excellently in Italy because (we would call them patronesses) there are so many rich (really rich) women who did not learn professions but who are sorry about that now & would like to compensate. These women with their donations ... keep the Italian assoc. going financially. ... On the other hand it has not helped to get the younger women (MDs) in in Italy. The situation in England is similar. Really rich women have donated much to the Brit Fed.... There is not one woman in Sweden able to do this. There are no tax exemptions for such things - and on the whole the Swedish men would be careful not to put the extra money in their wives' hands. They make fun of those "sissy" American men who do that. Please exclude my Folke.*

8/15/72   Leone produced a quantitative analysis of MWIA's revenues and expenses worthy of an MBA in advance of her presidential meeting in Paris.

The top line: *At present (since 1968) capitation fee = 6 sch/71 cents. 10,169 members pay per annum GBP3,050 = $7,442.*

8/19/72 *I agree with Alma in a way - in that I am sure that we as individuals & even the whole idea of MWIA is "worthy" - but we have let it drop down to a "quilting bee" (which probably was great fun & enjoyed by the best women 75 years ago).* In the draft her proposed presidential address enclosed with this letter, Leone mentions that she has attended six MWIA-related congresses in six countries in the last two years.

10/25/72 Leone reported to the girls her progress promoting MWIA in discussions with the Soviet, Indian and Israeli ambassadors. *Had to dress up and go to a big (36) women's dinner last night. I have one Jewish woman friend - she is also a widow now - & it was she who gave this dinner. Sat beside the wife of the Israeli ambassador who is very nice.*

5/20/73 *The Pres of MWIA has commanded me to have available for each member of the Exec - the figures for paying MWIA members for 1971, 72 & 73. You have already sent me for 69 & 70. Would you please hypnotize X... into producing these figures. ... Isn't it wonderful that Alma got the $50,000?*

11/1/73 Leone recognized that the massive population of Asia would dominate the future. *It is also very important for MWIA to have congresses in <u>Asia</u>. We'll never get medical women educated to internationalism if they just meet in Europe & the U.S.*

Promoting Girls in Medicine

7/3/68 *Don't you think that we older women (for instance 2 or 3 from each country) could write up a short story of how we landed in medicine? It is perhaps of little interest to the young MDs of the moment - but if kept in the records of the association - I feel sure it would be of great interest in one hundred years.*

4/12/70 *As the main problem with all these national associations is - how to get the younger women doctors to join. I think we ought to have available in our secretariat a few more facts - which the individual associations might be able to use as propaganda.*

Shouldn't we know for each country:
I   How many women MDs are there in the country?
II   Are girls admitted to medical schools on marks - or is there a sex quota?

III Is there equal pay for equal work for men & women MDs?

IV Are married women MDs allowed to keep their jobs in the same clinics as their husband MDs if they wish to?

V How many women MDs have leading posts? Or perhaps how many have docent or professors competens?

I think we should control these figures every 2 years to see if conditions are improving and where. The improvement could be briefly noted at each Congress.

Have you some suggestions as to how to better this questionnaire? Do give me our opinion.

1/23/71 It is sad about Korea & their schools. It is, however, quite outside our realm of action. We will be <u>geniuses</u> if we get permission for girls to study medicine on equal terms with boys in all developed countries. We simply cannot even aim at more. As yet in the world, I am convinced that it is better to try to educate gifted & highly gifted children. When the latter group, who are now neglected, are under control, we might consider retarded children. That will take 100 years or more.

2/23/72 Now about WINGO (Womens Internat Non Gov Org). It meets again in Geneva June 25 this year. It will be presided over by a Jewish woman (Internat Council of Jewish Women) - a nice type. Leone related the names and affiliations of various women who attended the conference and the prospects for United Nations action and funding for medical education of girls. *There was one Pres. (Peace & Freedom Commission) from East Berlin. She is Prof in Iranian - clever, looks dreadful - long black hair, herself short & <u>very very</u> bosomy. She did not utter a word about politics.*

There were presidents of about 5 Jewish Women`s Internat Org., Pres of Women Lawyers of the World, Pres. of about 5 Catholic Women`s Internat Associations - all <u>very</u> nice. The most capable was probably Mrs. P... (English - terrible accent), about 50, Pres of the Country Women of the World. This is an <u>enormous</u> organization. She is trained in politics & office holding from childhood & has a heart of gold.

Leone proposed a means for MWIA to relate to WINGO, then wrote: *Our interests are all so varied. What we all want is better education for girls & women.*

9/72 President's report to the executive, from page eight: *You will remember that I have proposed collecting for our archives the autobiographies of the early pioneer women in medicine in each country. This plan should have been better organized. A questionnaire could be used for the basic biographical data. Then the potential authors would only need to concentrate on the really valuable material, that is, those events in their childhood and youth which they believe led them to study medicine. I am certain that such accounts from pioneer medical women will be invaluable in the history of women and of our profession. I would also suggest that each national association be encouraged to donate examples of already existing biographies of their medical women in any language. A number of autobiographies have come in but with one or two exceptions they have not contained the desired material. This I consider is entirely the fault of insufficient planning on my part. I now propose that the project committee take over this plan and work out a better technique, perhaps with experienced medical interviewers, to get the desired material.*

6/30/73 I'll enclose in this letter 2 letters from Prof. Arasteh of George Washington U. in Washington DC, head of research in Graduate School. I read 2 new books by him - "Creativity in the Life Cycle" (meaning how do we destroy & how should we encourage the native creativity in children, adolescents and adults?). This subject has interested me since I was a child - & is the kernel of my interest in the history of women - & the essence of meaning in "The Emergence of the Medical Woman in Different Cultures". If we knew what released the creativity of little girls in Japan from 1880-1900 so that so many dared to study medicine - (& similar data with answers from each of our regions) - we would have made a great contribution to the history of women - and we could offer any gov. (in the developing countries) the facts of our study to apply in their country.

3/7/73 I'm not the type to run a PR program, so I would be helpless. I think the issue is much deeper. Why don't all women MDs belong to us - at such a minimal fee? Why don't we have definite "aims" which apply <u>solely</u> to women MDs or girl students anywhere who desire to study medicine. What can MWIA do to deflect a portion of those girls' sexual mania onto intellectual development?

5/8/73 Stephanie is christened. Had a very nice party lunch. The clergyman (Lutheran) was charming - about 60. He asked me why it is so difficult to get girls to study for a profession - (exactly the question we should study as a project). He has done a lot of teaching in the schools &, as he says, he so often advises girls to study med. - be children's doctors or gynaecologists. They always look surprised & seldom do anything about it. He asks, "What is wrong with girls?" It is of course the psychic environment - not the benzene or the polluted streams or viruses.

12/9/73 Leone wrote several pages to the girls on the responses of various MWIA members and academics to her proposal of an international study of why and how girls enter medicine.

11/22/75 *What is Fe del Mundo's age? What is Vera Peterson's age? Have you a U.S. address for Vera Peterson? I* must *have one black woman MD....* Most of Leone's letters to the girls in 1974-1976 concerned the book she edited, "Women Physicians of the World" - finding names and address for her solicitation of autobiographies of pioneer medical women.

Self - analysis

4/9/70 *I am not by nature "statute-minded."*

5/24/70 *In any case in view of my "leg", I hope you will excuse me if I don't come to Vienna in June. If I should suddenly look more normal by the end of June I'll come anyway. At the moment I have a sort of grapefruit hematoma on that lower leg - so you can imagine my feelings (vanity).*

6/6/70 Leone said she liked the Sacher Hotel in Vienna, possibly to please the girls, because she later called it "shabby."

9/15/70 Leone cast her vote in favour of a fashion show as part of the upcoming Paris congress.

10/3/70 *I have no "midi" clothes. Hate them* on me. *Will* allow *my two sisters to wear whatever they like. Should we have a fur coat with us? Unfortunately I was so dumb that I let the furrier turn down the hem on my fur coat. I look like my own great grandmother in it.*

12/5/70 *Although I don't want to struggle with politics myself, I realize that this is cowardly of me & I think it is a blessing that some women can and will.*

12/22/70 On the stationery of the hotel, "Los Monteros   Marbella":

Los Monteros

MARBELLA

Tuesday
Dec 22/70

Dear girls!
Here we are in a pretty hotel in the sunshine - Anne is riding & Marta is roasting herself in the boiling sun at the beach. In half an hour I walk down (10 min) to the Cabane & there we have a buffet lunch - I prefer sight-seeing trips - but last night things looked up a bit - I got into conversation with a lovely French couple of my age (or more) - He is a foundation engineer (whatever that is) & a darling & reminds me of my father - & can you imagine - he has been out in Edmonton to give special lectures several times! His wife is head (for France) for the social organization which arranges for care of cancer patients in the homes — after their clinical treatment - She has been doing this for 20 years - Distinguished people & "modest" - Then I dragged into the conversation a very nice American - a little (not much) too young for me

TELEGRAMAS: MONTEROS - TELEFONO 823894 - TELEX 77059

278

...but just right for Hertha - However
his wife is arriving today - Has a 21
yr old daughter at the Sorbonne & is
some sort of international financial
adviser - Really charming - & also modest.
I can't bear people who aren't modest -
    This is the extent of my adventures
so far -
    There are 2 young Swedish girls here
(18 & 16) with their Mother - Long blonde hair
& both have maxi   Breitschwang !!!
Horrible
    In Cardin's shop in Marbella we
overheard the owner say "No we don't
buy or sell maxis.
    This letter requires no answer
from my dear little friends in Vienna.
    It is only to tell you that I am
still alive & think of you & wish
you both a happy holiday -
        affectionately
            Leone

("Breitschwang" is what Canadians called "Persian lamb")

1/4/71 Fashion conscious: *Alma also wants the French to have Congress*
plates made in France to sell ($25 each).   This seems to be a fashion. I see
there are glass (crystal) plates which I personally think would be "less

offensive" to put it mildly. .... Have you seen recent "Elle" numbers? French women are apparently determined to bring about some changes. I'll enclose for you to look over, these. Please return them.

1/23/71   *I had 30 women friends to a gala dinner.* (Actually Leone's traditional birthday dinner, started when her mother had her invite the neighbourhood for Leone's fourth birthday). *Had the Canadian Ambassador as guest of honour. She is about 55-60, very clever & attractive - Miss Meagher - pronounced Mar believe it or not. Avocados filled with grapefruit & thousand island dressing. Boiled salmon. Hollandaise sauce. Gurken salate. & scalloped potatoes. Angel pie. .... Long dresses.*

6/6/71   *Was at a fantastic party in the country about 100 miles away in a small manor house built 1775 and furnished by Europe's best ebonists. Everything still in place. A dream. 30 of us. Host hostess MDs. ....*

Am sitting in the sun on my balcony the morning after the night before - with much champagne!

6/18/71   Leone reports frenetic travels and philanthropic activities.

24/6/71   The proposed new emblem for MWIA Leona thinks gaudy.

29/6/71   *The most distinguished Indian woman I have met at Congresses was Dr. Pasricha, 20B Ganga Ram Hosp., New Delhi - A lady.*

8/3/71   *This is not for the archives!   ....   Now about the fashions. There were no long coats in England nor even midis - not even in the shop windows on Bond St. Very few pants suits. Latest smart outfit is a cape - plus dress - the cape the same length as the dress. ....*

Are there any other obligations I ought to know about - & which you two are too tactful to mention?   ....

Have been intending for a long time to mention that I get a nightmare when I think of Herta having to eat & drink <u>alone</u> after she had been out to the theater with me. It wasn't stinginess. It is only that I've never been what we call here the "supé type". I don't get hungry late in the evening - & unfortunately I seem to be so egocentric that it never occurred to me that Hertha might be. Forgive me.

8/13/71   *If my writing looks peculiar it is because (1) I'm writing on my knees and (2) I've just had a boiling hot bath. After the latter, which I love, I cannot write nicely or lacquer my nails for half an hour.*

9/16/71   *I have always been taught that one should <u>never</u> give in to "utpressning" ... auspressning? blackmail I think we say.*

1/1/72   *Eva Mader Macdonald in Toronto is working on a project to celebrate the 1974 jubilee of Canadian women MDs (the founders) ... This book is to be a history ... This is of course a good idea - <u>but </u>they are going* *to use a free-lance writer. I am terrified of journalistic writers - but hope they have chosen well. Something for our archives.*

1/2/72   Apropos of the American NA's auctions of donated items: *I have however tried to think out some way to raise money which would be (in my opinion) more dignified & no trouble.*

1/20/72   *72 years old! .... Thank you so much for your pretty & warm-hearted telegram. I had 28 friends & I think we all looked very elegant (considering!) & I feel very happy today. It's fun to be a child for <u>one</u> evening*

5/20/72   Sense of irony: *Am enclosing a picture of Donald taken in Washington last week to amuse you. Send it back to me please. He isn't a bit religious - but a* (church) *congress of 10,000 is quite a bit of business. He says both of the men in the picture are top business men - curious the difference in countries.*

7/18/72   *This pound & dollar & shilling business is too enervating, don't you think? I'll write to Ild Schindler & ask her which Swiss would be good on the Finance Committee. She won't do it herself because she is like me (we don't spend more than we have) and we two know so little about finances.*

8/4/72   *Alma just sent me a copy of her letter to the Pub. Rel. boy - Tough!*

Personally I don't know (am not competent to judge) how it is possible to combine making MWIA known & not make it seem like advertising. Maybe I'm dumb. <u>Experts</u> probably know <u>how</u> to do this. There are tricks in all trades. Better to let the U.S. people be responsible.

1/22/73   *Have finally decided to be operated on here by a Dr Stenport (about 45) sometime in the last two weeks of February. His nurse will ring me when he can squeeze me in. Am not at all hopeful as I seem to be worse after each op.   ....*

The party went off well. Margaret Meagher was here & 2 Russians & my usual 30 friends. 6 had broken bones. What an age group we are! So they could not come. Two came on their hip prostheses & walked quite well.

M... sent me a box of chocolates for Xmas or my birthday. I never eat them & she knows that.

7/20/73   *As to my hip - I am getting slowly better & I do hope I'll be at least normal for my age by Sept. It's 4 years now since I was myself.*

11/1/73   *First of all, burn this letter as soon as you have digested it.*
Critical analyses of various candidates for MWIA offices followed.

Have just read the book about Esther P. Lovejoy. It is of course in many ways a bore - as I find are all biographies - but the facts are overwhelming. When I met her in Manila I had no idea of how much she had really accomplished. At least I had the gumption to introduce myself. She was a sweet little person - 90 some years. It is curious to discover that I, between the ages of 6 mos & 2 years, lived in a village in the mountains about 25 miles from Portland where she was practicing. It would be marvellous to have a real biography of her. Maybe someone will collect her letters. The author of this book is apparently a hater of Japan & Germany & not clear about Germany & Austria - & says our MWIA 50 yr Jubilee was in Manila. I don't like books by journalists.

1/21/74 *Thank you for the birthday wishes. I had 23 persons including K... and H... & I think it went off very well. Anyway I enjoyed it very much myself. H... says she is coming to my 75th! Had a telegram from Margaret Meagher, now teaching in Dalhousie U. for one year. Also sweet letters from two of my beaux from the days of my youth.*

1/25/74 *Am struggling with my tax declaration. Can't do it myself but must control the figures before I sign the matter. Horrible job.*

2/12/74 *Am glad you approve of my stamp idea. Even if only 10 countries succeeded it would be good & decent advertizing.*

3/18/74 *Am now rested up after my rather strenuous safari. It was magnificent & I wouldn't have missed it for worlds. The new national parks with the brand new Hilton tree top hotels are fantastic. As Swedes we were not allowed to include the 2 parks on the border of Tanzania - but we saw all the others.*

7/13/74 *Arrived home yesterday at noon half dead from lack of sleep. Halifax-London flies only at night. The only compensation was that I sat beside a young darling of 34 from Düsseldorf who teaches higher mathematics at University College in London. The solicitor general (top) in Canada had invited him as an expert consultant - on recidivism in criminality. He is a genius - modest & adorable. If I had been 15 or even 20 I don't know how I would have survived.*

11/18/74 Leone describes her extensive correspondence - with friends, soliciting contributors for the autobiography book, etc. *I run out of paper faster than I can buy it!*

1/13/75 Regarding the autobiography collection: *Nice letter from Lore Antoine. Do tell her - in passing - that she can write 20 pages if she likes. I only dared to ask for 5 - did not know what enthusiasm the project would meet. It is of course extremely valuable to have detailed accounts of the life and motivations of those of us who managed to land at the top of MWIA. An analysis of us will undoubtedly reveal quite amazing facts.*

Honoured in Alberta

Leone flew to Alberta in 1977. She visited her sister Phyllis Bouck in Calgary and at Spring Convocation in late May she received an Honorary DSc from the University of Alberta.

Two days after her return to Stockholm, she entered hospital. Her illness was lymph cancer, ironically the subject of one of her post-doctoral research projects. She succumbed July 2, 1977 and was buried alongside Folke in Eskilstuna, near Stockholm.

Donald remembers his mother with admiration and affection:

My mother always made an immediate, significant impression on people, of all types, nationalities and social standing. She was also immediately compassionate, but always remained analytical and perhaps at first also came across as a bit intellectually aloof, before she was fully understood by the counterpart, who mostly became attached to her, often forever thereafter. She was never neurotic or complex, rather straightforward and honest and very reciprocal. She stayed away from political ideology and avoided debating political issues. She chose to concentrate on individuals as such and their unique personalities as well as their "raisons d'être". This probably also enabled her psychiatric and psychoanalytical development and approach to life in general, very far from pathology, her initial subject of medical interest.

Mona chose one word to characterize her mother: *courage*. Like her namesake, Leone had the heart of a lion.

The autobiographies that Leone collected and edited were published posthumously by the MWIA with the following dedication.

In Memory

Leone McGregor Hellstedt, M.D., Ph.D., D.Sc.

January 19, 1900–July 2, 1977

Dr. Leone Hellstedt dedicated her life to excellence in all aspects of her medical profession. It was a life rich in success, high honors, and well-deserved international recognition.

Dr. Hellstedt, past president of the Medical Women's International Association, devoted several years of her life to collecting the memoirs of prominent pioneer women physicians from many nations. This great woman was gratified to know that her efforts were to materialize and would be published. Members and friends of the Medical Women's International Association remember Dr. Hellstedt with the greatest affection and respect. We dedicate this volume to the memory of Leone McGregor Hellstedt, whose work will serve as a beacon to the future generations of medical women of the world.

I rode home ... having many barbed wire gates to open and a deep creek to ford, but feeling as if I had done a good job.

[1] Toynbee, Arnold, *A Study of History,* Oxford University Press, London, Eighth Impression, 1963, Volume one, p. 49.

[2] Hellstedt, Leone McGregor, editor, *Women Physicians of the World,* Hemisphere Publishing Corporation, Washington & London, 1978, p. 204.

[3] ibid, p. 203.

[4] ibid, p. 203.

[5] Dr. Mona Theorell (Leone's daughter Monica) told me that in 1939, among the group moving into the big apartment at Strandvägan 53 were a nurse maid, a cook and a house maid.

[6] ibid, p. 204.

[7] 10/4/71.

[8] In 1930 Jacob Wallenberg joined the board of directors of AB Separator, parent company of Bergedorfer Eisenwerk in Germany, where Folke Hellstedt was then working as a manager and director.

[9] 12/9/73.

[10] Koblik, Steven. *The Stones Cry Out: Sweden's Response to the Persecution of the Jews, 1933-1945,* Holocaust Library, New York, 1988, pages 190 and 258.

[11] The Swedish Who's Who English translation lists Folke as having an MBA.

[12] Donald Hellstedt thinks that Jacob Wallenberg played a role in having Folke repatriated from the hectic and dangerous Hamburg/Bergedorf scene.

[13] 6/22/72 and 2/12/74.

[14] In an email to the author from Mona Theorell July 2, 2012.

[15] Shipping manifests indicated Leone arrived in Southampton from Buenos Aires February 6, 1939 aboard the Royal Mail Lines Ltd. ship *Asturias.* Ernst Folke Hellstedt - occupation "industry"; Leone McGregor Hellstedt - occupation "housewife". Ports of voyage Southampton, Buenos Aires, Montevideo, Rio de Janeiro. Proposed address in the United Kingdom: Grosvenor House, London. Last permanent address: Sweden.

[16] 4/29/72.

[17] 6/23/71.

[18] 4/29/72.

[19] 4/12/72.

[20] 1/23/71, p. 4.

[21] 5/28/73 Telling the girls why rich women in the USA and Britain have contributed to the MWIA, but none in Sweden: *There is not one woman in Sweden able to do this. There are no tax exemptions for such things, and on the whole the Swedish men would be careful not to put the extra money in their wives' hands. They make fun of those "sissy" American men who do that. Please exclude my Folke.*

[22] 8/11/73.

[23] 8/16/71.

[24] September, 1972 report to the MWIA Executive, p. 5.

[25] 1/22/73.

[26] 22/5/73 and 27/5/73.

[27] 6/18/71.

[28] Roazen, Paul, *How Freud Worked: First-Hand Accounts of Patients,* Jason Aronson Inc., Northvale, New Jersey, 1995, p. 250.

[29] *People will be only too readily inclined to include among the psychical assets of a culture its ideals - its estimates of what achievements are the highest and the most to be striven after. It will seem at first as though these ideals would determine the achievements of the cultural unit; but the actual course of events would appear to be that the ideals are based on the first achievements which have been made possible by a combination of the culture's internal gifts and external circumstances, and that these first achievements are then held on to by the ideal as something to be carried further. The satisfaction which the ideal offers to the participants in the culture is thus of a narcissistic nature; it rests on their pride in what has already*

been successfully achieved. To make this satisfaction complete calls for a comparison with other cultures which have aimed at different achievements and have developed different ideals. On the strength of these differences every culture claims the right to look down on the rest. In this way cultural ideals become a source of discord and enmity between different cultural units, as can be seen most clearly in the case of nations. Freud, Sigmund, *The Future of an Illusion,* (originally published in 1927), translated by W.D. Robson-Scott; revised and newly edited by James Strachey; Doubleday Anchor Books 1964, pp. 16-17.

[30] Op cit, Hellstedt, Leone, editor, p. 204.

[31] Although her opponents in Medical Women's International Association politics probably had something disparaging to say about Leone, particularly the French (about whom Leone had disparaging things to say), I did not encounter anything along these lines.

[32] *Man and Mind: Collected papers of Jeanne Lampl- De Groot M.D.,* International Universities Press, New York, 1985.

[33] Morani, Alma Dea, "Alma Dea Morani: Pioneer Plastic Surgeon", in *In Her Own Words: Oral Histories of Women Physicians,* edited by Regina Markell Morantz, Cynthia Stodola Pomerleau, and Carol Hansen Fenichel, Yale University Press, New Haven and London, 1982, pages 73-98.

[34] Adele Bloch-Bauer died in 1925, in her will leaving her Klimt portraits to Austria. Her husband retained the works until he fled from Austria along with other Jews in anticipation of the Nazi regime. Long after the war was over, a New York lawyer undertook to show that the family had contracted to part with some of these art works under duress, and therefore they should be returned to the surviving members of the Bloch-Bauer family, an elderly woman in Los Angeles and a female physician in Vancouver, British Columbia. In order to deflect criticism, the Austrian government formed an arbitration committee which awarded return of four major Klimt pictures. These the ladies immediately (in 2006) sold for about $200 million, the lawyer's share reputedly 40%, or $80 million. Ronald Lauder, owner of the Neue Galerie, a museum in New York City where *Adele Bloch-Bauer I* is now displayed, confirmed that he paid $135 million for this picture in 2006. Source: *New York Times,* June 19, 2006 and June 27, 2006 and literature in the Neue Galerie.

[35] Vergo, Peter, *Art in Vienna 1898-1918: Klimt, Kokoschka, Schiele and their contemporaries,* Phaidon Press Limited, London, 1975, pp. 12-17; and Steffen, Barbara, editor, *Vienna 1900: Klimt, Schiele and Their Times, a Total Work of Art,* Hatje Cantz, 2011, p. 153.

[36] Maurice Strong, like Leone, grew up on the Canadian prairie. He made his fortune in Alberta following Leduc #1, with Ajax and Norcen Resources. He was president of Power Corp. of Canada 1961-1966, and in 1972 when he and his wife were visiting Leone, he was Secretary General of the U.N Conference on the Human Environment. Later he became Executive Director of the U.N. Environmental Programme, the head of Petro-Canada and Ontario Hydro, and the leader of international environmental organizations.

[37] Leone did not have the author's name quite right. It is Huntford, Roland, and the book is *The New Totalitarians,* Allen Lane A Division of Penguin Books Ltd, London, 1971. Huntford says the new totalitarians are the Swedes. He describes how the nightmares of George Orwell's *Nineteen Eighty-Four* and especially Aldous Huxley's *Brave New World* were being realized in Sweden. Science and technology had advanced to the point where the unchallenged political bosses of Sweden, the Social Democrats who had been in power for 40 years, could control via their army of bureaucrats, officials and police what Orwell described as "...a population of slaves who do not have to be coerced, because they love their servitude." *Of all people, it is the Swedes who have come closest to this state of affairs. They have the necessary background and predilections. Outside Russia, they alone have grasped the necessity of adapting politics to technology, untroubled by doubts or reservations. They offer the first example of a system that fulfills Huxley's prophecy.* pp. 8-9, First paperback edition, 1975.

[38] Alma Morani, the American who succeeded Leone as president of the MWIA.

[39] In the general election of 1973 Olof Palme's Swedish Social Democratic Party lost seats but remained in office as the leader of a minority government. The Social Democrats' 156 seats added to the Left Party Communists' 19 seats gave the socialist bloc a total of 175 seats, exactly equal to the 175 seats held by the centre parties: Centre Party, 90 seats; Moderate Party, 51 seats; and People's Party, 34 seats.

[40] This "cleverest patient" is very likely a reference to the woman Mona mentioned to me as being an example of the unattainable ideal that her mother had in mind for young Monica. That is, Leone's praise for this patient Mona construed as invidious comparison - "Why aren't you a dozent?" One of my failures in trying to understand Leone is obviously my lack of insight into mother-daughter relationships. Although I studiously watched a series of movies about mother-daughter relationships, a pathetic measure I admit,

apart from a greater appreciation of their subtlety and complexity, I remain grossly unqualified to analyze these (notably Leone's relationship with her mother or with her daughter). Some films probably helped (e.g. Autumn Sonata, The Joy Luck Club) and some didn't (e.g. Thirteen, Mommie Dearest). My best guess is that Leone's mother, Leone and Mona all employed the defense mechanism that Anna Freud called "identification with the aggressor". Leone provided an example of mother-daughter complexity here: the suicide of her patient's mother as coincident with the personal success of the patient through psychoanalysis called forth the most extreme passive-aggressive measure the mother could muster.

Chapter 22

Leone: The Movie

Earlier I wrote that Leone's life could merit four stock movies:
1. the rags to riches, local girl succeeds despite obstacles story;
2. the mother-daughter-mother-daughter domestic psychodrama;
3. the crusade to bring equality to women in medicine;
4. the dramatic conflicts inherent in her status during the Nazi era.

Regarding the first three of these, Leone and others have written and spoken freely; of them I have recorded what I think is helpful to an understanding of Leone's life and its historical significance.

Of the fourth, however, Leone said nothing directly - and even obliquely, nearly nothing. Most people who lived through WW2 preferred not to talk about it. First there was survivor guilt - the best and most honourable had given their lives so that the survivors could live better lives. Killing other human beings, even in the line of duty and in a great cause, sickened civilized people. The guilty were legion, from those whose gratuitous savagery was expressed in mass executions of civilians - to those who failed to express their misgivings regarding compulsory hatred for people of a different political persuasion. Those most worthy of guilt, the war criminals, destroyed evidence of their guilt in anticipation of the postwar Nürnberg Trials and the revenge of Jewry.[1] Ordinary citizens found it tempting to burn files containing evidence of their wartime activities - to warm their houses and apartments during the fuel shortages of the winter of 1944-1945. The Nazis kept voluminous records, only a fraction of which survived the war.

As for the Swedes, self-styled "innocent bystanders", the public availability of information (such as citizens' income tax records) did not extend into the realm of what government officials did during the war. Press censorship was implemented in 1942 when a Göteborg newspaper carried eyewitness accounts of the extermination of Jews [2] and closer to home, the transport of 700 Norwegian Jews to Poland for extermination was reported by Swedish press and radio.[3] German officials told the Swedish government that news placing them in a bad light would violate Swedish neutrality and force

Germany to invade Sweden, as they had Denmark and Norway. Sweden acceded to the German wishes for media censorship of news contrary to German interests. Ironically Sweden had been the first country to constitutionally guarantee freedom of the press (in 1766, along with the right of home distilling).[4]

Reports of atrocities were stifled. The US State Department also suppressed news of mass executions in Poland.[5] This contributed to the disbelief that was widespread, not only in Sweden but in Canada and the USA. Germans might be the enemy, but they were also fellow members of western civilization and therefore incapable of such behaviour.[6]

Postwar, some historians and journalists were unable to see their requests for information satisfactorily answered.[7] To visibly ameliorate one situation, the Swedish Minister for Foreign Affairs authorized in 1997 a commission to inquire into the disposition of Jewish assets in Sweden before and during WW2. In its report of about 500 pages (*Sweden and Jewish Assets*, Stockholm, 3rd March 1999) the commission regretted the loss of much relevant information but found no **current** active suppression by self-serving banks or government departments. However, earlier Swedish governments' behaviour was considered reprehensible:

Recently the accepted Swedish view of Sweden's role during the Second World War has been questioned. ... The Commission has therefore opted to devote the introductory chapters of its final report to a general discussion of refugee policy, the policy of neutrality, trade policy and relations between public opinion and the government. One finds that Sweden's policy towards the belligerent great powers for most of the war was based on considerations of power politics. Moral issues were excessively disregarded and actions were taken with the overriding purpose of keeping Sweden out of the war and maintaining essential supplies. Today, of course, such an attitude can seem deplorable.[8]

There was a conspiracy of silence during and following WW2. Insofar as Leone was affected we would like to know: Who were the conspirators and why were they silent? What did they not want to talk about? In this chapter I'll adduce facts and cite their sources. The significance of these I'll leave to the judgement of the reader. Leone wrote, *I become more and more convinced that to get valuable data on women - the autobiographies must be sealed until all the people involved are dead.[9]* As I write this, Leone has been dead for 35 years and Folke for 43 years. If, by selecting this set of facts and not another, I tendentiously wrong them, I apologize. My intention is simply to draw attention to matters which probably created **dramatic conflicts** in Leone's life, although she did not discuss them in the written materials to which I had access.

Leone's Nazi-era Chronology

1930: in Hamburg during the turmoil which brought the Nazis to power in Bergedorf and Hamburg local governments.

1931: Chancellor Brüning's conservative-led coalition rescinded individual freedoms of the German Constitution in order to suppress the Nazis. Leone and Folke were married in Hamburg.

1932: moved to Stockholm. Began annual summer motoring vacations in Germany and Austria.

1933: Hitler became chancellor in January; used the extraordinary powers of that office to persuade and coerce on his way to dictatorship.

1934: with Jean Halton and Kathleen Campbell, Leone drove her LaSalle through Europe and North Africa for three months - probably March, April and May. On returning to Stockholm, she received Folke's blessing to begin psychoanalytic training in Zürich.

1934-1935 academic year: training analysis with Gustav Bally, lectures from Jung and Pulver.

1935: returned to Stockholm, resolved to obtain a medical licence in Sweden in order to pursue her goal of becoming a psychoanalyst.

1935-1936 academic year: medical studies at the Karolinska Institut, Stockholm.

1936-1937 academic year: medical studies at the Karolinska Institut. Leone qualified to practice medicine in Sweden but remained unemployed. She and Folke decided that it was time to have children.

1937: summer trip to Bavaria and Austria in 1937 Lincoln Zephyr. Daughter Monica born in October.

1938: Leone recruited Nana from the Hamburg children's hospital and stayed close to Monica for her first year - until embarking on a three-month trip with Folke to Argentina and Brazil.

1939: moved into Strandvägan 53 with three servants and Monica. Donald born in October, nine months after Leone and Folke's voyage from Rio de Janeiro to Southampton and their stay at the Dorchester Hotel in London.

1939-1945: in a cold apartment (due to coal and wood rationing), boring food, studying psychoanalysis and drawing comfort from Toynbee's *A Study of History*.[10] Summers were spent with the children and Nana in a beach hotel on the west coast of Sweden. *Folke could only join us for a month each summer.*[11]

Ties to Alberta, Canada

Leone was a Canadian in 1933-1945.[12] She did not renounce her Canadian citizenship until 1974. When she was a teenager, during WW1, Leone had tried desperately to join the **10% of the total population of Alberta who enlisted.**[13] As a female she could not become a combatant, but a woman could be an ambulance driver; accordingly she took an evening course in auto mechanics (she taught school during the day to save money for university) in order to qualify as an ambulance driver.   Although technically qualified, Leone was rejected for service because she was too young.

Why were so many Albertans in general, and Leone in particular, willing to defend the British Empire, Canada and Alberta with their lives? Unexcelled freedom and opportunity are obvious answers: freedom defined in the British tradition of the individual's rights being limited only where they infringe on the rights of other individuals; and opportunity defined by the Alberta balance sheet - large resources divided by a small number of people equalled a large per capita share interest. Albertans were equal shareholders in a polity having great wealth and within it they had considerable freedom of action.

If we know nothing else about Leone, we know that she valued individual freedom. Her profession, psychoanalysis, was banned in Nazi Germany largely because of its emphasis on the importance of the individual (versus that of the collective).[14] When a heroine of her adolescence, Dr. Rosamund Leacock, in the company of Miss M. Muir of the Calgary Herald, was reported on July 4, 1917 to have set a new speed record (four hours and ten minutes) from Banff to Calgary, they did not encounter a multiplicity of police bent on curbing their enterprise; and the feat was praised, not blamed. In 1917 Dr. Leacock could legally carry a pistol - compulsory handgun registration and control by the RCMP did not arrive until 1934. Dr. Leacock did not pay income tax. Nobody in Alberta did until the federal "temporary" *War Tax Upon Income* was implemented later in 1917: 4% of single men's annual incomes of more than $2,000, other exemptions to $3,000, rates of 2% - 25% for incomes above $6,000 per year. Tolerance and respect for individual freedom were expressed in British traditions - the right to be presumed innocent until proven guilty (except in customs and tax matters), *caveat emptor* and *habeas corpus*.

As a Canadian from freedom-loving Alberta, Leone could be expected to be opposed to Germany's National Socialist ideology and its following in Sweden. As a Canadian in neutral Sweden during the war, her activities were monitored and her mobility restricted.[15] Like everyone else in Sweden, she lost her freedom of speech.

Ironically for Leone, issues surrounding political and religious freedom controlled her life during the Nazi era. From her typescript autobiography:

Usually friends of our parents came home to lunch after church and there were great discussions on religious beliefs and political questions. I had such an overdose of these discussions as a child that I have never interested myself in either problem as an adult and much less discussed them.[16]

I mentioned earlier the staggering effect of a beautiful leather-bound book, "Macaulay" in gold on the spine, in a Stockholm antiquarian book shop. It opened in the middle to a speech given by James Babington (later Lord) Macaulay on the 17th of April, 1833, to "A Committee of the Whole House of Commons to Consider the Civil Disabilities of the Jews".[17] The week before I had read hundreds of pages of German language newspaper articles and minutes of Bergedorfer Eisenwerk management meetings from the time of the Nazis, and I was struggling to formulate in my mind precisely what was different about our way of thinking in Alberta and Canada. In 1833 Jewish participation in the political life of Britain was circumscribed; most important, a Jew could not be elected to the House of Commons. Macaulay spoke to this resolution:

That it is the opinion of this Committee that it is expedient to remove all civil disabilities at present existing with respect to His Majesty's subjects professing the Jewish religion, with the like exceptions as are provided with respect to His Majesty's subjects professing the Roman Catholic religion.[18]

The eloquence, precision, scope and force of Macaulay's argument was a revelation to me (later I learned that this speech is a classic in the annals of parliamentary rhetoric). Macaulay described the rights and obligations of a British citizen, and the reasoning for full participation of Jews and Roman Catholics in this citizenship. The motion passed without a division. While reading this speech I was struck by a remarkable coincidence: exactly 100 years later, April, 1933, the right of Jews to participate in the German parliament was withdrawn.

Ties to Psychoanalysis

Of course April, 1933, was just the beginning for persecution of Jews in the Third Reich. [19]

Leone had Jewish friends, some of them in Germany. Her chosen profession, psychoanalysis, was, in the wake of Freud's influence, considered by some a "Jewish profession".[20] Many of her mentors and colleagues were Jewish. Their fate was her concern.

The widow Frau Friedheim in Hamburg, "...*became a real mother to me for that year.* [21]

In Hamburg: *I had never before been exposed to so many interesting groups of people. ... I had my landlady, Frau Friedheim, who invited me to all her parties so that I met many interesting Jews. Lastly, I had Wolfgang Rittmeister who fascinated me more than any man I had ever met. He had a brother who was a psychoanalyst. He lived with his father in a charming villa and I was invited to all their dinners and musical evenings .... I did not enjoy sailing because I always froze. I only went along to be with Wolfgang.[22]*

Leone's infatuation with Wolfgang was set aside quickly when she met Folke Hellstedt, her ideal of a husband. Continued contact with Wolfgang's brother John, however, would have been inevitable during Leone's training in Zürich when she and John were attending Jung's lectures at the same time.[23] John was inclined (like Leone, I believe) to closely follow Freud's psychology, distinguishing his brand of psychoanalysis from the Adler-, Jung- and other hyphenated heresies popular at the time.[24] She could have easily followed John's career as a psychoanalyst - because he was appointed to a prominent position, head of the outpatient clinic of the German Institute for Psychological Research and Psychotherapy (Göring Institute) in Berlin. John got into trouble because his writing *...revealed a strong Freudian point of view* and he was inclined to *... the traditional iconoclastic bent within psychoanalysis that had originated with Freud himself and to the tendency among many European psychoanalysts to adhere to the social and political left.*[25] His Freudian and communist sympathies resulted in arrest on a charge of treason in 1942 and his execution (by guillotine) in 1943.

In 1985 Geoffrey Cocks wrote: *Rittmeister has become a celebrated figure[26] among psychotherapists in both East and West Germany - in the East for his socialist struggle against "German fascism" and in the West for adding a needed luster* (sic) *to the presence and activities of psychoanalysts at the Göring Institute. He does indeed stand out in word and deed from his colleagues at the Göring Institute, but he was not completely divorced from those traditions that animated those psychotherapists in Germany who continued their professional campaign after 1933 on the basis of a shared allegiance to a particular German philosophical, cultural and national heritage.* John confessed to longing for a *Führer* **before** the Nazis came to power.[27] Why could he not maintain his position, despite his qualifications, conscientious work and the sponsorship of Matthias Göring, head of the eponymous Institute and cousin of Hermann Göring , next in power only to Hitler? *Rittmeister had embraced a broader, humanistic vision of mankind, united in its common humanity rather than divided by the narrow* *and parochial concerns of a mind set that Rittmeister's guide, the genius Freud, had labeled "the narcissism of small differences."* [28]

In 1943 Tore Ekman, Leone's training analyst, left his psychoanalytic practice and academic appointments in Leipzig and Berlin in order to return to Sweden. If Leone did not know of John Rittmeister's fate before Ekman's return, she must have known after.

Leone's time in Zürich also placed her in the middle of a notorious uproar in psychoanalysis.

In February 1934 the Swiss psychiatrist Gustav Bally attacked Jung's future credibility as editor of a coordinated periodical and pointed to what he considered to be the damning emphasis that Jung had placed on the supposed distinctions between Jewish and Germanic science, a common theme among Nazi intellectual apologists. At best, Bally concluded, Jung was, even if unwittingly, abetting National Socialism. [29]

Bally was Leone's training analyst in Zürich, where she was also taking lectures from Jung. Nazi propagandists sought to benefit from Jung's intellectual prestige - by using his assertion that the collective unconscious of Jews was different from that of Germans - to justify their treatment of Jews as subversive aliens in Germany. [30]

As she trained to be a psychoanalyst during WW2, Leone must have followed the tribulations of her chosen profession and been distressed by the fates of its leaders as they fled from Austria and Germany. Sweden's immigration policy discriminated against Jews in the time when Germany allowed them to leave.[31]

Germany and Sweden

The extermination of individualism is an enterprise of the totalitarian state.[32] In Germany and Sweden during the 1930s and 1940s repressive socialist [33] regimes were elected by popular vote, sometimes by huge majorities. The Social Democrats came into power in 1932; in 1973 when Leone recommended the book by Roland Huntford (*The New Totalitarians*) to her friends, they were still in power. [34]

From 1931 onward, Leone was surrounded by people whose world views were quite different from hers. Maintaining her mental health in this environment must have been difficult.

Destruction of the centre of Stockholm has had the effect of cutting off the past. It was done with a callousness and ruthlessness that suggests a fear or hatred of what had gone before. (before the Social Democrat regime) *... a socialist alderman in charge of housing says he insists on demolishing all older buildings because he wants everyone to have the same high standard (equality again). ...* In response to the pleas of people who liked living in their old buildings, a conference was called. *... A certain official ... explained how 'research' had decided what kitchens, shape of room and lighting installations were best for people, and that these would, willy-nilly, be provided for tenants. 'Do you mean to say,' asked a rare, rebellious delegate, 'that you are going to tell people how to live?' 'Yes,' was the answer, ' That's my job.'* [35]

Reading the literature of the period revised my understanding of the Nazi era. Before undertaking the research concerning Leone's time in Germany and Sweden, I believed, as I suspect most Canadians do, that Hitler and his Nazi cronies had duped the German people into giving them political power; then they used this power to progressively withdraw individual freedoms until they realized the radically intolerant, totalitarian regime of Hitler's dreams. The whole truth is more complicated.

One of my naive beliefs was negated accidentally. Being a golfer, I was interested in the Austrian golf hotel where Leone and Folke met the deposed King Alfonso XIII of Spain, and where she and Alfonso played a two-ball every morning for three weeks. On ebay I was able to buy copies of the *TIME* magazines having Alfonso on the cover. Browsing in the April 31, 1931 issue, under "Foreign News" I ran across an account of Chancellor Heinrich Brüning's success in the Reichstag in fashioning a coalition of his conservatives and the socialists against the fascists, who were *... definitely in the ascendant,* in order to pass a budget and avoid dissolution of the Reichstag. Chancellor Brüning *... had fashioned a sharp spit on which to cook the goose of Adolf Hitler, "the pocket Mussolini.".*

To crush every challenge to his power Chancellor Brüning, as soon as the Reichstag adjourned, went straight to his patron and got Old Paul to sign the most drastic decree ever issued by a German President.

Under this decree:

1)   The so-called "fundamental rights" of personal liberty granted by the German Constitution are suspended.

2)   The Government is empowered to disperse any meeting, censor any newspaper or stop any public utterance which it chooses to term "seditious".

3)   This is carried to the extreme of permitting the Government to suspend entirely any offending newspaper for periods up to eight weeks; and before a public meeting the police are empowered to demand the written text of every speech that is to be made.[36]

Hitler's *Nationalsozialistische Deutsche Arbeiterpartei* (NSDAP, in English "Nazi", National Socialist German Workers' Party) succeeded because it expressed the will of the people. Similarly, the Swedish regimes of the time, sympathetic to Germany, expressed the will of the Swedish people. Leone was an alien among these people, the general population. Her psychosocial support would have been from those closer to her: friends and family.

Bergedorfer Eisenwerk

Unfortunately Leone's husband's work implied further demoralisation. According to her daughter Mona (born in October of 1937), Papa traveled a great deal on business during the war. Ernst Folke Hellstedt was the representative of the owner (Separator AB, Stockholm) on the three-man board of directors of Bergedorfer Eisenwerk at least from 1933-1945.[37] I was not able to find evidence of his attendance at board meetings during the war. No minutes of board meetings, only some minutes of lower management director meetings have survived in Germany - in the Bergedorf Museum archives. Alfa Laval refused my research colleagues permission to view their archives in Sweden. It seems practically certain, however, that Folke traveled to Bergedorf, at least for board meetings, and that he was familiar with Eisenwerk's operations.[38] My guess is that he was appalled at some of these, but was powerless to change them.

Folke had been working for Separator AB of Stockholm perhaps since 1917, when he was a step ahead of the Bolsheviks in St. Petersburg, then Moscow, then Omsk, then across to Vladivostok on the Trans-Siberian Railway, then to New Zealand. He is mentioned as a Separator AB employee in 1919 by *Vem är Vem,* the Swedish Who's Who. In 1930 Folke had been in the daughter company Bergedorfer Eisenwerk in Germany for about five years when the chief died and Folke replaced him.[39] In December of 1931 he and

Leone moved to Stockholm where he took up his senior management post in the parent company.[40] Sales and profitability of Eisenwerk improved year after year from 1933-1945[41]; dividends were paid on common and preferred shares. In 1936 the Eisenwerk product line included equipment for ships, cooling machines and storage coolers, pumps, humidifiers, water heaters, purifiers, degassing equipment and accessories for all of the above.[42] In 1937 the staff numbered 1,607. [43] Hitler Youth membership became a pre-condition for apprenticeship in 1938.[44] The milk business was off again in 1939, but Department "Spezial" and Department "G" were doing well;[45] the works was named a defence industry operation and therefore pledges of secrecy were required from employees.[46] With the war in progress a Nazi party functionary joined the Eisenwerk *Vertrauensrat* meetings, the workers were referred to as *Arbeitskamaraden* (a totalitarian cliché) and meetings ended with the salutation *Heil Hitler!*

Increased sales and associated production, coupled with losses of personnel to the military, resulted in acute labour shortage. The nearby Neuengamme concentration camp held slave labour, and forced labour became available from Poland and Ukraine from Operation Barbarossa.[47]

The Eisenwerk typescript chronicle of 1945 does not mention a major event in 1937, the delivery of a huge order (400 separators). Much later, in the company's 100th anniversary publication, *Alfa-Laval Astra: 1859-1959, 100 Jahre Bergedorfer Eisenwerk,* this merited only a few words: *Grosslieferung von 400 Schlammseparatoren für Deutsche Hydrierwerke* (large delivery of 400 mud separators for a German hydrogenation works). It is more than likely that these separators were delivered to IG Farben for the manufacture from brown coal of synthetic oil,[48] a process which involves hydrogenation and for which IG Farben was under tremendous pressure from Hitler to implement, having agreed ... *by the end of 1937, it could produce 300,000 to 350,000 tons annually. The Reich, in turn, pledged to guarantee a price corresponding to the cost of production, including a five percent interest on invested capital and generous depreciation, and to take measures to assure the sale of all synthetic oil not sold by I.G. through its own outlets.*[49]

IG Farben had contributed a large sum to the Nazi party when it was struggling. Hitler was grateful. Fulfillment of the terms of this groundbreaking *Benzinvertrag* (gasoline agreement) would provide the strategic source of oil and fuel that would permit the invasion of Austria,

Czechoslovakia and Poland.[50] Neither my research colleague nor I was able to find invoices or bills of lading indicating the German hydrogenation works for which the 400 separators were destined in 1937. During the war Eisenwerk executives were screened in Berlin and attained the highest security status. Secrecy regarding the critical nature of some products could have prevailed; or the documents concerning separators for hydrogenation might have been casualties of a 1945 sanitation program. Buried in the hundreds of pages of minutes of the monthly management meetings, however, I found evidence of Eisenwerk's manufacture of separators for *ersatz* oil manufacture. It came in the form of an indignant response to gossip that Eisenwerk was not achieving enough for the German war effort: the Operations Leader boasted that Eisenwerk manufactured critical equipment for the winning of gasoline from coal (mud separator), winning beer from potatoes and making artificial rubber.[51]

Minutes of *Vertrauensratsitzung* meetings also confirmed the use of forced labour.[52] From internet sources I had learned that Bergedorfer Eisenwerk was on a United Nations list of about 2,500 companies that used forced labour and slave labour during WW2. In 2001 the Museum für Bergedorf und die Vierlande published a profusely illustrated 136 page history of forced labour in Bergedorf, *Zwangsarbeit in Bergedorf: Stationen einer vorlorenen Jugend* (Forced Labour in Bergedorf: Stopping-place of Lost Youth). Photos and interviews in this publication describe how, in the wake of the Wehrmacht's advance through Poland and the Ukraine in 1941,[53] the SS took young women (the young men had been killed, captured or defected to the German forces) from their homes and "railroaded" them to Germany,[54] where factories were desperately short of labour. These women received small wages. Those from Slavic countries were thought to be inferior to Aryans, less likely to be loyal to the Aryan cause, and therefore housed in secure dormitories, given less critical work and paid less than labour considered more Aryan - French, Dutch and Belgian workers were more likely to be billeted with German families and trusted with making weapons and ammunition.

Soviet prisoners of war were considered a sabotage risk and therefore used for tasks like mining clay, digging canals, road building and clearing dangerous bombed areas. The notorious Neuengamme concentration camp was in Bergedorf. Late in the war it was estimated to hold 80,000 prisoners and to have a death rate of 2,000 prisoners per month.[55] Neuengamme had more than 35 *Aussenkommondon,* groups of prisoners who worked outside the camp during the day. At night,

> *The barracks were crammed tight with people, and in some places there was so little room that these tormented creatures had no choice but to lie on their sides. The official bed space was a width of 30-40 centimetres per man. Healthy and sick had to lie the one next to the other. Those poor people who couldn't raise their bodies were forced to relieve themselves indoors and the stink was overpowering.*[56]

The following page from *Zwangsarbeit in Bergedorf* begins a list of companies using *sowjetische Kriegsgefangene als Zwangsarbeiter* (Soviet prisoners of war as forced labourers).

Anhang 2

1. Auflistung von Firmen im Raum Bergedorf/Vier- und Marschlande, die im Zweiten Weltkrieg KZ-Häftlinge und/oder ZwangsarbeiterInnen beschäftigt haben

Die folgende Auflistung erhebt keinen Anspruch auf Vollständigkeit. Sie ist das Ergebnis der Studien zum Thema Zwangsarbeit. Sofern genaue Quellen vorlagen, sind sie entsprechend vermerkt und teilweise in Teil b) dieses Anhanges abgebildet. Die Liste der Alliierten (Catalogue of Camps an Prisons in Germany and German occupied Terretories 1939-1945) steht unter www.zweitausendeins.de zum kostenlosen Download bereit.

Holzhandlung Behr
bis 1969 am Kupferhof
Nachfolgefirma heute: Baumarkt Behr am Curslacker Neuen Deich
Beschäftigung von 15 bis 20 KZ-Häftlingen, überwiegend Häftlingsgruppe: Zeugen Jehovas und sowjetische Kriegsgefangene
Quelle: Liste der KZ-Gedenkstätte Neuengamme
Spende für die Einladung ehemaliger Zwangsarbeiterinnen nach Bergedorf.
Beitritt zur Stiftungsinitiative der deutschen Wirtschaft „Erinnerung, Verantwortung und Zukunft" am 4. April 2000.

Emil Bentin, Betonwerk
Lohbrügge Nord
Bobergerstraße 5, Hamburg-Lohbrügge
40 sowj. Kriegsgefangene
Auf dem Betriebsgelände standen Baracken, in denen die sowjetischen Kriegsgefangenen untergebracht waren. Sie wurden sowohl im Betonwerk als auch in anderen Lohbrügger Firmen wie der Mercedes-Werkstatt Gehrike eingesetzt.
Quelle: Aufstellung der Polizei Hamburg Revier 57 von 1946, Liste der Alliierten

Bergedorfer Eisenwerk, Alfa Laval
Hauptwerk bis 1973 am Bahndamm in Lohbrügge, Wilhelm Bergner Straße.
Heute stehen auf dem ehemaligen Firmengelände die Wohnblocks des Billebogens am Ludwig Rosenberg Ring.
Ab 1974 zog die Firma Alfa Laval nach Glinde um.
Sowohl auf dem Gelände am Bahndamm als auch im Zweigwerk Kampchaussee 22 wurden sowjetische Kriegsgefangene als Zwangsarbeiter eingesetzt.
Quelle: Liste der Alliierten

97

Eisenwerk used Soviet POWs to build railway embankments & branch lines

The official Nazi policy toward Soviet prisoners of war was *Vernichtung durch Arbeit* (extermination through work). A plaque in the New Cemetery in Bergedorf describes the fate of 1,000 Soviet prisoners brought to Bergedorf in October, 1941, 652 of whom were dead seven months later.

Der jugendliche Bote Hans Schulz hat sich mehrere Male etwas zu-
schulden kommen lassen und trotz Verwarnungen nicht gebessert.
Schulz wird mit Einwilligung der DAF und des Arbeitsamtes ent-
lassen.

Die beiden Arbeitskameraden Heinrichs und Wilhelm erhalten nach-
träglich eine Leistungszulage, die ab 15. November 1941 nachge-
zahlt wird.

Alle Arbeitskameraden, die Neuland bebaut haben, erhalten hier-
für vom Betriebsführer eine Prämie mit einem passenden Schreiben
für ihre Mitarbeit in der Erzeugungsschlacht ausgehändigt.

--ooOoo--

Vertrauensratsitzung am 28. Juli 1942.

Der Betriebsführer berichtete über die Materialzuweisungen und
betonte, dass für die Giesserei keine Giessmarken bewilligt würden
und daher in verschiedenen Abteilungen die Arbeitszeit vorüber-
gehend auf 48 Stunden gesetzt wurde. Er betonte weiter, dass
Arbeiten aufgenommen sind, für die es Giessmarken gibt, dass es
aber 5 - 6 Wochen dauern kann, bis die Vorbereitungen erledigt
sind.

Der Betriebsobmann weist darauf hin, für die Russen Brausebäder
anlegen zu lassen und peinlich auf die Sauberkeit der Russen zu
achten, damit keine Krankheiten auf Deutsche übertragen werden
können.

Weiter wurde dem Betriebsführer vorgeschlagen, sich rechtzeitig
nach Ersatz für den Montageinspektor Illgen umzusehen, da der
Mann nicht mehr richtig mit den Monteuren umzugehen vermag und
nur noch auf sein Alter Rücksicht genommen wird. Auf die Dauer
geht dies aber nicht.

Der Arbeitskamerad Lohöfer, der seine Leistung nach Angabe des
Meisters und Kalkulators tüchtig gesteigert hat, erhält einen
zu niedrigen Lohn. Der Betriebsobmann betonte, dass Lohöfer die
Spitze von RM 1.2o erhalten müsste, wenn man ihm die Lust an der

Der Betriebsobmann weist ... "The shop steward stresses the layout of the
Russian shower baths and taking pains regarding the cleanliness of the
Russians so that no illnesses can be transmitted to Germans."

303

If God lived on earth, people would break his windows.

Jewish proverb

If we follow the trail of Jung's remarks to Matthew Halton regarding the significance of the halfway point of one's life, our attention is drawn, in Leone's case, to the last half of the year 1938. Her situation then? She was qualified to practise medicine in Sweden, but was unemployed. She could not do the work for which she was especially qualified, renal pathology, because there seemed a lack of facilities and funding for this science in Sweden, particularly for those without Swedish training. She had a husband whom she loved, but he was away most of the time, travelling the world on business. She had a year-old daughter whom she treasured and a registered German nurse to take care of her. She and her three servants occupied the fourth floor of a substantial nineteenth-century building with a handsome view over a wide boulevard and a scenic canal. She spoke Swedish poorly and was considered brash and ill-mannered by Stockholm society women; in turn she found them boring. Her ambition to become a psychoanalyst was frustrated by the lack of training analysts in Sweden; where there were training analysts - Vienna, Berlin and her beloved Hamburg - the events of November 10 (*Kristallnacht,* the Night of Broken Glass) and its aftermath dispersed them throughout the world. Swedish immigration restrictions regarding Jews did not help Leone to further her chosen career; the trajectory of the last half of her life was set during a three month trip with Folke to South America - they resolved to have another child.

Late 1938 was also a turning point for Germany and Sweden generally. Shortly after midnight, in the darkness of the early hours of November 10, 1938, a coordinated attack began on the Jews of Germany.

In hundreds of Jewish neighbourhoods, paramilitary stormtroopers of the SA 'Sturmabteilung', or Storm Division - some in their Brownshirt uniforms, others in civilian clothes - lit bonfires and threw furniture and books from synagogues and private homes into the flames. In the streets, Jews were chased, reviled and beaten up. Tens of thousands of Jewish shops and homes were ransacked.[57]

The day following "the night of broken glass" 30,000 Jewish men were arrested and taken to concentration camps.

Kristallnacht taught those German Jews who still retained hope that Nazism would modify its anti-Jewish stand that the time had come to leave, except those who still clung, as some did, to the belief that the norms of civilised behaviour could not be totally breached or abandoned....[58]

In ten months following, before the onset of war, 120,000 German Jews and 140,000 Austrian Jews (Freud had already gone to England, in June) fled their homes. Britain was the most welcoming destination, then the USA. Canada took not so many, Sweden even fewer.[59] Half of Germany's Jews emigrated during the 1930s; nearly all of the 250,000 who remained were murdered.

Sweden did not wish to be involved

Unlike women in England, Leone could not take her children to Canada for the duration of the danger and hardship. Perhaps she wouldn't have even if she could. [60] But I believe she was deeply unhappy for most of the war - physically uncomfortable, intellectually deprived and spiritually oppressed.

Sweden had been part of the German cultural sphere since the mid-nineteenth century. The German language, German technology and education, German music and art - all exercised greater influence on Sweden than did the culture of any other foreign country. Especially among the well-educated and upper classes of Sweden, Germany represented the finest traditions of Western culture. What German culture represented in broad and simplified sense was a combination of order, achievement, symmetrical forms, respect for the past, and Christian (Lutheran) tradition. ... the Bolshevik menace was ... the latest version of the traditional Russian threat to Sweden ....[61]

War with the Allies impelled Germany to strategic occupation of Scandinavia. Denmark, Norway and Finland resisted. Sweden didn't. Staying out of the war at any cost was the successful political platform put forward by Per Albin Hansson's Social Democrats. For example, the policy decisions regarding alternatives which might help Finland: *... doing neither*

was better than doing something that might turn out to be wrong[62]*; ...
present a unified front to the world, to protect Swedish neutrality, and to
avoid internal conflict...; ... a foreign policy that took the least possible risks.*

Although nominally neutral, having signed neutrality agreements with both
the Allies and Germany, Sweden nevertheless favoured Germany [63] until it
became clear, after El Alamein and Stalingrad, that Germany was going to
lose the war.[64] Swedish policy gradually changed, permitting such things as
the initiative of Raoul Wallenberg in Budapest (funded by the United
States), [65] until, by the end of the war, it favoured the Allies. Winston
Churchill remarked that Sweden would never recover its honour.[66]
*If we remove the realist interpretation of the foreign policy pursued during
the war, a traumatic national self-identity appears. The trauma consists of
the feelings of dismay, humiliation, indignation, shame, contempt for an
adaptation that placed Sweden outside the struggle between democracy and
dictatorship, humanism and barbarianism, bad and good.*[67]

Matthew Halton, the man from Pincher Creek, was with the forces fighting
Rommel. Of the Eighth Army, he wrote in 1944:

*The living have received their tribute from Churchill: "When after the war is
over a man is asked what he did, it will be enough for him to say 'I marched
with the Eighth Army'." For the dead, it will be useless for relatives to drive
along the desert road after the war to deck their crosses with flowers or
memories. The little crosses will already be hidden by the shifting sand. But
that will not matter if only the "realists" of the world have learned any
lesson from their idealism.*
     *   *   *
The lesson is that idealism is the only realism.[68]

From the last page but one of *Ten Years to Alamein.*

---

[1] Penkower, Monty Noam, *The Jews Were Expendable: Free World Diplomacy and the Holocaust,*
University of Illinois Press, Urbana & Chicago, 1983, pp. 22, 95, 194, 253.
[2] Torgny Segerstedt's newspapers. *The King pleaded directly with Segerstedt in 1940 to cease and desist
from his attacks on Hitler. K.G. Westman, minister of justice during the period and therefore responsible
for any action against the independence of the press, recorded in his diary a macabre explanation of
Segerstedt's un-Swedish behavior: "His Jewish mistress has removed his soul and replaced it with a Jewish
one." Koblik, Steven, The Stones Cry Out: Sweden's Response to the Persecution of the Jews 1933-1945,*
Holocaust Library, New York, 1988, pp. 23-24.

[3] *The departure of the ship that carried half of Norway's Jews (approximately 700 people) to Poland and their death was reported on all Swedish newspapers and on the radio. Public meetings were held to show solidarity for Norway's Jews. Many pastors gave sermons condemning Germany's policy toward the Jews, and all the bishops of Sweden issued a joint declaration protesting Germany's racial activities. A Gallup poll taken in mid-December indicated that 25 percent of the respondents named persecution of the Jews in Norway as the event they would most remember from 1942. Stalingrad was a distant second at 12 percent.* ibid.,, Koblik, Steven, *The Stones Cry Out: Sweden's Response to the Persecution of the Jews,* p. 60.

[4] *While the four estates, the royal house, and government offices, as well as religion, were protected from abuse, freedom of the press in principle was unrestricted. The freedom of the press act was incorporated into the constitution, which meant that it could be abolished or changed only after action at two meetings of the estates and with the agreement of all four estates. Elsewhere, only in Great Britain and the Netherlands was there freedom of the press at all in the modern sense, and, in being made part of the constitution, the Swedish freedom of the press act can be considered unique. The result of the act was open discussion in press and pamphlets without precedent in Sweden.* Koblik, Steven, editor, *Sweden's Development From Poverty to Affluence, 1750-1970,* U. of Minnesota Press, 1975, pp. 31-32 .

[5] op cit, Koblik, *The Stones Cry Out,* p. 196-198.

[6] In 1942 the *New York Times* published reports which were dismissed by many because of this newspaper's Jewish ownership. Lipstadt, Deborah, *Beyond Belief: The American Press and the Coming of the Holocaust, 1933-1945,* The Free Press, Simon & Schuster, New York, 1986.

[7] Highly visible more recent examples are Stieg Larsson's *The Millennium Trilogy* and the December, 2010 scandal regarding the father of the German-born Queen Silvia of Sweden lying about his background (documents found in Berlin and South America revealed his 1934 Nazi party membership).

[8] Page one of the Summary of *Sweden and Jewish Assets.*

[9] letter of November 22, 1971 to the girls in Vienna.

[10] Of the eventual twelve, in 1939 Toynbee had written six volumes: I & II Geneses of Civilizations (1934); III, Growths of Civilizations (1934); IV, Breakdowns of Civilizations (1939); V & VI, Disintegrations of Civilizations, (1939).

[11] Leone's typescript autobiography, p. 64.

[12] A British subject, actually, carrying a British passport until the Canadian Citizenship Act of 1947 resulted in the issue of Canadian passports.

[13] Dept. of National Defence, Ottawa (~ 45,136 men enlisted in Alberta plus approx. 2,000 who joined British units, women ambulance drivers, et al); Dept. of Municipal Affairs, Edmonton (total Alberta population 470,000 in 1914). Other sources more or less agree.

[14] Cocks, Geoffrey, *Psychotherapy in the Third Reich: the Göring Institute,* Oxford University Press, New York and Oxford, 1985, p. 59.

[15] The Swedish Secret Police monitored British citizens. Denham, Henry, *Inside the Nazi Ring: a Naval Attaché in Sweden 1940-1945,*Holmes & Meier, New York, 1984, pp. 27-28.

[16] typescript autobiography dated January, 1970, p. 20.

[17] Lady Trevelyan, editor, *The Complete Writings of Lord Macaulay in Twenty Volumes, Speeches, Vol. 1,* delivered April 17, 1833, The Brampton Society, New York, pp. 131-145, no date on volume.

[18] Abrahams, Israel and the Rev. S. Levy, *Essay and Speech on Jewish Disabilities by Lord Macaulay,* Jewish Historical Society of England, 1910, second edition, p. 42.

[19] Before the ascension of Hitler in January, the first wave of Jewish migration had already begun, led by Albert Einstein. He had left the intellectual gratification of the elite physics axis of Berlin-Copenhagen for the personal freedom and security of individual rights that he found at Princeton in the United States. Isaacson, Walter, *Einstein: His Life and Universe*, Simon & Schuster, New York, p. 379.

[20] Freud regretted the loss of Jung as a disciple (1913) in large part because Jung was not a Jew and Freud wished to enlarge his following by changing the perception of psychoanalysis as a "Jewish profession". Moreover, anti-Semitism hampered the profession: *Anti-Semitism was an all too common adjunct to the aristocratic German tradition of which men like Göring partook, and the many brilliant Jews in medicine, especially those who dominated the elite and exclusive corridors of the psychoanalytic movement, could only have served to add professional jealousy to common cultural bigotry.* op cit, Cocks, Geoffrey, p. 114

[21] Leone's typescript draft autobiography, p. 49.

[22] ibid, p.50. Leone's attraction to Hamburg can in part be attributed to the civilized behaviour she found there. Of John Rittmeister it was said, *Er hatte die typische Zurückhaltung des gebildeten Hamburgers*

(He had the typical reserve of educated Hamburgers). Bräutigam, Walter, *John Rittmeister: Leben und Sterben, 1898-1943,* Langewiessche-Brandt, Ebenhausen bei München, 1987, p. 41.

[23] In 1935 both were at the Burghölzli Clinic in Zürich. op cit, Cocks, Geoffrey, *Psychotherapy in the Third Reich: the Göring Institute,* Oxford University Press, 1985, p. 65.

[24] Leone and John Rittmeister had the same training analyst in Zürich, the Freudian Gustav Bally: *...schon unter dem Einfluss der bei Gustav Bally 1935 begonnen Lehranalyse, das Studium der Theorien Sigmund Freuds.* Op cit Bräutigam, Walter, p. 24.

[25] ibid, p. 65.

[26] The John-Rittmeister Institut (psychoanalysis, psychotherapy) was founded in 1989 in Kiel, Schleswig-Holstein. John 's close friend in Zürich, Alfred Storch, the Jewish psychiatrist and philosopher, wrote about and publicized John's work following the war. The current head of the Institut was aware of John's brother Wolfgang, but she was unable to tell me what happened to him. Donald Hellstedt met Wolfgang after the war and quickly came to trust him almost as a father.

[27] For those who are curious but don't wish to take on the books on the topic (some in German), a summary of the entanglement of psychoanalytical and Nazi politics by Bernd Nitzchke is available online in an English translation by Channing Bates: *Psychoanalysis and National Socialism. Banned or Brought into Conformity? Break or Continuity?* International Forum of Psychoanalysis 12, 2003, pp. 98-108.

[28] op cit, Cocks, Geoffrey, p. 68. The Rittmeister family helped many Jews to escape Germany in the time between Kristallnacht and the Endlösung. (op cit Bräutigam, p.31).

[29] op cit, Cocks, Geoffrey, p. 132.

[30] Hitler, Adolf, *Mein Kampf,* translated by Ralph Manheim, Sentry Edition C, Houghton Miflin Company, Boston, The Riverside Press, Cambridge, 1943, pp. 282-296.

[31] The Wannsee Conference of National Socialist party members and government ministers, January 20, 1942, formulated the "final solution to the Jewish question." For a thorough treatment of this phenomenon, see: Penkower, Monty Noam, *The Jews Were Expendable: Free World Diplomay and the Holocaust,* University of Illinois Press, Urbana and Chicago, 1983.

[32] *Brave New World* by Aldous Huxley and *1984* by George Orwell are well known dramatizations. *Economic security by itself does not necessarily imply a love of servitude. Other conditions are required: on the side of the rulers, a thorough understanding of the interaction between economics and power; and on the side of the ruled, submission to authority and a reverence for the expert. Also, in both cases, an aversion to individuality, an instinct for the collective, a suspicion of parliamentary institutions, a worship of the state, and a preference for government by bureaucrat rather than by politician. ... the Swedes have consistently fulfilled these specifications.* Huntford, Roland, *The New Totalitarians,* Allen Lane, A Division of Penguin Books, London, 1971, p. 9.

[33] The Nazi (National Socialist German Workers') party claimed to represent ordinary Germans, although Hitler made deals advantageous to German big business and courted the old aristocratic military class with huge appropriations for arms. The Nazis hated Communists but conspicuously celebrated Labour Day, May 1st. To round out his appeal to a maximum of German voters, Hitler ended speeches with "Amen."

[34] ibid, Huntford, p. 10.

[35] ibid, Huntford, p. 283.

[36] *TIME Magazine,* April 6, 1931, p. 20

[37] The financial pages of Berlin newspapers for this period are online. Because Bergedorfer Eisenwerk was a public company, its results were published in these and other newspapers. Sales and profits climbed steadily from 1933 until 1943, the last of these newspapers that I was able to find. The 1943 Eisenwerk report shows Ernst Hellstedt, Stockholm, as Supervisory Board President. His fellow directors were Dr. Wilhelm Grethe, lawyer and notary public, Ludwig Vogel of Hamburg-Bergedorf and Dr. Hans Ohle of Reinbek.

[38] He is listed as a director in the Berlin financial newspapers until 1943. The *Bergedorfer Eisenwerk Vorstandes* report for 1944 is signed by Hellstedt.

[39] From the typescript in-house chronicle of Bergedorfer Eisenwerk, *Geschichte des Bergedorfer Eisenwerkes Aktiengesellschaft Astra-Werke vom Gründungsjahr 1859 bis zur Gegenwart* (present ,1945), p. 78:

1930: In der ganzen Welt über 4 Millionen Alfa-Laval Separatoren verkauft. Die Maschinen erhielten uber 1500 höchste Auszeichnungen. ... Dieses Jahr wird von einschneidender für die Leitung des Werkes.

Direktor Wenck stirbt am 11.October in Bad Neuheim, Direktor Ernst Folke Hellstedt übernimmt die Leitung. (Worldwide over 4 million Alfa-Laval separators sold. The machines achieved more than 1500 high honours. This year saw change in the leadership of the works. Director Wenck died on the 11th of October in Bad Neuheim and Director Ernst Folke Hellstedt took over the leadership).

[40] *Direktor Hellstedt geht im Dezember nach Stockholm zurück. Direktor Voges und Direktor Ohle kommen in den Vorstand.* ibid, p. 81.

[41] From Berlin financial newspapers and the Bergedorfer Eisenwerk *Gemeinschaftsbuch* (a sort of company diary which included minutes of the monthly meetings of the *Vertrauensratszitzung,* newspaper clippings mentioning Eisenwerk, orders from *der Führer* affecting Eisenwerk, results of sports competitions for the staff, reviews of concerts sponsored by Eisenwerk, reports of amounts contributed to the Christmas fund, amounts contributed to the Adolf Hitler fund, etc.).

[42] op cit, *Geschichte des Bergedorfer Eisenwerkes,* p. 87.

[43] ibid, p. 89.

[44] *Gemeinschaftsbuch,* 9.May.1938.

[45] ibid, 20.June.1939 meeting of *Vertrauensrat.*

[46] ibid, 5.September.1939 meeting of *Vertrauensrat.*

[47] The attack on Russia June - December, 1941.

[48] In the newspaper *Hamburger Fremdenblatt* of June 11, 1937, under the headline, *Bergedorfer Eisen voll beschäftigt* (Bergedorfer Eisenwerk fully occupied), sales increases to the food industry and for ship's coolers are reported. In addition: *Starkes Interesse bestand für die Spezialseparatoren für die Gewinnung von wichtigen Produkten aus einheimischen Rohstöffen* (Strong interest exists for the special separators for the winning of important products from domestic raw materials). The same report, presumably a press release by Bergedorfer Eisenwerk, was carried in the *Frankfurter Zeitung* (Frankurt am Main) of June 13, 1937.

[49] Borkin, Joseph, *The Crime and Punishment of I.G. Farben,* The Free Press, Collier Macmillan, New York, 1978, p. 60.

[50] *From now on the IG's fate and fortunes would be inextricably tied to those of the Third Reich. The future was not yet visible but the cartel had in essence committed to providing Hitler with the means to launch the most devastating conflict in human history. The agreement Bosch* (Director of IG Farben) *had signed was far more than the fulfillment of his long-held ambitions. It was also a pivotal moment in a sequence of events that would lead inexorably to the blitzkrieg, to Stalingrad and to the gas chambers at Auschwitz. Many years later the US Army's General Telford Taylor would accuse IG Farben's bosses of making World War II possible, of being 'the magicians who made the nightmare of Mein Kampf come true.'* Jeffreys, Diarmuid, *Hell's Cartel: IG Farben and the Making of Hitler's War Machine,* Bloomsbury Publishing, London, 2008, p.163.

[51] *Vertrauensratsitzung 19.8.1943,* Minutes of the monthly trust advisors' meeting (labour and management representatives), August 19, 1943.

[52] For example, the *Vertrauensratsitzung* minutes of 18 October 1943 note that it was necessary to commandeer the Polish eating room for apartments to house victims of the Hamburg bombing.

[53] On June 22, 1941, Germany attacked Russia without warning: three million men (with 3,350 tanks, 7,000 field guns, 2,000 aircraft and 600,000 horses towing guns and wagons) killed two million Russians in three weeks. (Beevor, Anthony, *Stalingrad,* Penguin Books, 1998, pp. 12-14). Following the Luftwaffe - Wehrmacht advance through Ukraine and Poland, SS men commandeered girls in their late teens for rail transport to Germany and forced labour. They also rounded up Jews for confinement in ghettos, or killed them forthwith if they resisted. Anti-Semitic locals provided the SS with lists of Jews and helped to build and man the death camps, the biggest of which were in Poland because that is where most of the Jews were: in 1939, four million Jews in Poland, 700,000-900,000 in Hungary, 250,000 in Germany, 200,000 in Austria, 300,000 in France, 10,000 in Sweden, 8,000 in Denmark, 1,800 in Norway, 700 in Finland. Soviet prisoners of war were confined in concentration camps and treated according to the official Nazi policy toward them: *Vernichtung durch Arbeit* (extermination through work).

[54] *Zwangsarbeit in Bergedorf: Stationen einer Verlorenem Jugend,* Museum für Bergedorf und die Vierlande, Bergedorf 2001, p. 12.

[55] Persson, Sune, *Escape from the Third Reich,* translated by Graham Long, Skyhorse Publishing, New York, 2009, p.95.

[56] ibid, p. 122.

[57] Gilbert, Martin, *Kristallnacht: Prelude to Destruction*, Harper Perennial, London, 2006, p.15

[58] Ibid, p. 268. The night of November 9-10 is still marked by "lest we forget" gatherings. For example, the partner of the late Stieg Larsson (*The Millennium Trilogy*) celebrated his memory by inviting his friends active in opposition to Sweden's neo-Nazis to a November 9 party. Gabrielsson, Eva, *Stieg and Me*, Orion Books Ltd., 2011, pp. 184-187.

[59] Sweden's Alien Act of 1927 severely restricted immigration of Jews. Responding to international pressure regarding the hundreds of thousands of Jews trying to leave Germany and Austria, the Alien Act was revised in 1937 to allow Swedish officials to admit political refugees. When Germany began disallowing entry of Jews, Switzerland and Sweden had Germany stamp a large red "J " on German Jews' passports - so that they could refuse entry to Jews from Germany and thus avoid the problem of what to do with them when the German border guards would not allow them to return. Following Kristallnacht, at the end of 1938, 300 Jews had been admitted to Sweden as refugees. Political protests by physicians (!) and demonstrations by hundreds of students in Uppsala carrying signs "Protest mot Judeimporten" (Protest against Jewish Immigration) and "Sverige åt Svenska" (Sweden for Swedes) raised government concern that immigration of too many Jews would not only cause resentment over Jews taking Swedish jobs in a time of high unemployment, but it could aggravate anti-Semitism to dangerous levels. After the Wannsee Conference of January, 1942, Jews were not allowed to leave the Reich and " ... thus the immigration ceased to be a problem for the Swedish authorities." Lindberg, Hans, *Svensk flyktingspolitik under internationelt tryck 1936-1941* (Swedish refugee policy under international pressure), p. 301.

[60] Donald said his mother thought about taking the children to Canada: *I know for sure that she had a British passport until after the war and then a Canadian. I remember I heard that my parents had been seriously considering that my mother, Mona and I should leave Sweden for Canada immediately before and after the war. One of these occasions can have been shortly after the war, when my mother traveled to Canada ... I also remember that Mona and I would immediately become Canadian citizens.*

[61] op cit, Koblik, *The Stones Cry Out*, pp. 12-13.

[62] ibid Koblik, p. 20.

[63] German troops travelled on Swedish railways to facilitate movement to Norway and Finland without risk of attack. Swedish air space was open to German fliers. Allied forces had no like privilege. Germany remained Sweden's biggest trading partner. Iron ore from Sweden was critical to the German war effort. When strategic Allied bombing succeeded in destroying Germany's capacity to manufacture ball bearings (necessary for aircraft and vehicles), Sweden's SKF filled large German orders.

[64] In late 1942 the Allied Eighth Army took 30,000 Axis prisoners at El Alamein and forced Rommel's Afrika Korps into a series of retreats which culminated in the surrender of 238,000 men near Tunis in May, 1943. The siege of Stalingrad cost Russia 155,000 dead and 320,000 wounded; but the Russian winter campaign of 1942-1943 killed 1,000,000 Germans and it gave Russia time to mobilize 6,000,000 men and re-arm with the help of American aid (427,000 vehicles, 2,000 railway locomotives, 15,000 aircraft, 247,000 telephones, four million tires and half the boots worn by the Red Army). Hastings, Max, *All Hell Let Loose: The World At War 1939-45*, Harper Collins, London, 2011, pp. 320-322 .

[65] Raoul Wallenberg worked in the Swedish Embassy in Budapest, Hungary. In 1944 Adolf Eichmann, having succeeded in organizing the killing of nearly all of the Jews in Europe, Ukraine and Poland, was given the job of exterminating as many of Hungary's 900,000 (by Nazi definition) Jews as possible. In seven weeks, May 18 - July 8, 148 trains transported 437,402 Jews from Hungary to Auschwitz. Countering Eichmann, Wallenberg issued thousands of phony Swedish passports to get Jews past Nazi police and onto ships bound for neutral countries or America. The Swedish government approved of his activity as long as it was financed from America. By some reckonings Wallenberg saved 45,000 lives before he was arrested by Soviet forces in 1945, taken to a prison camp in Russia and never heard from again. Kershaw, Alex, *The Envoy: the epic rescue of the last Jews of Europe in the desperate closing months of World War II*, Da Capo Press, Perseus Books Group, Philadelphia, 2010.

[66] Weinburg, Gerard L., *A World at Arms: A Global History of World War II*, Cambridge, 1994, p. 396

[67] Ekman, Stig and Klas Emark, editors, *Sweden's relations with Nazism, Nazi Germany and the Holocaust: a survey of research*, Almquist & Wiksell International, Stockholm, 2003, from the *Introduction* by Stig Ekman, p. 28.

[68] Widespread recognition of the obsolescence of idealism and the folly of honour is considered a cause of the absence of major wars since 1945. Pinker, Steven, *The Better Angels of Our Nature: Why Violence Has*

Declined, Penguin Books, New York, 2011, 802 pages. Of course the problem of dealing with Adolf Hitler (which caused Albert Einstein to abandon pacifism) has not arisen in our time.

INDEX